Oxford Studies in European Law

General Editors: Paul Craig and Gráinne de Búrca

RACISM AND EQUALITY IN THE EUROPEAN UNION

Racism and Equality in the European Union

MARK BELL
Professor of Law, University of Leicester

OXFORD
UNIVERSITY PRESS

OXFORD
UNIVERSITY PRESS

Great Clarendon Street, Oxford OX2 6DP

Oxford University Press is a department of the University of Oxford.
It furthers the University's objective of excellence in research, scholarship,
and education by publishing worldwide in

Oxford New York

Auckland Cape Town Dar es Salaam Hong Kong Karachi
Kuala Lumpur Madrid Melbourne Mexico City Nairobi
New Delhi Shanghai Taipei Toronto

With offices in

Argentina Austria Brazil Chile Czech Republic France Greece
Guatemala Hungary Italy Japan Poland Portugal Singapore
South Korea Switzerland Thailand Turkey Ukraine Vietnam

Oxford is a registered trade mark of Oxford University Press
in the UK and in certain other countries

Published in the United States
by Oxford University Press Inc., New York

First published 2008

British Library Cataloguing in Publication Data
Data available

Library of Congress Cataloging in Publication Data
Data available

Typeset by Newgen Imaging Systems (P) Ltd., Chennai, India
Printed on acid-free paper in the UK
by the MPG Books Group

ISBN 978–0–19–929784–9

1 3 5 7 9 10 8 6 4 2

For Maurice

Acknowledgements

The research which culminated in this book commenced during a Jean Monnet Fellowship at the Robert Schuman Centre for Advanced Studies, European University Institute, Florence. It was largely completed during a subsequent period of research leave granted by the University of Leicester. I am grateful to both institutions for the generous support which they provided.

A number of individuals kindly read and commented upon draft chapters of this book. Their constructive feedback was extremely beneficial and I thank them for the time invested: Neil Chakraborti, Pascale Lorber, Virginia Mantouvalou, Sue Millns, Valsamis Mitsilegas, and Lisa Waddington. My understanding of the law, and how it operates in practice, has been greatly enhanced by a range of projects that I have been involved with during the lifespan of this book. Specifically, I have learnt a lot from my fellow participants in the European Network of Legal Experts in the Non-Discrimination Field. I have also had my knowledge enriched through the chance to work with various NGOs; given the topic of this book, I particularly benefited from opportunities to participate in events and projects of the European Network Against Racism. A wide variety of people supplied me with information that contributed to the writing of this book; gratitude is especially due to Tansy Hutchinson and Vadim Poleshchuk. I am also grateful to Stelios Andreadakis for excellent research assistance.

Throughout the process of writing this book, I have been fortunate to enjoy the support of Gwen Booth and her colleagues at Oxford University Press, as well as the general editors of this series. Gwen was very helpful in always responding swiftly and precisely to my many queries along the way. In addition, I received constructive comments and suggestions from four anonymous reviewers of the book proposal.

Support of an academic nature is certainly required for writing a book, but equally essential (if not more important) are the personal relationships which have given me encouragement to see this project to its completion. I am constantly grateful to my parents and family who, although mostly across the Irish Sea, remain immensely close to me. I am greatly appreciative of the active interest they have taken in the progress of this book, which has been a wonderful source of motivation. As life has developed in Leicester, I have enjoyed the benefits of working in a friendly environment at the School of Law and I thank my colleagues for their continued support. Maurice FitzGerald has probably had to endure more than anyone else my ruminating about the contents of this book. His support has been invaluable and it is to him that this book is dedicated.

Contents

List of Abbreviations

AG	Advocate General
Art	Article
CA	Court of Appeal
CERD	Committee on the Elimination of Racial Discrimination
CETS	Council of Europe Treaty Series
CJEL	Columbia Journal of European Law
CML Rev	Common Market Law Review
CRE	Commission for Racial Equality
Dec	Decision
DG	Directorate-General
Dir	Directive
EAPN	European Anti-Poverty Network
EAT	Employment Appeals Tribunal
EC	European Community
ECHR	European Convention on Human Rights
ECR	European Court Reports
ECRI	European Commission on Racism and Intolerance
ECSR	European Committee of Social Rights
EEA	European Economic Area
EEC	European Economic Community
EES	European Employment Strategy
EHRLR	European Human Rights Law Review
EHRR	European Human Rights Reports
EJML	European Journal of Migration and Law
ELJ	European Law Journal
ELR	European Law Review
ENAR	European Network Against Racism
EOC	Equal Opportunities Commission
EP	European Parliament
EPL	European Public Law
ERRC	European Roma Rights Centre
ESF	European Social Fund
ETUC	European Trade Union Confederation
EU	European Union
EUMC	European Union Monitoring Centre on Racism and Xenophobia
EUMF	European Union Migrants' Forum
EU-SILC	European Survey on Income and Living Conditions
FCNM	Framework Convention on National Minorities
FLS	Feminist Legal Studies
FRA	Fundamental Rights Agency
GC	Grand Chamber of the European Court of Human Rights

HL	House of Lords
ICERD	International Convention on the Elimination of All Forms of Racial Discrimination
ICLQ	International and Comparative Law Quarterly
IJCLLIR	International Journal of Comparative Labour Law and Industrial Relations
ILJ	Industrial Law Journal
IRJ	Industrial Relations Journal
JCER	Journal of Contemporary European Research
JCMS	Journal of Common Market Studies
JEPP	Journal of European Public Policy
JESP	Journal of European Social Policy
LTR	Long-term resident
MJ	Maastricht Journal of European and Comparative Law
MLR	Modern Law Review
NAP	National Action Plan
NGO	Non-Governmental Organisation
NRP	National Reform Programme
OECD	Organisation for Economic Cooperation and Development
OJ C	Official Journal of the European Union (Communication Series)
OJ L	Official Journal of the European Union (Legislation Series)
OJLS	Oxford Journal of Legal Studies
OMC	Open Method of Coordination
OOPEC	Office for the Official Publications of the European Communities
OUP	Oxford University Press
PRIAE	Policy Research Institute on Ageing and Ethnicity
QB	Queen's Bench Division, English High Court
Reg	Regulation
Res	Resolution
RRA	Race Relations Act
S Ct	United States Supreme Court
TCN	Third country national
TFEU	Treaty on the Functioning of the European Union
YEL	Yearbook of European Law

List of Tables

Table of Cases

A. EUROPEAN UNION

Court of Justice

Court of First Instance

B. COUNCIL OF EUROPE

European Court of Human Rights

European Committee of Social Rights

C. OTHER JURISDICTIONS

France

Netherlands

UK

USA

Table of Legislation

A. EUROPEAN UNION

European Community Treaty

Decisions

Directives

Regulations

European Union Treaty

Framework Decisions

Introduction

The role of the European Union in combating racism has been the subject of debate and analysis for around two decades. From the mid-1980s until 1997, the dominant question was whether it was appropriate for the Union to intervene in this field, or whether it should remain purely a matter for national authorities. In 1997, the Member States agreed to amend the founding Treaties in order to confer a specific legal competence on the EU 'to take appropriate action to combat discrimination based on sex, racial or ethnic origin, religion or belief, disability, age or sexual orientation' (EC Treaty, Article 13). Simultaneously, 'combating racism and xenophobia' was added to the EU Treaty as a core objective of the Union's project to create 'an area of freedom, security and justice' (Article 29). Those Treaty amendments largely resolved any lingering doubts over *whether* this was a topic apt for EU intervention. Instead, the debate shifted towards the question of *how* EU law and policy could be most effectively deployed to combat racism.

The Treaty amendments came into effect in 1999 and on 29 June 2000 the Council of Ministers adopted Directive 2000/43 implementing the principle of equal treatment between persons irrespective of racial or ethnic origin.[1] This Directive was ground-breaking in various respects. Notably, it moved beyond the EU's traditional focus on discrimination within the labour market, tackling key social policy subjects such as education, housing, and healthcare. In addition, it marked a significant evolution in the content of anti-discrimination law, as illustrated by the inclusion of an express prohibition of harassment or the duty on all states to establish a body or bodies for the promotion of equal treatment. A large body of academic literature relating to this Directive, as well as to the further anti-discrimination legislation adopted in its wake,[2] has

[1] [2000] OJ L180/22.

[2] Council Directive (EC) 2000/78 establishing a general framework for equal treatment in employment and occupation [2000] OJ L303/16; EP and Council Directive (EC) 2002/73 amending Directive (EEC) 76/207 on the implementation of the principle of equal treatment for men and women as regards access to employment, vocational training and promotion, and working conditions [2002] OJ L 269/15; Council Directive (EC) 2004/113 implementing the principle of equal treatment between men and women in the access to and supply of goods and services [2004] OJ L373/37; EP and Council Directive (EC) 2006/54 on the implementation of the principle of equal opportunities and equal treatment of men and women in matters of employment and occupation (recast) [2006] OJ L204/23.

accumulated in recent years.[3] Consequently, the main aim of this book is not to add yet further commentary and reflection on those Directives. Looking back to the debate in the mid-1990s, a Directive on racial discrimination was intended to be just one element of a much broader policy agenda through which the EU would combat racism. The European Council's Consultative Commission on Racism and Xenophobia,[4] which paved the way to the Treaty amendments, recommended a host of measures across EU law and policy, in areas such as police and judicial cooperation, education, and employment. This horizontal perspective was taken up by the Commission in 1998 when it launched an 'Action Plan Against Racism':[5]

> Many Community policies and programmes could contribute positively to the fight against racism. As part of this Action Plan, the Commission will actively develop a mainstreaming approach to combating racism and discrimination and promoting integration across all sectors, in particular in areas of employment, the European Structural Funds, education, training and youth programmes, public procurement policy, research activities, external relations, information actions and cultural and sports initiatives.[6]

This idea of 'mainstreaming' entails the mobilization of all areas of EU law and policy in order to combat racism and promote equality. In practical terms, this implies that policy-makers in all fields should ensure: (1) that any measures taken do not discriminate on grounds of racial or ethnic origin; and (2) law and policy instruments are actively used to promote equality for all persons, irrespective of racial or ethnic origin. The mainstreaming approach was clearly borrowed from gender equality policy, where it had been publicly endorsed by the Commission in 1996.[7] Since then, a considerable body of literature has amassed around the adequacy and effectiveness of gender mainstreaming by the EU institutions.[8] Few authors, however, have analysed the Union's use of mainstreaming as part of policy against racism. This is probably best explained by the half-hearted nature with which this strategy has been pursued. As discussed further in Chapter 4, the 1998 Action Plan did not herald a 'new dawn' for anti-racism policy; rather it faded away and became just one of many initiatives that have been embarked upon over the years. Writing in 2004, Jo Shaw commented that 'despite the rhetoric and these paper policies, there has been little solid

[3] eg H Meenan (ed), *Equality Law in an Enlarged European Union—Understanding the Article 13 Directives* (Cambridge: Cambridge University Press, 2007). For an extensive bibliography of academic literature on the Directives, see: <http://europa.eu.int/comm/employment_social/fundamental_rights/pdf/pubst/crirev.pdf> accessed 9 May 2008.

[4] Consultative Commission on Racism and Xenophobia, 'Final Report' Ref 6906/1/95 Rev 1, RAXEN 24 (Brussels: General Secretariat of the Council of the European Union, 1995).

[5] COM (1998) 183. [6] ibid 3. [7] See further Ch 3.

[8] eg T Rees, *Mainstreaming Equality in the European Union—Education, Training and Labour Market Policies* (London: Routledge, 1999). See also journal special issues: (2000) 7 JEPP 346; (2002) 10 FLS 209.

action in practice to bring the fight against racism to the forefront of the EU's policy concerns'.[9]

The idea of mainstreaming has, though, persisted in various forms. Since 2002, the Commission has subjected an increasing range of law and policy initiatives to 'impact assessment', a type of pre-legislative scrutiny designed to uncover potentially negative economic, social, or environmental impacts.[10] In 2005, a Group of Commissioners on Fundamental Rights, Non-Discrimination and Equal Opportunities was established with a mandate to 'ensure the coherence of Commission action in the areas of fundamental rights, anti-discrimination, equal opportunities and the social integration of minority groups'.[11] More recently, the Treaty of Lisbon, if ratified, will include the following article in the Treaty on the Functioning of the European Union (TFEU):

> In defining and implementing its policies and activities, the Union shall aim to combat discrimination based on sex, racial or ethnic origin, religion or belief, disability, age or sexual orientation.[12]

It would be misleading to suggest that the Union has been consciously committed to mainstreaming as a tool of anti-racism policy since 1998; nevertheless, the idea has lingered.

Purpose, scope, and structure

The principal research question which this book seeks to explore is the extent to which the interlocking objectives of combating racism and promoting equality have been mainstreamed across EU law and policy. In order to answer this overarching question, a number of sub-questions arise. First of all, it is necessary to clarify what is meant by 'racism' and 'equality' in today's enlarged European Union. As discussed in Chapters 1 and 2, these are multifaceted concepts. Racism can be understood as encompassing both overt theories that certain 'races' are biologically superior, and subtle institutional practices which perpetuate inequality for minority groups. Within Europe, the social groups vulnerable to racism are heterogeneous in nature, including migrants, Roma, or historic national minorities. In addition, research increasingly draws attention to the relevance of 'intersectionality', that is, the cumulative effect of combinations of characteristics, such as ethnicity and gender. The flip side of combating racism is promoting equality. Yet there is little consensus on what 'equality' entails,

[9] J Shaw, 'Mainstreaming equality in European Union law and policymaking' (Brussels: ENAR, 2004) 5.

[10] Commission, 'Communication on impact assessment' COM (2002) 276.

[11] Commission, 'A roadmap for equality between women and men, 2006–2010' (Luxembourg: OOPEC, 2006) 34.

[12] Art 10, Consolidated version of the TFEU [2008] OJ C115/53.

most notably the extent to which this requires society to adapt in response to cultural diversity or whether equality can be reduced to a flat sameness of treatment.

The second sub-question concerns the meaning of mainstreaming in the context of promoting ethnic equality. Chapter 3 explores the competing models of mainstreaming which exist, such as 'elite-bureaucratic' or 'democratic-participatory' approaches. Alongside these models, debate surrounds the appropriate instruments through which mainstreaming can be implemented. This ranges from creating legally enforceable duties to more technical instruments such as impact assessment or data collection. As mentioned earlier, a great deal of literature has already been devoted to analysing mainstreaming in relation to gender equality, so a key point of inquiry is whether the models and techniques of mainstreaming need adjustment when applied to combating racism and promoting equality for ethnic minorities.

Having established the theoretical framework, the remainder of the book considers the evidence of mainstreaming in EU law and policy. In so doing, it seeks to explore how the concepts of 'racism' and 'equality' are articulated, as well as what model, if any, of mainstreaming has been pursued. Mainstreaming is not designed to be a replacement or alternative to specialized measures against discrimination. In the context of gender equality, the Commission refers to a 'dual approach' of gender mainstreaming coupled with specific measures (such as anti-discrimination legislation).[13] Similarly, mainstreaming to promote ethnic equality cannot be detached from specific measures taken under the aegis of anti-discrimination policy (most notably Directive 2000/43). Consequently, Chapter 4 provides the context for mainstreaming by examining the position of racism within anti-discrimination policy.

The subsequent four chapters each consider an area of EU law and policy and seek to identify evidence of the extent to which issues relating to racism have already been mainstreamed. Given the vast scope of EU law and policy, it was evident from the outset that a number of case studies had to be selected. In making this selection, several factors were instrumental. First, a range of policy fields had been designated by the Commission in its 1998 Action Plan as target areas for mainstreaming. Preliminary research allowed identification of policies where there was at least some tangible evidence of activity on issues relating to racism. It would, of course, have been possible to select some fields where hitherto little or no connection has been made to combating racism, such as environmental policy.[14] Yet by limiting the inquiry to those areas where there had been a concrete engagement, it was felt that this would yield more substantial evidence about how racism, equality, and mainstreaming were being

[13] Commission (n 11 above) 7.

[14] Capacity Global, 'Environmental justice and race equality in the European Union' (London: Capacity Global, 2007): <http://www.capacity.org.uk/downloads/CC-EJ%20in%20EU.pdf> accessed 9 May 2008.

constructed. Second, the material scope of Directive 2000/43 prohibits racial discrimination in various aspects of social life, such as employment, education, healthcare, and housing. If mainstreaming is to operate in a complementary fashion to specific measures on racism, then it would be reasonable to expect to find evidence of mainstreaming in EU policies which touch on these fields. Third, studies of racism in European states have flagged up the most sensitive areas of law and policy.[15] Immigration and the criminal justice system feature prominently, so it was deemed important to include an analysis of these aspects of EU law and policy. Finally, the discussion of mainstreaming in Chapter 3 links its rise, in part, to the spread of 'new governance'. In brief, this trend moves away from a reliance on traditional, binding legal instruments as the dominant method of regulation. Instead, new governance invokes more flexible strategies, such as guidelines, benchmarking, and peer review. In the context of the EU, this is manifested in the rise of the 'open method of coordination'. Therefore, the choice of case studies was influenced by a desire to examine different styles of regulation in order to consider whether this had any impact on the functioning of mainstreaming.

The four cases selected for examination were: employment (Chapter 5); education, health, and housing (Chapter 6); immigration and integration (Chapter 7); and criminal law (Chapter 8). Although Chapter 6 groups together a number of topics, these fall under the shared umbrella of the EU's Strategy for Social Protection and Social Inclusion. The choice of case studies inevitably meant that a number of potentially interesting areas were not examined. Perhaps the most notable omission is public procurement policy; however, this has recently been the subject of a highly comprehensive analysis by Christopher McCrudden.[16] Similarly, some existing publications have considered cultural policy[17] and asylum.[18] In the light of the geographic scope of Directive 2000/43, the decision was also taken not to examine EU external relations policies.

[15] eg the research reports of the EU Monitoring Centre on Racism and Xenophobia or the regular 'shadow reports' published by the European Network Against Racism.

[16] C McCrudden, *Buying Social Justice—Equality, Government Procurement, and Legal Change* (Oxford: OUP, 2007).

[17] T Ahmed and T Hervey, 'The European Union and cultural diversity: a missed opportunity?' in European Centre for Minority Issues (eds), *European Yearbook of Minority Issues Vol 3, 2003/04* (Leiden: Koninklijke Brill NV, 2005) 43.

[18] M Bell, 'Mainstreaming equality norms into European Union asylum law' (2001) 26 ELR 20.

1

'Race', Ethnicity, and Racism in Europe

Since the mid-1980s, the issue of racism has gradually assumed greater prominence within European Union law and policy discourse. Nevertheless, the meaning of core concepts has always been hedged with ambivalence. This is excellently demonstrated within Directive 2000/43. This forbids discrimination on grounds of 'racial or ethnic origin',[1] but the preamble declares:

> The European Union rejects theories which attempt to determine the existence of separate human races. The use of the term 'racial origin' in this Directive does not imply an acceptance of such theories.[2]

At the same time, the European Commission commonly refers to this Directive as the 'Racial Equality' Directive. This book aims to identify the extent to which the objectives of combating racism and promoting equality have been integrated across various areas of EU law and policy. To this end, it is essential to clarify at the outset the meaning of 'racism'. Legal and policy documents often use this term in a rather loose fashion as if its meaning was self-evident and uncontested. In contrast, this chapter will illustrate the variety of issues potentially falling under the broad category of racism. From a European perspective, it is particularly important to consider the historic and geographic context in which racism is manifested.[3] Expressions of racism are not necessarily consistent across the (enlarged) EU. The chapter begins by considering theoretical critiques of 'race', ethnic origin, and the concept of racism. It proceeds to consider how these terms have been used within legal instruments. The final sections examine the principal groups vulnerable to racism within the EU.

[1] Art 1, Council Directive (EC) 2000/43 implementing the principle of equal treatment between persons irrespective of racial or ethnic origin [2000] OJ L180/22. This Directive prohibits discrimination on grounds of racial or ethnic origin in employment, vocational training, education, social protection, social advantages, and access to goods and services, including housing.

[2] Recital 6.

[3] E Howard, 'Race and racism—why does European law have difficulties with definitions?' (2008) 24 IJCLLIR 5, 11.

A. 'Race' and Racism

The origins of the term 'racism' lie in a critique of scientific theories on 'race'.[4] Such theories came to prominence during the nineteenth century and sought to categorize the human population into a number of biologically distinct 'races'. These were often identified by reference to physical characteristics, such as skin colour and facial appearance. Crucially, it was purported that these racial categories were aligned with different levels of intellectual capacity, leading to the view that some 'races' were superior to others.[5] The supposed objectivity of such scientific analysis originally provided a veneer of legitimacy for imperialism and the slave trade.[6] It also provided an ideological underpinning for the emergence of race laws in the 1930s and the subsequent Holocaust.[7]

A critique of the concept of biologically distinguishable human 'races' can be traced back to the 1920s and 1930s.[8] This accelerated in the post-war period under the auspices of several inquiries conducted by UNESCO. These concluded that, in fact, there was no scientific basis for the proposition that the human population was composed of a number of distinct 'races', as opposed to a spectrum of human diversity. The 1978 Declaration on Race and Racial Prejudice summarizes this viewpoint:

> 1. All human beings belong to a single species and are descended from a common stock. . . .
> 5. The differences between the achievements of the different peoples are entirely attributable to geographic, historical, political, economic, social and cultural factors. Such differences can in no case serve as a pretext for any rank-ordered classification of nations or peoples.[9]

This international consensus on the scientific falsity of 'race' persists, although there is some return to this debate in the context of contemporary genetic profiling.[10] Within academic literature, the artificial nature of the concept is often indicated by placing 'race' within inverted commas. The corollary of rejecting 'race' as an objective criterion is the recognition that perceptions of 'race' are social constructions. As such, perceptions of 'race' are likely to vary 'over time and across

[4] R Miles and M Brown, *Racism* (2nd edn, London: Routledge, 2003) 58.

[5] C Hirschman, 'The origins and demise of the concept of race' (2004) 30 *Population and Development Review* 385, 393.

[6] ibid 395.

[7] A Lentin, *Racism and Anti-racism in Europe* (London: Pluto Press, 2004) 60.

[8] Miles and Brown (n 4 above) 58; Howard (n 3 above) 10.

[9] Art 1, Declaration on Race and Racial Prejudice, 20th General Conference of UNESCO, 27 November 1978.

[10] R Bhavnani, H Safia Mirza, and V Meetoo, *Tackling the Roots of Racism—Lessons for Success* (Bristol: Policy Press, 2005) 9; R Carter, 'Genes, genomes and genealogies: the return of scientific racism?' (2007) 30 *Ethnic and Racial Studies* 546.

space'.[11] Historical and geographic circumstances will determine the process through which racialization occurs; in other words, the way in which physical characteristics can become imbued with social meaning.[12] In a multinational polity such as the EU, this implies that perceptions of 'race' are likely to differ between states.

The discrediting of 'race' can be associated with a shift in vocabulary towards ethnicity. Whilst scientific theories on 'race' attempted to place the human population into a small number of biologically determined categories, ethnicity is viewed as more fragmented and pluralistic.[13] Ethnicity is informed by cultural differences, such as language, dress, religion, literature, and music. It is often premised on individuals' *belief* in a shared, common origin.[14] Solomos and Schuster argue that ethnic groups are also social constructions; they are imagined communities based on selective memory and perceived common heritage.[15] In principle, the cultural nature of ethnicity suggests that individuals can alter their ethnicity. McVeigh and Lentin argue that ethnicity is an inherently shifting characteristic which arises from a combination of internal self-definition and external perception.[16] Consequently, it holds the potential to be a better way of signifying the socially constructed nature of perceived difference or 'otherness', rather than the biological notion of 'race'. Nevertheless, there are certain drawbacks to a focus on ethnicity. Bhavnani et al. suggest that there is a tendency to regard the cultural qualities represented by ethnicity as static and unchanging.[17] In particular, ethnic groups risk being viewed as relatively homogeneous entities with little recognition of their internal diversity.[18] If ethnicity becomes viewed as a fixed trait beyond individual control, then it may be little more than a 'politically correct code word for "race"'.[19] This tendency is reinforced by the habit of viewing only the 'other' as bearing ethnic qualities.[20] The label 'ethnic' is often used only in conjunction with minorities and it is associated with that which is exotic and different.[21]

B. Scientific, Cultural, and Institutional Racism

Belief in the existence of superior, biologically separate 'races' can be summarized under the label of 'scientific racism'. Whilst this outlook declined in the post-war

[11] K Tyler, 'The genealogical imagination: the inheritance of interracial identities' [2005] *The Sociological Review* 476, 479.

[12] Miles and Brown (n 4 above) 100.

[13] S Fenton, *Ethnicity* (Cambridge: Polity Press, 2003) 52.

[14] ibid 62.

[15] J Solomos and L Schuster, 'Citizenship, multiculturalism and the politics of identity: contemporary dilemmas and policy agendas' in R Koopmans and P Statham (eds), *Challenging Immigration and Ethnic Relations Politics* (Oxford: OUP, 2000) 74, 79.

[16] R McVeigh and R Lentin, 'Situated racisms: a theoretical introduction' in R Lentin and R McVeigh (eds), *Racism and Anti-racism in Ireland* (Belfast: Beyond the Pale Publications, 2002) 1, 5.

[17] Bhavnani et al. (n 10 above) 14.

[18] Fenton (n 13 above) 68.

[19] Miles and Brown (n 4 above) 93.

[20] Lentin (n 7 above) 30.

[21] The Runnymede Trust, *The Future of Multi-ethnic Britain—The Parekh Report* (London: Profile Books, 2002) xxiii.

period, it was not, however, accompanied by the disappearance of racism as a phenomenon. For example, issues such as Apartheid or segregation in the USA propelled the adoption of the International Convention on the Elimination of Racial Discrimination (ICERD) in 1966.[22] In an effort to explain ongoing manifestations of racism, attention increasingly focused on 'cultural racism'.[23] This perspective argues that discrimination and prejudice arise not because of individuals' belief in the biological superiority of their perceived 'race', but rather from conflicts between different ethnic groups. A cultural perspective on racism suggests that individuals have an innate tendency to prefer their own cultural community and that a mixing of cultures inevitably produces conflicts in inter-ethnic relations.[24] As overt opposition to persons of a different 'race' becomes less common and widely assumed to be unacceptable discourse, this is replaced with stealthy 'race' talk coded in terms of concern about 'too much' cultural diversity.[25] Naturally, this concept of racism implies a strong nexus between racism and discourse on immigration. For example, McMaster highlights how extreme right-wing political parties in Europe shifted away from the use of overt language expressing ideas of racial superiority. Instead, their discourse became couched in terms of opposition to immigrants and immigration.[26] As a result, racism has become intertwined with the concept of xenophobia (literally, the fear of foreigners). Kundnani notes how hostility to foreigners (and foreign culture) is often presented as inevitable or natural, thereby invoking xenophobia as an 'alibi for racism'.[27]

A concept of cultural racism leads to an anti-racist strategy premised on changing *individual* attitudes and behaviour. People have to be persuaded to overcome suspicion and hostility to those of a different culture. On the one hand, law may be deployed to penalize individual acts of racial discrimination. On the other, policy is directed towards learning about other cultures and encouraging people to value diversity.[28] This approach seems evident in the EU's anti-discrimination media campaign. It centres on slogans such as 'for diversity, against discrimination' or 'our differences make the difference'.[29]

One of the limitations in the culturalist vision of racism is its emphasis on individual prejudice as a cause of racism.[30] This tends to characterize racism as a

[22] International Convention on the Elimination of All Forms of Racial Discrimination (New York, 7 March 1966); K Boyle and A Baldaccini, 'A critical evaluation of international human rights approaches to racism' in S Fredman (ed), *Discrimination and Human Rights—The Case of Racism* (Oxford: OUP, 2001) 135, 150.

[23] Lentin (n 7 above) 76.

[24] T Modood, '"Difference", cultural racism and anti-racism' in B Boxill (ed), *Race and Racism* (Oxford: OUP, 2001) 238.

[25] A Kundnani, 'In a foreign land: the new popular racism' (2001) 43 *Race & Class* 41, 52.

[26] N McMaster, *Racism in Europe 1870–2000* (Houndmills: Palgrave, 2001) 210.

[27] Kundnani (n 25 above) 50. [28] Lentin (n 7 above) 81.

[29] <http://www.stop-discrimination.info> accessed 26 April 2007.

[30] E Bonilla-Silva, 'Rethinking racism: towards a structural interpretation' (1996) 62 *American Sociological Review* 465, 467.

behavioural aberration which should fade away with the passage of time and individual enlightenment. Critics have argued that this does not pay sufficient attention to the deep-seated nature of stereotypes which are shaped by public discourse and are consequently difficult to dislodge.[31] This ranges from the casual linking in the media of immigration and terrorism, through to workplace assumptions about who would 'fit in'. Moreover, the focus on individuals downplays the role of structural factors which go beyond the actions of any given individual. McCrudden notes how the persistence of inequality eventually provoked commentators to question whether individual prejudice was a sufficient explanation for racism.[32] An alternative perspective, 'institutional racism', rose in prominence, dating from the 1960s in both the UK and USA.

The precise meaning of institutional racism has been the subject of considerable academic debate.[33] As a concept, its strength lies in departing from the idea of racism as purely intentional prejudice on the part of individuals towards those of a different culture. Instead, it recognizes that racism occurs even in the absence of conscious discriminatory motivation. To this end, it attributes great importance to whether equal outcomes are ensured in practice for all ethnic groups; where unequal outcomes persist, this is taken as evidence of institutional racism.[34] The concept of institutional racism famously entered mainstream public policy discourse in the UK through the findings of an official inquiry into the mishandling by police of an investigation into the racist murder of a young black man, Stephen Lawrence. The inquiry's report provided the following definition of institutional racism:

> The collective failure of an organisation to provide an appropriate and professional service to people because of their colour, culture, or ethnic origin. It can be seen or detected in processes, attitudes and behaviour which amount to discrimination through unwitting prejudice, ignorance, thoughtlessness and racist stereotyping which disadvantage minority ethnic people.[35]

In this case, institutional racism was detected in the organization's collective failure to treat his murder in the manner that would have been adopted for a white victim. Institutional racism draws attention to the power of 'routines and everyday practices'.[36] For instance, when police or immigration officers exercise discretion and assess how 'suspect' an individual is, there is a strong risk of stereotyping.

[31] Bhavnani et al. (n 10 above) 17.

[32] C McCrudden, 'Institutional discrimination' (1982) 2 OJLS 303, 305.

[33] M Verlot, 'Understanding institutional racism' in The Evens Foundation (eds), *Europe's New Racism: Causes, Manifestations and Solutions* (Oxford: Berghahn Books, 2002) 27; Miles and Brown (n 4 above) 66–71.

[34] M Rowe, *Policing, Race and Racism* (Cullompton: Willan Publishing, 2004) 10.

[35] para 6.34, W MacPherson, 'The Stephen Lawrence Inquiry—report of an inquiry' (Cm 4262-I, 1999).

[36] Runnymede Trust (n 21 above) para 5.26.

The idea that racism can arise from taken-for-granted institutional practices can be applied beyond the sphere of criminal justice. McCrudden notes how typical labour market practices can institutionalize disadvantage for ethnic minorities.[37] Recruitment of new workers by relying on 'word-of-mouth' or the family and friends of the current workforce will tend to reproduce the existing ethnic profile. An alternative example of institutional racism arises from *DH v The Czech Republic*.[38] In this case, children were allocated to special schools for those with learning disabilities on the basis of supposedly neutral psychological tests. In practice, Roma children in the town of Ostrava were more than 27 times more likely to be allocated to such schools than a similarly situated non-Roma child.[39] Crucially, the European Court of Human Rights held that it was not necessary to show that any individual Roma child had been subject to prejudicial treatment in the conduct of the tests. The 'disproportionately prejudicial effect on the Roma community' was sufficient evidence to support a finding of unlawful discrimination.[40] Although the Court does not expressly refer to the concept of institutional racism in its judgment, this may be viewed as implicit both in the emphasis attached to the presence of manifestly unequal outcomes and in the Court's conclusion that the system of testing was inherently discriminatory.[41]

The breadth of the concept of institutional racism has, though, been a source of criticism. Miles and Brown refer to 'conceptual inflation' in the analysis of racism and the difficulty of determining the limits to racism if it is completely disconnected from motivation.[42] If the focus is purely on effects and outcomes, then any difference in the socio-economic position of ethnic groups will be potentially attributed to racism. Some authors also draw a distinction between institutional racism, which concentrates on racism arising from the actions and processes of institutions, and a broader concept of structural racism, which embraces all socio-economic structures that may give rise to inequality.[43] Given that this book focuses on the role of the EU (and its institutions), the term institutional racism will be maintained.

In short, sociological debates on the meaning of racism present a spectrum of options. The next section turns to consider the role that law plays in defining racism.

C. 'Race', Ethnicity, and Law

When law is deployed to combat racism, certain choices have to be made in the language used within the law; these convey how the law defines racism. In fact, it is rather rare to find an express definition of 'racism' within legal instruments.

[37] McCrudden (n 32 above) 314.
[38] *DH and others v The Czech Republic* [GC] (2008) 47 EHRR 3.
[39] para 134. [40] para 209. [41] para 201.
[42] Miles and Brown (n 4 above) 71. [43] Bonilla-Silva (n 30 above) 466.

This may reflect an assumption that racism refers merely to a state of mind, as opposed to specific acts which could be the subject of legal regulation.[44] Indeed, legal instruments typically concentrate on defining the concept of discrimination.[45] ICERD, for example, contains no definition of 'racism', but does define 'racial discrimination'. In relation to the latter, a key question for all anti-racism laws is what constitutes 'racial' discrimination. Here, the use of the term 'race' is an initial dilemma. On one side, the sociological critique of 'race' discussed above has exposed the artificiality of 'race' as a means of categorizing the human population. Given the consensus that there is no scientific basis for the existence of 'race', one aim of anti-racism laws should be to undermine this perceived category. Haney López warns that using 'race' as a category within the law tends to legitimize its existence in the popular imagination.[46] For example, ICERD refers to 'promoting understanding among all races'[47] or the 'protection of certain racial groups'.[48] In the European context, the historical resonance of 'race' underscores its problematic nature.[49] In some states, it is strongly associated with laws promulgated by the Nazi and Fascist governments in Europe during the 1930s and 1940s. Indeed, in 1996, the European Parliament adopted a resolution stating that 'the term should therefore be avoided in all official texts'.[50]

On the other side of this debate, it can be argued that anti-racism laws are designed to prohibit discrimination based on perceptions about 'race', therefore, legal texts need to engage expressly with this concept. In other words, it needs to be clear that if someone treats another less favourably and this is based on their belief about that other's 'race', then this act must be forbidden by law. This rationale is adopted in the general policy recommendation of the European Commission against Racism and Intolerance (ECRI), the Council of Europe's specialized body working on racism and related issues. The explanatory memorandum states:

> Since all human beings belong to the same species, ECRI rejects theories based on the existence of different «races». However, in this Recommendation ECRI uses this term in order to ensure that those persons who are generally and erroneously perceived as belonging to «another race» are not excluded from the protection provided for by the legislation.[51]

[44] E Howard, 'The road to equality—developing the protection against discrimination on racial or ethnic grounds within the European Union' Ph.D. thesis, Queen Mary, University of London, February 2007.

[45] Howard (n 3 above) 27.

[46] I Haney López, *White by Law—The Legal Construction of Race* (New York: New York University Press, 1996) 111.

[47] Art 2(1).

[48] Art 2(2). The preamble of ICERD states that 'any doctrine of superiority based on racial differentiation is scientifically false'.

[49] Howard (n 3 above) 12.

[50] para K, Resolution on the communication from the Commission on racism, xenophobia and anti-Semitism [1996] OJ C152/57.

[51] fn 1, ECRI general policy recommendation no 7 on national legislation to combat racism and racial discrimination, CRI (2002) 41, 13 December 2002.

This balance also seems to be the logic within the EC Racial Equality Directive, given the statement in Recital 6, mentioned at the outset of this chapter. An alternative approach in some states has been to qualify the term 'race' within national legislation. For instance, in France, 'race' is often prefaced by the words 'real or assumed'.[52] These strategies fit comfortably with the prohibition of direct discrimination or harassment, where the actual characteristics of the victim are not determinative of the existence of the unlawful act. Article 2(1) of the Racial Equality Directive defines direct discrimination as 'where one person is treated less favourably than another is, has been or would be treated in a comparable situation *on grounds of racial or ethnic origin*' (emphasis added).[53] The law can claim to reject the existence of 'race', yet penalize situations where someone is treated less favourably on this ground. The key is the reason for the discriminator's action, not the actual characteristics of the victim. Greater difficulties arise in respect of indirect discrimination. Article 2(2)(b) of the Racial Equality Directive states:

> Indirect discrimination shall be taken to occur where an apparently neutral provision, criterion or practice would put *persons of a racial or ethnic origin* at a particular disadvantage compared with other persons, unless that provision, criterion or practice is objectively justified by a legitimate aim and the means of achieving that aim are appropriate and necessary (emphasis added).

The nature of indirect discrimination is that the rule or practice does not overtly distinguish on grounds of perceived 'race'. Instead, the complainant is seeking to demonstrate that a group of people of a particular racial origin compared with persons not of that racial origin are placed at a particular disadvantage. It is very difficult to mount such a complaint without implicitly accepting the existence of groups that can be defined according to racial origin. Banton observes that 'the introduction of the concept of *racial group* was in Britain seen as the price to be paid for the prohibition of indirect discrimination'.[54] He criticizes this trade-off, arguing that in the long term the continued use of such terminology 'breathes new life into the obsolete idea of race'.[55]

Given the contested nature of 'race', it is not surprising many legal instruments against racism have sought to identify alternative conceptual categories. This also reflects the shift from a focus on scientific racism towards cultural racism. If cultural difference is viewed as the catalyst for contemporary manifestations of racism, then it is necessary to capture the various markers through which cultural difference is signified. This is already evident in ICERD, which defines racial discrimination as 'any distinction, exclusion, restriction or

[52] eg Art L. 1132-1 Labour Code.

[53] Admittedly, not all language versions of the Directive adopt this expression: eg the Italian version refers to less favourable treatment 'because of his race' ('a causa della sua razza').

[54] M Banton, *The International Politics of Race* (Cambridge: Polity Press, 2002) 201.

[55] ibid.

preference based on race, colour, descent, or national or ethnic origin'.[56] More than 35 years later, ECRI's general policy recommendation advocated a longer, open-ended list: '«direct racial discrimination» shall mean any differential treatment based on a ground *such as* race, colour, language, religion, nationality or national or ethnic origin' (emphasis added).[57] The advantage of the open list approach is that it recognizes the dynamic quality of racism. It is not a stable phenomenon, but rather one which varies in its manifestation according to context.[58] Specifically, the groups vulnerable to racism are likely to vary due to factors such as the process of state formation or the history of migration. Two contemporary examples are asylum-seekers and Muslims. Asylum as an avenue for migration grew sharply in political sensitivity during the 1980s and 1990s and consequently asylum applicants became a key group vulnerable to racism.[59] Similarly, the period since the 1990s has witnessed an increasing political focus on the situation of Muslims in Europe, a debate accentuated post-9/11. Modood argues that hostility to Muslims, often summarized in the term Islamophobia, is a present-day expression of racism.[60]

The difficulty encountered in defining racism in law is striking the balance between recognition of its changing form with identification of its outer limits. At one end of the spectrum, it is possible to point to discrimination on grounds such as age, gender, or sexual orientation. Although these can be combined with racism, it is rarely argued that discrimination on these grounds is an aspect of racism. In contrast, there are grounds such as religion or nationality where there is considerable variation between legal sources as to whether these should be placed under the umbrella of racism. In contrast to ICERD or ECRI's recommendation, the Racial Equality Directive adopts the relatively narrow formula of discrimination on grounds of 'racial or ethnic origin'. Moreover, it specifies that this does not cover a difference of treatment based on nationality,[61] whilst discrimination on grounds of religion or belief is regulated in a separate Directive.[62] As discussed above, the concept of racial origin is inherently problematic, so this seems a limited vehicle for capturing the meaning of racism. Instead, ethnic origin is likely to be the centre of judicial scrutiny in interpreting the scope of the EC Directive.

The category of ethnic origin sits comfortably with a strategy designed to combat cultural racism. Ethnicity captures a range of cultural variables that leads to internal or external perception of difference. This view has been affirmed by

56 Art 1(1). 57 para I(1)(b), ECRI (n 51 above).

58 Bonilla-Silva (n 30 above) 475.

59 C Lynch, 'Racism in Europe—ENAR Shadow Report 2005' (Brussels: European Network Against Racism, 2006) 7.

60 Modood (n 24 above) 247. 61 Art 3(2).

62 Council Directive (EC) 2000/78 establishing a general framework for equal treatment in employment and occupation [2000] OJ L303/16. This Directive prohibits discrimination on grounds of religion or belief, disability, age, and sexual orientation, but only in respect of employment and vocational training.

the European Court of Human Rights. In *Timishev v Russia*, the Court considered alleged discrimination by Russian security services against persons of Chechen ethnicity. It took the opportunity to offer the following definition:

> Ethnicity and race are related and overlapping concepts. Whereas the notion of race is rooted in the idea of biological classification of human beings into subspecies according to morphological features such as skin colour or facial characteristics, ethnicity has its origin in the idea of societal groups marked by common nationality, tribal affiliation, religious faith, shared language, or cultural and traditional origins and backgrounds.[63]

Interestingly, this definition explicitly acknowledges the interaction of nationality and religion in the construction of ethnicity. Pinning down the limits to ethnicity has troubled courts and law-makers in various Member States. In the UK, Sikhs[64] and Jews[65] have been accepted as ethnic groups, whereas Rastafarians[66] have not. In the Netherlands, case law from the Equal Treatment Commission has recognized that discrimination related to ethnic origin can cover Jews[67] and, in certain circumstances, Rastafarians and Muslims.[68]

The importance of identifying the groups protected by anti-racism laws is perhaps most significant with a view to combating institutional racism. This shifts the focus away from sanctioning individual unlawful acts (although this is still required), towards tackling patterns of inequality. This implies an identification of those groups which currently experience unequal outcomes and in respect of which interventions to redress inequalities are needed. Within EU official documents, the term 'ethnic minorities' is often adopted as a catch-all label for those groups in society which experience inequality arising from racism. For example, beginning in 1999, the EU Employment Guidelines have identified 'ethnic minorities' within the category of groups vulnerable to disadvantage in the labour market.[69] Yet, the scope of this expression is not always clear. A 1996 comparative study of anti-racism policies for the European Foundation for the Improvement of Working and Living Conditions found a great variation in the terms used to refer to those vulnerable to racism (ethnic minorities, immigrants, foreigners) which overlapped with differences between national policy approaches to racism.[70]

[63] para 55, *Timishev v Russia* (2007) 44 EHRR 37.
[64] *Mandla v Dowell Lee* [1983] 2 AC 548, HL.
[65] *Seide v Gillette Industries Ltd* [1980] IRLR 427, EAT.
[66] *Dawkins v Department of the Environment* [1993] IRLR 284, CA.
[67] Opinion 1998/48, Equal Treatment Commission.
[68] Opinion 1998/57, Equal Treatment Commission. See further, M Gijzen, *Selected Issues in Equal Treatment Law: A Multi-layered Comparison of European, English and Dutch Law* (Antwerp: Intersentia, 2006) 317.
[69] Guideline 9, Council Resolution on the 1999 Employment Guidelines [1999] OJ C69/2. See further Ch 5.
[70] J Wrench, Preventing racism at the workplace—a report on 16 European countries (Luxembourg: OOPEC, 1996) 7–10.

D. Groups Vulnerable to Racism

Compiling a list of groups vulnerable to racism in Europe is a potentially vast task and it could quickly become a rather arid discussion. This section does not, therefore, aim to provide an exhaustive taxonomy, but instead to identify some key differences between the categories of persons vulnerable to racism. These differences will have implications for determining the appropriate legal and policy responses. All European states contain some elements of ethnic diversity, yet the source and nature of this diversity vary greatly. Kymlicka proposes a basic distinction between historic national minorities and migrant communities (he calls the latter 'ethnic groups').[71] Whilst both are vulnerable to discrimination on grounds of their ethnicity, there are important differences in the context in which this occurs and the way in which it is manifested.

Kymlicka defines national minorities as 'groups that formed complete and functioning societies on their historic homeland prior to being incorporated into a larger state'.[72] These can be further distinguished between national minorities with an ethnic 'kin' state[73] (such as Polish minorities in Lithuania, Danish minorities in Germany, or Hungarian minorities in Romania) and those groups almost wholly contained within a broader state, such as Sami in Finland or Catalans in Spain. This handful of examples illustrates that national minorities can be found in both western and eastern Europe. Nevertheless, the sensitivity of the European Union to the situation of national minorities can be linked to the 2004 and 2007 enlargements.[74] In some central and eastern European states, national minorities constitute a very significant proportion of the population.[75]

Migrant communities can also be found across the EU Member States. In 2007, the Commission estimated that there were 18.5 million third country nationals resident in the EU.[76] The relative size of this population group varies considerably across the Member States, ranging from 0.1% of the population of Slovakia and Poland to 8.4% in Estonia and Spain (see Table 1.1). There are also significant differences in the extent to which these minorities have become established components of the domestic society. In some states, such as the UK and France, post-war immigrant communities have been present for several

[71] W Kymlicka, *Multicultural Citizenship* (Oxford: OUP, 1995) 10.

[72] W Kymlicka, 'Western political theory and ethnic relations in Eastern Europe' in W Kymlicka and M Opalski (eds), *Can Liberal Pluralism be Exported? Western Political Theory and Ethnic Relations in Eastern Europe* (Oxford: OUP, 2001) 13, 23.

[73] ibid 64.

[74] G Sasse, 'EU Conditionality and Minority Rights: Translating the Copenhagen Criterion into Policy' EUI Working Papers, RSCAS No 2005/16 (Florence: European University Institute, 2005); B de Witte, 'Politics versus law in the EU's approach to ethnic minorities' RSC No 2000/4, EUI Working Papers (Florence: European University Institute, 2000).

[75] eg in Slovakia, the Hungarian minority forms around 10% of the population: Commission, 'Equality, diversity and enlargement' (Luxembourg: OOPEC, 2003) 104.

[76] Commission, 'Third annual report on migration and integration' COM (2007) 512, 3.

Table 1.1 Proportion of working age non-EU nationals and foreign-born nationals relative to total working age population, 2005

Member State	Non-EU nationals	Foreign-born nationals
Austria	7.1	5.9
Belgium	2.8	6.2
Cyprus	7.4	3.6
Czech Republic	0.4	1.2
Denmark	2.5	2.5
Estonia	8.4	4.6
Finland	0.9	1.3
France	3.6	6.3
Hungary	0.5	1.2
Germany	5.4	7.9
Greece	5.3	2.1
Ireland	2.7	4
Italy	4.1[a]	n/a
Latvia	(0.4)	10.9
Lithuania	(0.4)	3
Luxembourg	3.2	3.5
Malta	1.7	2.3
Netherlands	2.6	9
Poland	0.1	0.5
Portugal	2.6	4.1
Spain	8.4	n/a
Slovakia	(0.1)	0.7
Slovenia	(0.4)	7.7
Sweden	3.1	11.5
UK	4	4.8
EU10	0.5	1.5
EU15	4	4.6
EU25	3.4	4.1

[a] Data for Italy concern the entire population and are taken from ISTAT, 'La presenza straniera in Italia: caratteristiche socio-demografiche' (Rome: ISTAT, 2007) 35.

Notes: Data in brackets indicate lack of reliability due to small sample size. Data were not available for Bulgaria and Romania.

Adapted from: Commission, 'Employment in Europe 2006' (Luxembourg: OOPEC, 2006) 214.

generations and in many cases have acquired nationality of the host state. For example, 11.5% of the working age population in Sweden are 'foreign-born' Swedish nationals (see Table 1.1). As immigration is a dynamic phenomenon, new communities are steadily being created, whilst old communities may be altered by fresh sources of migration. In this light, it is important to recognize diversity within migrant groups. The situation of a second generation Pakistani woman holding British nationality may be very different from that of a Pakistani man recently arrived on a temporary work permit. Finding an appropriate all-encompassing term to refer to such groups is difficult in a multilingual European context.[77] Whilst 'foreigners', 'immigrants', or 'migrants' may be common terms in many European countries, these labels can be regarded as inappropriate for those descendants of migrants who are now EU citizens and may have lived their entire lives within the EU. At the other end of the spectrum, in the UK, the nuanced term 'black and minority ethnic' is frequently used. Yet this has less resonance in a European context.[78] Whilst recognizing its limitations, this book will generally use the term 'ethnic minority' to encompass both migrants and descendants of migrants.[79]

Not all groups vulnerable to ethnic discrimination fit neatly within the two categories discussed above. Notably, Roma communities, who have been described as Europe's largest ethnic minority,[80] appear to straddle both categories.[81] Historically, the Roma are traced back to migration from the Indian sub-continent in a period between the eleventh and fifteenth centuries.[82] Some present-day Roma communities are nomadic, but equally many are now settled communities. Within individual states, there is often diversity within the Roma population; in Italy, for example, there are both established communities of long historical standing, and Roma migrants coming from the Balkans since the 1990s.[83] The size of the Roma population varies considerably across the Member States, although the exact figures are often a matter of debate (see Table 1.2).

There is some inconsistency between EU states on whether Roma constitute a national minority and, accordingly, are entitled to benefit from the specific legal protections accorded to such groups. Traditionally, many eastern European states denied Roma access to national minority status, placing them in the less privileged legal category of 'ethnic minority'.[84] The relevance of this debate to anti-racism policies lies in the strategies adopted to combat inequality. In some

[77] S Allen and M Macey, 'Race and ethnicity in the European context' (1990) 41 *British Journal of Sociology* 375.

[78] C Neveu, 'Is "black" an exportable category to mainland Europe? Race and citizenship in a European context' in J Rex and B Drury (eds), *Ethnic Mobilization in a Multi-cultural Europe* (Aldershot: Averbury, 1994) 97.

[79] As discussed below in relation to the Roma, some 'historic' national minorities were also originally migrants and the two categories are not always clear-cut. Migrant generally refers here to migration since the Second World War.

[80] Commission, 'Equality and non-discrimination in an enlarged European Union' COM (2004) 379, 20.

[81] P Barsa, 'Ethnocultural justice in East European states and the case of Czech Roma' in W Kymlicka and M Opalski (eds), *Can Liberal Pluralism be Exported? Western Political Theory and Ethnic Relations in Eastern Europe* (Oxford: OUP, 2001) 243, 254.

[82] Commission, 'The situation of Roma in an enlarged European Union' (Luxembourg: OOPEC, 2004) 7. See further, A Bancroft, *Roma and Gypsy-Travellers in Europe—Modernity, Race, Space and Exclusion* (Aldershot: Ashgate, 2005).

[83] N Sigona, 'Locating "the Gypsy problem". The Roma in Italy: stereotyping, labelling and "nomad camps"' (2005) 31 *Journal of Ethnic and Migration Studies* 741, 744.

[84] R Guglielmo and T W Walters, 'Migrating towards minority status: shifting European policy towards Roma' (2005) 43 JCMS 763, 765. It should be noted that 'ethnic minority' in this context does not extend to contemporary immigration.

Table 1.2 National estimates of the Roma population

Member State	Roma population
Austria	15–20,000
Belgium	10–15,000
Bulgaria	371,356
Cyprus	700
Czech Republic	32,903–200,000[a]
Denmark	2,000–4,500
Finland	5–8,000
France	250–300,000
Germany	85–120,000
Greece	250–300,000
Hungary	570,000 (higher and lower estimates also exist)
Ireland	20–27,000
Italy	85–120,000
Lithuania	2,571
Luxembourg	200–500
Netherlands	30–40,000
Poland	12,900–20,000[a]
Portugal	40,000
Romania	1,400,000–2,500,000 (lower estimates also exist)
Slovakia	90,000–350,000[a]
Slovenia	3,246–10,000[a]
Spain	90–100,000 (some estimates are up to 600,000)
Sweden	15–20,000
UK	200–300,000

[a] The lower figure is taken from the national census, but the real figure is believed to be much higher.

Note: No data were available for Estonia, Latvia, or Malta. The data derive from a variety of sources and from different periods since the mid-1990s.

Reproduced with permission from: European Commission, Directorate-General for Employment, Social Affairs and Equal Opportunities, 'Gender inequalities in the risks of poverty and social exclusion for disadvantaged groups in thirty European countries' (Luxembourg: OOPEC, 2006) 101–102.

instances, measures normally associated with national minorities have been extended to Roma. For example, in Slovenia, Roma representatives have been guaranteed seats within certain local municipalities, even though they are not officially classified as a national minority.[85] There are also examples of positive action schemes which might be more typically associated with ethnic minorities. Notably, the European Commission has an internship programme reserved to Roma.[86] The combination of such initiatives suggests a *sui generis* status for the

[85] M Tratar and M Hot, 'Report on measures to combat discrimination: Slovenia' (Brussels: European Commission, 2007) 50.

[86] <http://ec.europa.eu/employment_social/fundamental_rights/roma/rtrain_en.htm> accessed 16 June 2008.

Roma. Indeed, both the Parliamentary Assembly of the Council of Europe[87] and the European Parliament[88] have proposed recognizing the Roma as a 'European minority', whilst the European Court of Human Rights has described the Roma as 'a specific type of disadvantaged and vulnerable minority'.[89]

Jewish communities are another example of a group which does not easily fit within the dichotomy between national and ethnic minorities. Jewish communities have a long historical tradition within Europe, but their territorial location was shattered by the Holocaust. It is evident that the manifestation of racism in respect of Jewish people is quite distinct from, for example, its form in respect of the Roma. Anti-Semitism is characterized by negative stereotyping of Jewish people, including linking Jews to conspiracy theories about the exercise of power.[90] It remains intertwined with Holocaust denial or trivialization.[91] Moreover, the intensity of anti-Semitic acts appears to be partially related to the prevailing political situation within the Middle East.[92]

This section has focused on the diversity hidden behind broad terms such as 'ethnic minority'. Groups vulnerable to discrimination because of their ethnic origins differ in their characteristics and this needs to be taken into account when designing anti-racism law and policy. Whilst the principal distinction may be between national minorities and ethnic minorities, not all groups are easily placed within these categories. Aside from Jewish people and the Roma, it is also possible to point to other groups that do not fit within this typology, such as Russian minorities in the Baltic states.[93] This diversity leads some commentators to refer to 'racisms', rather than a monolithic notion of a single racism.[94] This pluralistic approach opens the door to recognizing also the interaction of race with other variables, such as gender or disability. This is considered further in the next section.

E. Intersectionality and Racism

One of the criticisms of terms such as 'ethnic group' is that they suggest a uniformity of experience, with all members assumed to share similar characteristics. Yet an individual's ethnic origin will be combined with their other personal characteristics such as gender, age, physical/mental abilities, and sexual orientation. It is almost trite to say that a black woman can face both racial and sexual discrimination, an idea frequently summarized in the umbrella term

[87] para 2, Recommendation 1203 (1993) on Gypsies in Europe, 44th Ordinary Session.

[88] para 2, Resolution on the situation of Roma in the European Union [2006] OJ C45E/129.

[89] para 182, *DH and others v The Czech Republic* [GC] (2008) 47 EHRR 3.

[90] McMaster (n 26 above) 212–16.

[91] European Union Monitoring Centre on Racism and Xenophobia (EUMC), 'Antisemitism: summary overview of the situation in the European Union 2001–2005' (Vienna: EUMC, 2006) 19.

[92] ibid.

[93] Kymlicka (n 72 above) 76–9.

[94] eg S Fredman, 'Equality: a new generation?' (2001) 30 ILJ 145, 148.

'multiple discrimination'. This can be broken down into several strands. To the extent that different forms of discrimination operate concurrently, then this may be described as 'additive discrimination'.[95] For example, if there are barriers to promotion for both women and ethnic minorities, then a black woman faces a dual set of barriers. This is the addition of ethnicity *plus* gender. Whilst this notion is relatively straightforward, the more complex concept is that of 'intersectional discrimination'.[96] This suggests that the combination of different forms of inequality results in a distinct experience.[97] Therefore, the situation of a black woman is not akin to the sum of a white woman and a black man. This can be attributed to a number of factors. Intersectionality may give rise to specific stereotypes, such as the assumption that women wearing a headscarf will lack self-confidence or that young Muslim men pose a security risk.[98] Alternatively, intersectionality can expose tensions within minority communities.[99] For instance, lesbian, gay, and bisexual (LGB) persons from minority communities can find themselves distant both from LGB communities and from their own ethnic community.[100] An empirical study of South Asian disabled women in the UK emphasized the barriers to independence for such women.[101] Physical barriers sometimes made it difficult to participate in collective religious events in the community, whilst there were considerable social barriers for a disabled woman to marry within the community and this heightened dependence on parental support.

Whether characterized as additive or intersectional, there is a growing body of evidence which indicates heightened levels of disadvantage for those vulnerable to multiple discrimination. Considerable research on the interaction of gender and ethnicity was undertaken by the former British Equal Opportunities Commission (EOC). This revealed, *inter alia*, higher unemployment rates, lower pay rates, and increased occupational segregation for women from ethnic minority communities.[102] Very substantial differences existed between the situations of

[95] S Hannett, 'Equality at the intersections: the legislative and judicial failure to tackle multiple discrimination' (2003) 23 OJLS 65, 68; A McColgan, 'Reconfiguring discrimination law' [2007] PL 74, 83.

[96] ibid.

[97] K Crenshaw, 'Demarginalizing the intersection of race and sex: a black feminist critique of antidiscrimination doctrine, feminist theory, and antiracist politics' in A Phillips (ed), *Feminism and Politics* (Oxford: OUP, 1998) 314, 315.

[98] Commission, 'Tackling multiple discrimination—practices, policies and laws' (Luxembourg: OOPEC, 2007) 17.

[99] S Fredman, 'Double trouble: cumulative discrimination and EU law' (2005) 2 *European Anti-Discrimination Law Review* 13.

[100] F Colgan, C Creegan, A McKearney, and T Wright, 'Lesbian, gay and bisexual workers: equality, diversity and inclusion in the workplace' (London: Comparative Organisation and Equality Research Centre, London Metropolitan University, 2006) para 4.9.

[101] Y Hussain, 'South Asian disabled women: negotiating identities' [2005] *The Sociological Review* 522.

[102] L Buckner, S Yeandle, and S Botcherby, 'Ethnic minority women and local labour markets' (Manchester: EOC, 2007).

women from different ethnic communities; whilst Black Caribbean women in England had an economic activity rate of 73%, this figure was just 27% for Bangladeshi women.[103]

Although gender and ethnicity might be the best documented illustration of intersectionality, other ground combinations can be linked to disadvantage. The British HIV/AIDS charity, Crusaid, reported that 60% of applicants to its hardship fund were of African ethnic origin and 54% were 'at some stage in the asylum or immigration process'.[104] A 2001 study in the UK reported that Black Africans were twice as likely as white people to fear discrimination because of their HIV status.[105] Alternatively, recent research in the UK revealed differences in the treatment of children with autism according to ethnicity.[106]

Taking intersectionality into account has a number of implications for anti-racism law and policy. First, there are some grounds which are very difficult to disentangle from 'race' and ethnicity. Differences in treatment due to nationality, religion, and language are often interlinked with discrimination on grounds of ethnic origin. In many instances, direct discrimination on these grounds will constitute indirect discrimination on grounds of ethnic origin. Given the proximity between grounds such as nationality, religion, language, and ethnicity, there is a strong argument in favour of a comprehensive response in law and policy.

Other grounds are less intimately bound up with 'race' or ethnicity, but may give rise to multiple discrimination. Difficulties are likely to arise where the basic scope of anti-discrimination law varies. Currently, EC legislation prohibits discrimination in education on grounds of racial or ethnic origin,[107] but not on grounds of gender.[108] This leaves an obvious gap where multiple discrimination cannot be addressed. In contrast, EC employment discrimination legislation does cover a range of grounds: gender, racial or ethnic origin, religion or belief, disability, age, and sexual orientation. Notwithstanding the disparities between the various Directives applying to these forms of discrimination, this provides a first step in enabling multiple discrimination to be tackled. Therefore, an Asian gay man harassed on grounds of ethnic origin and sexual orientation can bring a case citing both aspects of his harassment. Yet, the fragmented legislative framework does not facilitate an integrated analysis of such complaints. Roseberry cites

[103] ibid 20.

[104] Crusaid and National AIDS Trust (NAT), 'Poverty and HIV—findings from the Crusaid Hardship Fund 2006' (London: Crusaid/NAT, 2006) 6–7.

[105] Terence Higgins Trust (THT), 'Prejudice, discrimination and HIV' (London: THT, 2001) para 4.5.

[106] C Corbett and P Perepa, 'Missing out? Autism, education and ethnicity: the reality for families today' (London: The National Austistic Society, 2007).

[107] Dir 2000/43, Art 3(1)(g).

[108] Art 3(3), Council Directive (EC) 2004/113 implementing the principle of equal treatment between men and women in the access to and supply of goods and services [2004] OJ L373/37.

the experience in the United States where multi-ground discrimination claims are in practice often broken into separate components by the courts.[109]

Responding to the nuances of intersectionality also poses challenges for policy frameworks. The history of EU initiatives on equality has been characterized by a strong distinction between gender equality on the one hand, and other forms of discrimination on the other. Whilst this dichotomy has shifted in recent years, there is a risk that rigid policy boundaries hinder recognition of intersectionality. This also permeates into participation and consultation processes. An intersectional perspective will query whether NGOs representing 'women' or 'ethnic minorities' will adequately convey the perspective of minority women. Given the risk that intersectional minorities remain isolated, their voices may be difficult to reach.

F. Conclusions

The aim of this book is to assess the extent to which the objectives of combating racism and promoting equality have been mainstreamed across EU law and policy. A first step to answering that question is to deconstruct what is meant by racism, particularly in the geographic context of the EU. This chapter has illustrated that no single definition of racism can be provided; instead, it is essential to recognize the multiple forms that racism takes, varying across time and place. Specifically, racism extends beyond the notorious belief in the biological superiority of certain 'races' (scientific racism). Contemporary forms of racism encompass prejudice based on cultural difference (cultural racism), but also ethnic inequalities arising from organizational culture and practice (institutional racism). Like most legal systems, EC legislation has not attempted to provide a specific definition of racism; however, it has prohibited discrimination on grounds of 'racial or ethnic origin'. This chapter found that the concept of racial origin is inherently problematic, being grounded in the scientifically false notion that human beings can be separated into biologically distinct 'races'. Whilst the inclusion of terms such as 'race' or 'racial origin' in legislation may be necessary to ensure that protection is comprehensive, they will be generally avoided in this book. In the diverse geographic context of Europe, ethnicity and ethnic origin are arguably more resonant and are less encumbered by the ideological baggage associated with 'race'.

In the enlarged EU, discrimination on the grounds of ethnic origin potentially affects two broad categories. The term 'ethnic minorities' has been adopted to refer to migrants and their descendants, whilst the term 'national minorities' is

[109] L Roseberry, *The Limits of Employment Discrimination Law in the United States and European Community* (Copenhagen: DJØF Publishing, 1999) 337. See also, G Moon, 'Multiple discrimination—problems compounded or solutions found?' (London: Justice, 2007) 6.

used to refer to Europe's historic minorities. These categories are not hermetically sealed and it is necessary to be cognizant of groups such as Jewish and Roma Communities who are vulnerable to ethnic discrimination, but who do not fit neatly within the above dichotomy. The understanding of what constitutes an ethnic group is geographically contextual, with the European Court of Human Rights pointing to cultural markers, such as nationality, religion, and language.[110] This indicates the blurred boundary between ethnic discrimination and discrimination on grounds of such characteristics. Therefore, measures to combat racism need to take account of discrimination on related grounds, such as religion or nationality. Rather than delving into a long and arid debate about the extent to which Islamophobia is or is not racism, it seems more productive to proceed from an acknowledgement that an effective strategy for combating racism needs to address related forms of religious discrimination.

The above observations on the concept of racism and the groups most vulnerable in Europe to ethnic discrimination provide a framework against which subsequent chapters can analyze EU law and policy in this field. Nevertheless, combating racism is just one element of the objectives normally pursued by mainstreaming. The flip side of combating racism is the positive goal of achieving equality. This is particularly true in the light of the concept of institutional racism, which places the spotlight on whether equal outcomes are being ensured for ethnic minority groups. Therefore, Chapter 2 examines what is meant by equality, especially when placed in the context of combating racism.

[110] para 55, *Timishev v Russia* (2007) 44 EHRR 37.

2

Racism and Equality

The central inquiry pursued by this book is to explore the extent to which the objectives of combating racism and promoting equality have been mainstreamed across EU law and policy. Combating racism might be described as a negative objective; it concerns the repression of an unwanted phenomenon. In contrast, the objective of promoting equality offers a more positive horizon. The two objectives are inherently intertwined; equality cannot be realized where racism persists. Chapter 1 provided analysis of what the term 'racism' means in today's Europe, identifying several different forms of racism, as well as a range of groups which are especially vulnerable to racism. This chapter turns to examine the term 'equality', an altogether broader field of study. Equality is a highly contested political and philosophical concept, so this chapter can only scratch the surface of the extensive debates on this topic which exist within academic literature. In the context of the current book, the primary purpose of this chapter is to examine what the objective of equality means in the specific context of combating racism and how the different readings of equality relate to the competing concepts of racism identified in Chapter 1.

Equality is a pluralistic concept, one which is capable of bearing a number of different interpretations. In official documentation and academic literature, 'equality' is used alongside other terms, such as 'equal opportunities', 'non-discrimination', 'equal treatment', and 'diversity'. The precise meaning of these terms is often difficult to pin down, especially in the context of European research where different jurisdictions (and languages) have adopted their own forms of equality-speak. For example, in EU jargon, 'equal opportunities' traditionally equates to gender equality, whereas 'non-discrimination' is understood as discrimination based on other grounds. Theoretical critiques of equality conventionally begin with a dichotomy between *formal equality*, sometimes called individual justice, and *substantive equality*, sometimes called group justice. This chapter will consider each of these concepts, but with a specific accent on how they relate to racism. Whilst much of the debate around the formal/substantive dichotomy can be applied to various manifestations of inequality (gender, disability, age, etc), certain issues which arise are peculiar to combating racism or are at least of greater salience in this context.

A. Formal Equality

Formal equality is underpinned by ideas of consistency and rationality.[1] Consistency relates to the way in which different categories are treated. This is essentially the Aristotelian principle that 'likes should be treated alike'.[2] Equality as consistency is an approach which has widely permeated European legal orders, especially interpretations of equality within constitutional law. The Court of Justice also adopts this formula in explaining its general principle of respect for fundamental rights:

> It is in this regard settled case-law that the principle of non-discrimination requires that comparable situations must not be treated differently and that different situations must not be treated in the same way.[3]

Within anti-discrimination legislation, formal equality is principally tackled through the prohibition of direct discrimination. The standard definition of direct discrimination within EC legislation follows that found in the Racial Equality Directive: 'direct discrimination shall be taken to occur where one person is treated less favourably than another is, has been or would be treated in a comparable situation on grounds of racial or ethnic origin'.[4] Therefore, the scope of formal equality will depend upon when situations are regarded as 'comparable'. This connects to the idea of equality as rationality. If, in considering job applicants, an employer rejects a person because of her ethnic origin, then this will normally be contrary to formal equality. A difference in ethnic origin is not relevant to her ability to do the job, so it is viewed as irrational to take this into consideration.

Equality as consistency and rationality holds an initial appeal in combating racism. By stripping away irrelevant characteristics, it promises to focus on individual abilities and merit.[5] The emphasis on rationality is consonant with the market logic of efficiency. Moreover, perceived 'race' and ethnicity are characteristics which are rarely connected to an individual's ability to do a job or to use a service; consequently, the application of formal equality is less contentious than in respect of other grounds, such as age or disability, where the suspect

[1] C McCrudden, *Buying Social Justice—Equality, Government Procurement, and Legal Change* (Oxford: OUP, 2007) 513; E Howard, 'The European Year of Equal Opportunities for All—2007: is the EU moving away from a formal idea of equality?' (2008) 14 ELJ 168, 170.

[2] D Schiek, 'Torn between arithmetic and substantive equality? Perspectives on equality in German labour law' (2002) 18 IJCLLIR 149, 150; L Waddington and A Hendriks, 'The expanding concept of employment discrimination in Europe: from direct and indirect discrimination to reasonable accommodation discrimination' (2002) 18 IJCLLIR 403, 406.

[3] para 31, Case C-148/02 *Garcia Avello v Belgium* [2003] ECR I-11613.

[4] Art 2(2)(a), Council Directive (EC) 2000/43 implementing the principle of equal treatment between persons irrespective of racial or ethnic origin [2000] OJ L180/22.

[5] C McCrudden, 'Theorizing European equality law' in C Costello and E Barry (eds), *Equality in Diversity—The New Equality Directives* (Dublin: Irish Centre for European Law, 2003) 1, 21.

characteristic can, sometimes, impact upon a person's capacity.[6] Considering the concepts of racism identified in Chapter 1, formal equality correlates with opposition to scientific racism, by clearly rejecting the notion that 'race' can be relevant to determining individual intellect and ability. It also serves to counter cultural racism. Formal equality presupposes that cultural differences are normally not relevant considerations and that individuals should not be treated less favourably on this basis.

Pursuing formal equality has significant consequences for how claims from ethnic and national minorities are approached. Its emphasis on according the *same* treatment tends towards an assimilationist model of integration.[7] Minorities will be entitled to be protected from less favourable treatment because of their ethnic origins, but claims for different or separate treatment are unlikely to be successful. Formal equality emphasizes the protection of individuals from irrational discrimination, rather than recognition of collective disadvantage. France is often held up as the paradigm of this approach, where the Republican model of integration rests on the universal equality of all citizens under the Constitution.[8] Accordingly, France has not signed the Council of Europe's Framework Convention on National Minorities (FCNM).[9]

The limits of formal equality

The simple attractiveness of formal equality rests on its sense of justice through the identical treatment of individuals irrespective of background. Whilst appearing fair and adequate on the surface, this conceals its limited utility for tackling the roots of inequality. It assumes that the pre-existing norm (in respect of which equal treatment is granted) is inherently neutral.[10] A good illustration is workplace rules about personal appearance and dress, which often reflect the conventions of the majority ethnic group. The Irish police previously had a 'no beards' rule. Whilst this applied in the same way to all officers, it had the effect of excluding some ethnic groups, in particular Sikhs, where growing a beard was a cultural norm.[11] Formal equality fails to place the norm into a wider social

[6] M Bell and L Waddington, 'Reflecting on inequalities in European equality law' (2003) 28 ELR 349, 359; E Howard, 'The case for a considered hierarchy of discrimination grounds in EU law' (2006) 13 MJ 443.

[7] B Parekh, 'Integrating minorities' in T Blackstone, B Parekh, and P Saunders (eds), *Race Relations in Britain – A Developing Agenda* (London: Routledge, 1998) 1, 2.

[8] M Wieviorka, 'Racisme, racialisation et ethnicisation en France' (1996) 1195 *Hommes & Migrations* 27, 33; D Borrillo, 'Les instruments juridiques français et européens dans la mise en place du principe d'égalité et de non-discrimination' [2002] *Revue français des affaires sociales* 113.

[9] FCNM (Strasbourg, 1 February 1995; CETS 157). Within the EU, Belgium, Greece, and Luxembourg have signed but not ratified the FCNM.

[10] S Fredman, *Discrimination Law* (Oxford: OUP, 2002) 94.

[11] J Burke, 'Move to allow gardaí to wear religious head gear' *Sunday Tribune* (Dublin 14 November 2004) 7. See later in this chapter, however, on the refusal to allow Sikh officers to wear turbans.

context in order to assess its real consistency with equality.[12] Dress codes that require men to be clean-shaven or women to wear skirts often have little functional rationale, but reflect cultural assumptions about what constitutes a tidy or attractive appearance. Although such policies or requirements can, in principle, be complied with by all persons (a Sikh man could shave off his beard), formal equality fails to take into account their exclusionary effect in practice. This blindness to the context of seemingly neutral practices also ignores the effects of a history of socio-economic inequality. This is most striking in relation to Roma communities, who have experienced substantial educational disadvantage.[13] For example, a study in Spain found that 70% of Roma over 15 were either completely or functionally illiterate.[14] Inequality in educational outcomes means that Roma are often not in a position to compete equally in the labour market. Even if formal equality succeeded in stripping away irrational anti-Roma prejudice, this would not result in equal labour market participation due to the legacy of educational disadvantage.

The flip side of equal treatment of comparable situations is the requirement that 'different situations must not be treated in the same way unless such treatment is objectively justified'.[15] This holds greater potential to respond positively to difference. In *Thlimmenos*,[16] the European Court of Human Rights found a violation of Articles 9 (freedom of religion) and 14 (non-discrimination) of the European Convention on Human Rights (ECHR) where a Jehovah's Witness was excluded from chartered accountancy because of his criminal record. Whilst not contesting this general rule, the Court emphasized that his case was distinguished because his criminal conviction was due to a refusal to perform military service based on a religious belief in pacifism. It held that the right to non-discrimination is 'violated when States without an objective and reasonable justification fail to treat differently persons whose situations are significantly different'.[17] Following this logic, the European Committee of Social Rights (ECSR)[18] has held that simply treating Roma communities in the same way as the general population will not deliver equality. As a result of socio-economic disadvantage and, in some cases, the continued pursuit of a nomadic lifestyle,

[12] B Parekh, 'Equality in a multicultural society' in J Franklin (ed), *Equality* (London: Institute for Public Policy Research, 1997) 142.

[13] Commission, 'The situation of Roma in an enlarged European Union' (Luxembourg: OOPEC, 2004) 18–20.

[14] B Sánchez-Rubio, 'A comparative research study on Roma and employment in Spain' (2006) 16 *ENARgy* 27.

[15] para 57, Case C-300/04 *Eman and Sevinger v College van burgemeester en wethouders van Den Haag* [2006] ECR I-8055.

[16] *Thlimmenos v Greece* (2001) 31 EHRR 15.

[17] ibid para 44.

[18] The Committee is the specialist supervisory body which makes legal assessments of national compliance with obligations under the European Social Charter (Turin, 18 October 1961; CETS 35) and the European Social Charter (Revised) (Strasbourg, 3 May 1996; CETS 163).

there can be a need for states to treat Roma differently in matters such as the consequences of unlawful occupation of land.[19]

The difficulty with the above approach is the absence of any guiding principle to determine what type of different treatment should be provided once it is determined that the individual or group is in a different situation.[20] The case of *DH v The Czech Republic*[21] illustrates the risk that difference is used to reinforce disadvantage. This case concerned a group of Roma children who had been placed in 'special schools', a type of school intended for children with learning disabilities. Statistical evidence demonstrated that Roma children were much more likely to be placed in special schools than non-Roma children. In some special schools, 80–90% of the children were Roma. When the case first reached a chamber of the European Court of Human Rights, it held that there was no breach of Article 14 ECHR. The majority judgment emphasized that the children had been individually assessed by educational specialists and their educational needs were deemed to require allocation to special schools.[22] As these children were viewed as 'different' from the standard, then it was legitimate to treat them differently. This decision was overturned on appeal to the Grand Chamber of the Court;[23] however, it indicates the risk of an unguided principle of treating different situations differently.

B. Substantive Equality

Formal equality has been criticized for being relatively empty in terms of its underlying values and objectives.[24] The emphasis on consistency and rationality tends to focus on the situation of individuals and draws no distinction between majority and minority groups. In this respect, formal equality is symmetrical; discrimination against a white European is viewed in the same terms as discrimination against a black African. Substantive equality takes a different approach. Its goal is to eliminate inequality. This encompasses socio-economic disadvantage, but also cultural recognition and representation within public arenas (such as media and government).[25] The idea of moving beyond formal

[19] In *European Roma Rights Centre (ERRC) v Greece* (2005) 41 EHRR SE14, the ECSR noted that there was a shortage of suitable accommodation for Roma and consequently they were often forced into illegal occupation of land. Therefore, when evicted, Roma were left with no alternative accommodation. The Committee concluded that special measures were required to take into account the actual situation of Roma (paras 19–20). See also, *ERRC v Italy* (2006) 43 EHRR SE7; *ERRC v Bulgaria* (2008) 46 EHRR SE10.

[20] Schiek (n 2 above) 150.

[21] *DH and others v The Czech Republic* (2006) 43 EHRR 41.

[22] ibid para 49.

[23] *DH and others v The Czech Republic* [GC] (2008) 47 EHRR 3. See further Ch 1.

[24] L Betten, 'New equality provisions in European law: some thoughts on the fundamental value of equality as a legal principle' in K Economides, L Betten, J Bridge, A Tettenborn, and V Shrubsall (eds), *Fundamental Values* (Oxford: Hart Publishing, 2000) 69, 73.

[25] S Fredman, 'The future of equality in Britain' EOC Working Paper Series No 5 (Manchester: EOC, 2002) 10.

equality is conveyed in EC legislation by referring to the goal of 'full equality in practice'.[26]

Substantive equality entails a shift away from the individualistic focus of formal equality, towards an emphasis on collective experiences of inequality. This acknowledges the rather obvious fact that discrimination does not occur against random individuals, instead it is predominantly experienced by individuals sharing similar characteristics. The consequences of discrimination are, accordingly, demonstrated through evidence of group inequalities, be it in terms of lower educational attainment, weaker performance in the labour market or under-representation in public institutions. This concern with group inequalities illustrates contiguity between substantive equality and the concept of institutional racism, which is also focused on group outcomes.[27] Moreover, the diagnosis of discrimination as a problem experienced on a collective basis means that substantive equality places a priority on tackling the sources of group inequality.

Within anti-discrimination legislation, a first step in this direction is often the prohibition of indirect discrimination.[28] Therefore, practices which apply equally to all persons, but which put certain groups at a particular disadvantage, can be held to be unlawful. The prohibition of indirect discrimination is normally moderated, though, by the possibility to justify the measure or practice where it is an appropriate way of pursuing a legitimate aim.[29] This opens the door for existing norms and structures to be challenged based on their effects in practice. For example, Amnesty International has documented the widespread use of Estonian language requirements for jobs in both the public and private sector in Estonia.[30] These requirements place at a disadvantage persons from minority communities who do not speak Estonian as a first language; this will principally affect the 25% of the population from the Russian-speaking minority. Of course, there will be many jobs within Estonia where being able to speak Estonian is an objectively justified requirement. Nevertheless, Amnesty argues that this is difficult to sustain in towns where the great majority of the population are Russian-speaking and it might not be necessary in practice to be fully competent in Estonian.[31]

Indirect discrimination claims will frequently be the mechanism through which claims for accommodation of cultural diversity are played out. In the context of combating racism, the extent to which substantive equality is pursued

[26] Art 5, Dir 2000/43. This expression was drawn from EC Treaty, Art 141(4) on positive action in the context of gender equality.

[27] See Ch 1.

[28] D Schiek, 'Indirect discrimination' in D Schiek, L Waddington, and M Bell (eds), *Cases, Materials and Text on National, Supranational and International Non-discrimination Law* (Oxford: Hart Publishing, 2007) 323.

[29] Art 2(2)(b), Dir 2000/43.

[30] Amnesty International, 'Linguistic minorities in Estonia: discrimination must end' (Amnesty International, 2006) <http://web.amnesty.org/library/index/engeur510022006> accessed 16 June 2008.

[31] ibid para 5.

will therefore be closely related to the dominant model of integration vis-à-vis ethnic and national minorities. At the national level, the responses of European states have varied greatly. Some have adopted an approach premised on recognition of difference, thereby accepting the prima facie legitimacy of challenges to traditional cultural norms. In the UK, multiculturalism has been the prime orientation of law and policy since the 1970s, albeit increasingly contested in recent years. An illustration of how this fits with a substantive equality perspective can be seen in the disposition to accommodate turban-wearing by Sikhs. Therefore, exemptions have been provided from obligations to wear safety headgear[32] or motorcycle helmets.[33] In contrast, the French Conseil d'Etat rejected a challenge in 2006 from a Sikh association to the requirement that a driving licence required the submission of a photograph of the individual with nothing covering the head.[34] Similarly, in 2007, the Irish police refused permission for a potential Sikh recruit to wear a turban alongside the official uniform.[35] Such contrasting approaches indicate the difficulty of unravelling the meaning of equality from broader policies relating to immigration.

Finding a resolution of such disputes at EU level poses a particular dilemma. EU policy contains only a rather loose consensus about how the integration of minorities should be approached (see further Chapter 7). Nevertheless, Shaw draws attention to the signals provided in the EU Charter of Fundamental Rights.[36] The right to non-discrimination found in Article 21 is immediately followed by Article 22, which states: 'The Union shall respect cultural, religious and linguistic diversity'. Shaw suggests that this offers 'the possible seeds of a multicultural vision for the Union'.[37] The Treaty of Lisbon, should it be ratified, gently strengthens this direction. Article 2 of the Treaty on European Union will state:

> The Union is founded on the values of respect for human dignity, freedom, democracy, equality, the rule of law and respect for human rights, *including the rights of persons belonging to minorities* (emphasis added).[38]

Two points flow from this provision. First, it makes it highly difficult to maintain that minority groups do not exist within the Union and, second, the wording tends to imply that persons belonging to minorities may have specific rights which are distinct from those of the majority population.

[32] Reg 26(1) of the Employment Equality (Religion of Belief) Regulations, SI 2003/1660, specifies that requiring a turban-wearing Sikh to wear a safety helmet is indirect discrimination that cannot be justified.

[33] Parekh (n 12 above) 128.

[34] *Association United Sikhs and Mann Singh*, Case no 289947, 6 March 2006. The Conseil d'Etat held that the rule was justified on grounds of public security, such as the prevention of fraud.

[35] C O'Brien, 'Gardaí deny turban ban is based on race or religion' *Irish Times* (Dublin, 24 August 2007) 7.

[36] J Shaw, 'Mainstreaming equality and diversity in European Union law and policy' in J Holder and C O'Cinneide (eds), *Current Legal Problems 2005. Vol 58* (Oxford: OUP, 2006) 255.

[37] ibid 292.

[38] Consolidated version of the Treaty on European Union [2008] OJ C115/17.

Another significant aspect of substantive equality is its asymmetrical perspective.[39] Group disadvantage is, by definition, not experienced in the same way by all groups. Therefore, substantive equality endorses the legitimacy of measures designed to end inequalities through conferring advantages on disadvantaged groups. At this point, the formal equality and substantive equality models come into conflict.[40] Take, for example, the European Commission's programme of internships for Roma.[41] Both Roma and non-Roma can compete for the general internships, but Roma are given an additional opportunity to compete for a small number of reserved internships. This conflicts with formal equality, because (superficially) non-Roma have less opportunity to obtain an internship than Roma. Yet, the context of socio-economic inequality amongst Roma implies that, in practice, they face much greater hurdles in order to obtain an internship in the Commission, given their weaker starting point. Setting aside a limited number of internships may be the only way to guarantee some access to internships for Roma and to challenge a self-perpetuating cycle of exclusion. Although there is a great variety of terminology in this area, at EU level, these sorts of compensatory measures have been labelled 'positive action'. Article 5 of the Racial Equality Directive provides:

> With a view to ensuring full equality in practice, the principle of equal treatment shall not prevent any Member State from maintaining or adopting specific measures to prevent or compensate for disadvantages linked to racial or ethnic origin.

Most European states accept the role for public policy intervention in order to combat ethnic inequalities; dedicated initiatives for Roma are a common example, especially in central and eastern Europe.[42] Nevertheless, positive action often remains contentious. The Slovak Constitutional Court, for example, annulled a provision in domestic anti-discrimination law which merely incorporated almost identical language to Article 5 of the Racial Equality Directive.[43] Stronger forms of positive action, sometimes referred to as 'positive discrimination', have been largely eschewed within Europe (in relation to ethnic minorities).[44] For instance, Uppsala Law School in Sweden sought to promote ethnic minority participation by reserving 10% of places for students where both parents were born outside Sweden. This measure was eventually held by the Swedish

[39] M Gijzen, *Selected Issues in Equal Treatment Law: A Multi-layered Comparison of European, English and Dutch Law* (Antwerp: Intersentia, 2006) 65.

[40] H Collins, 'Discrimination, equality and social inclusion' (2003) 66 MLR 16, 17.

[41] <http://ec.europa.eu/employment_social/fundamental_rights/roma/rtrain_en.htm> accessed 16 June 2008.

[42] Notably, nine countries in central and south-eastern Europe are participating in the 'Decade of Roma Inclusion' programme: <http://www.romadecade.org> accessed 16 June 2008.

[43] O de Schutter, 'Positive action' in D Schiek, L Waddington, and M Bell (eds), *Cases, Materials and Text on National, Supranational and International Non-discrimination Law* (Oxford: Hart Publishing, 2007) 757, 830.

[44] C O'Cinneide, 'Positive action and the limits of existing law' (2006) 13 MJ 351, 355.

Supreme Court to be unlawful direct discrimination.[45] In contrast, in the United States, there has been greater openness to the use of preferential treatment schemes, both in the labour market and in other contexts, notably higher education.[46] Over time, the US Supreme Court's attitude to positive action (normally referred to there as 'affirmative action') has shifted, generally in a more restrictive direction.[47] It has, though, approved a more flexible approach to merit. When considering the use of 'race'-based criteria in admissions to a law school, it accepted that 'race' could be taken into account in an effort to combat the under-representation of ethnic minorities.[48] The majority emphasized that positive educational benefits flowed from maintaining diversity.[49]

In part, the reluctance of European law-makers and courts to go further with positive action can be traced to the approach developed by the Court of Justice in relation to gender equality. The Court has baulked at measures conferring automatic and unconditional preferential treatment for women, at least at the point of selection for employment.[50] The Court of Justice has yet to indicate whether it will simply extend the principles of its gender equality case-law to other grounds of discrimination and to non-labour market activities. Whilst this would provide a veneer of consistency, it would neglect the underlying function of substantive equality, which is to address entrenched inequalities. The causes and manifestations of those inequalities are not identical across all grounds, or even within grounds. Ware emphasizes the link between US affirmative action programmes and the history of slavery and segregation of African Americans.[51] The rationale of compensation, as well as the difficulties in overcoming the legacy of segregation, underpinned the need for strong intervention. Based on this logic, Kymlicka argues for a nuanced approach to positive action as a means of combating racism.[52] He contrasts the situation of black Canadians and Arab Canadians. Whilst both categories are vulnerable to racism, empirical evidence

[45] A Numhauser-Henning, 'Report on measures to combat discrimination: Directives 2000/43/EC and 2000/78/EC: Sweden' (Brussels: European Commission, 2007) 16.

[46] R Dworkin, 'Bakke's case: are quotas unfair?' in B Boxill (ed), *Race and Racism* (Oxford: OUP, 2001) 297; S Fredman, 'Affirmative action at the Court of Justice: a critical analysis' in J Shaw (ed), *Social Law and Policy in an Evolving Union* (Oxford: Hart Publishing, 2000).

[47] L Ware, 'Strict scrutiny, affirmative action, and academic freedom: the University of Michigan cases' (2004) 78 *Tulane Law Review* 2097.

[48] *Grutter v Bollinger* 539 US 306, 123 S Ct 2325 (2003), *Gratz v Bollinger* 539 US 244, 123 S Ct 2411 (2003).

[49] *Grutter v Bollinger*, 333. In a subsequent case, the Supreme Court emphasized that strict scrutiny would be applied to any racial classification and declined to apply the *Grutter* principle to a scheme where 'race' was used in the allocation of children to particular high schools: *Parents involved in community schools v Seattle School District No 1 et al* 551 US, 127 S Ct 2738 (2007).

[50] eg Case C-158/97 *Badeck* [2000] ECR I-1875. See further, C Tobler, 'Positive action under the revised second equal treatment Directive' in Association française des femmes juristes and European Women Lawyers Association (eds), *L'égalité entre les femmes et hommes et la vie professionnelle—le point sur les développements actuels en Europe* (Paris: Dalloz, 2003) 59.

[51] Ware (n 47 above) 2112.

[52] W Kymlicka, *Politics in the Vernacular—Nationalism, Multiculturalism, and Citizenship* (Oxford: OUP, 2001) 197.

reveals that black Canadians experience much higher rates of disadvantage.[53] A similar picture emerges within the EU where there is evidence of significant disparities in the socio-economic experience of different ethnic minority groups. For example, in Hungary, the unemployment rate of persons of African or Arabic origin is comparable to or lower than that of the majority ethnic population. In contrast, the unemployment rate of Roma is five times higher.[54] Such findings support a case-sensitive approach when using positive action. The evidence that some EU states followed policies which systematically segregated Roma into inferior schools presents a compelling argument for positive action to overcome the legacy of disadvantage which has been created. Indeed, in this particular context, there is a stronger case for preferential treatment schemes as a means of remedying the effects of segregation.[55]

The limits of substantive equality

The discussion above has illustrated how substantive equality addresses some of the weaknesses found within formal equality. Nevertheless, it contains its own difficulties. Below three main limitations to substantive equality are examined: accommodating difference; equality of opportunity or outcome; reflecting diversity.

Accommodating difference

A first point of criticism relates to setting parameters in the accommodation of difference. Whilst substantive equality allows supposedly neutral practices to be challenged, it struggles to pinpoint when it will be appropriate to accept or reject such claims. The organization of state and society is riddled with culturally determined practices all of which are potentially open to challenge within a substantive equality framework. This ranges from requirements to speak a particular language to the dates of public holidays. Parekh argues that certain limits to difference claims can be accepted on the basis of maintaining cultural cohesion.[56] Consequently, he accepts that certain aspects of the way in which the UK is organized flow from its history as a predominantly Christian country and that equality does not compel the erasure of any trace of that cultural influence.[57] Yet, drawing these boundaries in a European context is particularly thorny. Member States hold widely varying perceptions of what constitutes a legitimate

[53] ibid 188.

[54] High Level Advisory Group of Experts on the social integration of ethnic minorities and their full participation in the labour market, 'Ethnic minorities in the labour market—an urgent call for social inclusion' (Brussels: European Commission, 2007) 38–9.

[55] B Hepple, 'Race and law in Fortress Europe' (2004) 67 MLR 1, 8; O de Schutter and A Verstichel, 'Integrating the Roma into European society: time for a new initiative' in European Centre for Minority Issues (eds), *European Yearbook of Minority Issues, Vol 4, 2004/05* (Leiden: Koninklijke Brill, 2006) 429, 432.

[56] Parekh (n 12 above) 153.

[57] ibid 147.

requirement of integration into national society as opposed to unacceptable ethnic discrimination.

In addition, substantive equality does not seem to provide any clear signpost for the relative treatment of claims from national and ethnic minorities. Many European states extend specific rights to those groups recognized as national minorities, such as an entitlement to use a minority language when dealing with public services. Typically, such rights have not been extended to ethnic minorities. The extent to which it is legitimate to distinguish between national and ethnic minorities is an important issue in the context of the enlarged EU,[58] but one which is not easily resolved by a simple reference to substantive equality.

Equality of opportunity or outcome

The previous point connects to a second criticism of substantive equality, which is the difficulty in defining its ultimate goal. In principle, the aim is to eliminate inequalities, but that is open to a number of interpretations. A distinction can be drawn between equality of opportunity and equality of outcome.[59] The former seeks to put ethnic minorities in a position to compete on an equal basis for access to jobs, educational opportunities, and services. The focus is on remedial measures, such as targeted training programmes. These do not guarantee jobs for under-represented groups. Rather, they are designed to compensate for present or past disadvantages, thereby creating a level playing field.[60] Equality of outcome instead aims to ensure the proportionate representation of all groups, for example, within the labour market.

Both equality of opportunity and equality of outcome can be difficult to pin down. In relation to equality of opportunity, it seems difficult to measure progress without using benchmarks that focus on outcomes. If certain ethnic groups remain under-represented in the labour market, then it will be hard to be confident that equality of opportunity has been secured. Yet, if equal representation is the benchmark for evaluating equality of opportunity, then this merges into the goal of equal outcomes. In essence, equality of opportunity is not concerned with securing equal outcomes; rather it seeks to ensure that any differences which remain are not attributable to discrimination. Olli and Kofod Olsen refer to the need to identify 'unjustifiable outcome gaps'; however, they acknowledge the complexity of sifting discriminatory from non-discriminatory factors in explaining differences in the socio-economic outcomes of ethnic groups.[61]

[58] R Cholewinski, 'Migrants as minorities: integration and inclusion in the enlarged European Union' (2005) JCMS 695.

[59] Howard (n 1 above) 171.

[60] S Fredman, *Human Rights Transformed—Positive Rights and Positive Duties* (Oxford: OUP, 2008) 178.

[61] E Olli and B Kofod Olsen, 'Towards common measures for discrimination: exploring possibilities for combining existing data for measuring ethnic discrimination' (Copenhagen: Centre for Combating Ethnic Discrimination and the Danish Institute of Human Rights, 2005) 95.

On the surface, equality of outcome is more straightforward, implying that all social groups should enjoy proportionate participation in the enjoyment of socio-economic goods or within decision-making bodies. Operationalizing that objective in the context of racism in Europe quickly encounters certain obstacles. First, there is an implicit need to define the groups in respect of which proportionate representation must be secured. As regards gender equality, this is comparatively straightforward as the obvious distinction is between women and men. In contrast, there is no shared definition of ethnic group within Europe. Looking at national minorities, it is telling that the FCNM foregoes any definition of national minority and experience of state reporting under the Convention has revealed starkly different national interpretations.[62] Similarly, any catalogue of ethnic groups is contingent upon both time and place. The 2001 UK census included the question: 'what is your ethnic group?' The optional answers distinguished, under the heading 'White', between 'British', 'Irish', and 'any other White background'.[63] The prominence given here to British and Irish as separate ethnic groups would have little resonance in, say, Romania. This difficulty in defining ethnic groups is connected to the broader debate on the collection of ethnic data.

Generally speaking, most European states have not systematically collected data relating to ethnic origin, be it in the context of a national census or other official datasets. Several reasons can be identified which explain the reticence of European states to collect ethnic data in a manner similar to other less controversial categories, such as gender or age. First, there is an underlying philosophical objection in those states, such as France, where the existence of ethnic minority groups remains contested.[64] This links into a wider debate around whether the collection of data reinforces a categorization mentality, whereby individuals are encouraged to think of their identity as rigidly defined according to certain ethnic boxes.[65] Ethnic categories tend to become taken-for-granted, unalterable statuses, whereas the idea of ethnicity was originally distinguished from 'race' by its rejection of a biologically determined outlook in favour of one based on socially constructed identities.[66] Second, collecting ethnic data has sometimes been interpreted as contrary to data protection legislation. The EC

[62] H Heintze, 'Article 3' in M Weller (ed), *The Rights of Minorities in Europe—A Commentary on the European Framework Convention for the Protection of National Minorities* (Oxford: OUP, 2005) 107.

[63] Commission, 'Comparative study on the collection of data to measure the extent of discrimination within the United States, Canada, Australia, the United Kingdom and the Netherlands' (Luxembourg: OOPEC, 2004) 65.

[64] A Blum, 'Resistance to identity categorization in France' in D Kertzer and D Arel (eds), *Census and Identity—The Politics of Race, Ethnicity and Language in National Censuses* (Cambridge: Cambridge University Press, 2002) 121.

[65] F Caestecker, 'Registration of allochthonous persons, the experience of Flanders' in J Cormack (ed), 'Proving discrimination: the dynamic implementation of EU anti-discrimination law—the role of specialised bodies' (Brussels: Migration Policy Group, 2003) 11, 15.

[66] See further Ch 1.

Data Protection Directive establishes a presumption that such data processing should be unlawful:

Member States shall prohibit the processing of personal data revealing racial or ethnic origin, political opinions, religious or philosophical beliefs, trade-union membership, and the processing of data concerning health or sex life.[67]

Nevertheless, there are significant exceptions to this prohibition.[68] In addition, the Directive defines 'personal data' as 'information relating to an identified or identifiable natural person'.[69] As a consequence, data which have been rendered anonymous will fall outside its scope. Although it is thus possible to organize ethnic data collection in a manner which complies with the Data Protection Directive, national legislation is sometimes more stringent or imposes procedural obstacles which are likely to deter such data collection.[70]

Finally, there are persistent concerns surrounding the potential for misuse of ethnic data. In some European states, such as the Netherlands or France, this is informed by unhappy historical echoes relating to the registration of Jewish persons during the Second World War. More generally, the interpretation applied to data carries a risk of reinforcing negative stereotypes. This is particularly sensitive in relation to crime statistics. If these show an over-representation of ethnic minorities, immigrants, or Roma amongst those appearing in the criminal justice system, then this may reinforce prejudices about the supposed criminal proclivity of such groups. FitzGerald and Sibbitt emphasize the need for refined scrutiny of statistics on crime and ethnicity, controlling for other key factors, such as age or socio-economic status.[71] In practice, elements of the popular media frequently fail to present a nuanced analysis. Fear surrounding the misuse of ethnic data may also be one explanation for under-reporting, where individuals decline to identify with ethnic minority categories. This has been especially noted in relation to Roma communities, where official data have been criticized for substantially underestimating the real size of the population.[72]

In short, it is clear that ethnic data collection in Europe is a complex process which faces considerable challenges. Yet, in the absence of data, it will be difficult to make an accurate assessment of whether equal outcomes (or equal opportunities) have been achieved. Data reveal more clearly the contours of inequality,

[67] Art 8(1), EP and Council Directive (EC) 95/46 on the protection of individuals with regard to the processing of personal data and on the free movement of such data [1995] OJ L281/31.

[68] eg where the data subject consents to their data being processed (Art 8(2)). See de Schutter (n 43 above) 861.

[69] Art 2(a).

[70] P Simon, '"Ethnic" statistics and data protection in the Council of Europe countries' (Strasbourg: Council of Europe, 2007) 42.

[71] M FitzGerald and R Sibbitt, 'Ethnic monitoring in police forces: a beginning' Home Office Research Study 173 (London: Home Office, 1997) 91.

[72] F Babuisk, 'Legitimacy, statistics and research methodology – who is Romani in Hungary today and what are we (not) allowed to know about Roma' (2004) *Roma Rights Quarterly* Issue 2.

as well as tracking how the picture is changing over time. This is obviously essential in making an evaluation of whether current law and policy instruments are actually effective. At the same time, even if comprehensive data were available, this does not fully resolve the difficulty of interpreting what equal outcomes demand. Should, for example, democratic institutions be an exact mirror of the society they represent? Another challenge to determining what constitutes an equal outcome is segregation. Some instances of segregation are easily identifiable as detrimental to the goal of substantive equality, such as where immigrants are systematically allocated low status work within an organization. There can, though, be voluntary dimensions to segregation. This is evident in relation to housing and spatial segregation. On the one hand, ethnic minority communities are unlikely to 'choose' to live in urban districts which are characterized by crime, poor housing, or low environmental quality. On the other hand, congregating in a particular area may be voluntary where this facilitates the life of cultural and religious institutions or even commercial enterprises such as specialist food stores. The general goal of 'equal outcomes' does not provide a clear indication of how far, if at all, the state should intervene to dismantle such segregation.

Reflecting diversity

A final criticism of substantive equality is that by focusing on *group* inequalities, it emphasizes overly rigid characteristics of group membership. This risks essentializing the experience of individual members of ethnic groups and downplaying internal diversity.[73] For example, university selection schemes that attach merit to a person's membership of an under-represented ethnic group could reinforce assumptions that a person from that group will behave in a certain way, hold a particular set of beliefs and so on. Such assumptions tend to neglect intersectionality and the strong differences in experience between, for instance, a young man and an older woman who happen to share the same ethnic origin. Indeed, Schiek draws attention to the 'deeply individualistic' dimension to equality: 'no one shall be judged on the basis of assumptions in line with group characteristics'.[74] An appreciation of intersectionality also underscores the difficulty in defining equal outcomes. Proportionate representation will demand attention to combinations of characteristics such as ethnicity with gender or disability. Given that some of these sub-groups will be relatively small, a focus on exact numerical representation may be unrealistic.

The increasing influence of an intersectionality perspective leads some authors to suggest that diversity is emerging as an alternative concept of equality,

[73] Y Alibhai-Brown, *After Multiculturalism* (London: The Foreign Policy Centre, 2000) 45.

[74] D Schiek, 'Broadening the scope and the norms of EU gender equality law: towards a multidimensional conception of equality law' (2005) 12 MJ 427, 436.

challenging the traditional dichotomy of formal/substantive equality.[75] Whilst there is no settled interpretation of what the diversity model entails, Squires notes that it readily accepts the need to accommodate difference and implies greater participation of affected persons in the process of negotiating accommodation claims.[76] In this way, it could be said that the diversity model begins by recognizing that 'equality' is a complex objective which may mean different things in different contexts.[77] For Roma families, it might involve gaining access for their children to mainstream schools, whilst for (some) Muslims it could be viewed as the ability to establish separate schools with an Islamic ethos, on the same terms as those already afforded to Christian ethos schools. The diversity model appears to place less emphasis on socio-economic outcomes, instead drawing attention to other dimensions of equality claims, such as 'recognition' or 'dignity'.[78] This is particularly apposite in the context of individuals or groups which are vulnerable to discrimination, but without this giving rise to an overall pattern of socio-economic disadvantage. For example, some historic national minorities in central and eastern Europe appear to have broadly similar patterns of labour market performance to the majority ethnic population.[79]

The diversity model implies that one of the major contemporary challenges in pursuing equality is dealing with a multiplicity of claims for *different* treatment, often flowing from diverse cultural or religious practices. It places considerable emphasis on the *process* for resolving such claims. The opportunity for genuine participation in the decision-making process may have the result that the final outcome, whatever this should be, is viewed as more legitimate.[80] This focus on the deliberative process is particularly salient where conflicts between equality grounds arise. For example, should an employer accede to a request from a Muslim female employee not to work alongside male employees?[81] Moller Okin warns against accommodations which reinforce traditional hegemonies with minority groups.[82] The difficulty in finding the appropriate response to potential conflicts between equality grounds once again exposes some of the limitations of simply pursuing a general goal of substantive equality.

[75] eg L Barmes and S Ashtiany, 'The diversity approach to achieving equality: potential and pitfalls' (2003) 32 ILJ 274; E Howard, 'The road to equality—developing the protection against discrimination on racial or ethnic grounds within the European Union' Ph.D. thesis, Queen Mary, University of London, February 2007. For a critical perspective, see J Wrench, 'Diversity management can be bad for you' (2005) 46 *Race & Class* 73.

[76] J Squires, 'Is mainstreaming transformative? Theorizing mainstreaming in the context of diversity and deliberation' (2005) 12 *Social Politics* 366.

[77] Howard (n 1 above) 173.

[78] S Fredman, 'Changing the norm: positive duties in equal treatment legislation' (2005) 12 MJ 369, 378; McCrudden (n 5 above) 28.

[79] High Level Group (n 54 above) 37.

[80] Fredman (n 78 above) 379.

[81] eg para 9, *Azmi v Kirklees Metropolitan Borough Council* [2007] IRLR 484, EAT.

[82] S Moller Okin, 'Is multiculturalism bad for women?' in J Cohen, M Howard, and M Nussbaum (eds), *Is Multiculturalism Bad for Women?* (Princeton: Princeton University Press, 1999) 9, 23.

C. Conclusions

Combating racism ultimately leads to a search for 'equality'. As with racism, equality is also a multi-dimensional concept. Formal equality views racial discrimination as fundamentally irrational, the taking into account of irrelevant characteristics. In this fashion, it resonates with the concepts outlined in Chapter 1 of scientific racism and cultural racism. Although formal equality appears neutral, insofar as it seeks to remain blind to ethnicity, its effect is to enshrine pre-existing cultural hierarchies. Ethnic or national minorities are only entitled to the same treatment in comparison to that already afforded to the dominant ethnic group(s). In reality, ethnic and national minorities often seek recognition of their difference and adaptation of the prevailing norm. Formal equality ultimately offers a meagre response to the cultural complexity of contemporary European societies.

Substantive equality opens the door to probing the necessity of traditional practices and challenging assumed norms. The concept of cultural racism suggests that discrimination is mainly due to individual prejudice, which can be combated by promoting understanding of cultural diversity. If this extends to adapting individual behaviour in response to cultural diversity, then it may find an echo in the concept of substantive equality. The more obvious link is between substantive equality and institutional racism. In both concepts, the supposed neutrality of taken-for-granted practices is called into question. Moreover, both institutional racism and substantive equality are intrinsically concerned with ensuring equal outcomes and use this as an indicator of progress.

The full articulation of substantive equality remains contested. In the context of racism, there is an ongoing debate surrounding the appropriateness of ethnic data collection, the use of positive action, and the extent to which accommodating difference might be outweighed by promoting the integration of migrants and minorities. Indeed, the wider political debate on immigration often looms in the background of any discussion of ethnic equality. Whilst these issues are distinct priorities for combating racism, they are not unique. Data collection is also controversial in relation to sexual orientation, whilst positive action in the context of gender equality has been the source of recurrent litigation at the Court of Justice. An intersectionality perspective recalls the need to weave together analysis of the different equality strands. Debates around ethnic data collection will have a narrow horizon if they do not also consider the need for data to shine light on the particular experience of minority women.

Having examined the multiple dimensions to racism and equality, as well as the interaction between these concepts, Chapter 3 turns to the other element of this book's analytical framework: mainstreaming.

3

Mainstreaming Ethnic Equality

Mainstreaming is premised on the idea that equality needs to be taken into account and actively pursued throughout all areas of law and public policy. At its core, it rejects the assumption that specific laws or policies on equality are sufficient. Instead, it is based on the premise that targeted initiatives need to be accompanied by the infusion of equality objectives across law and policy boundaries. In practice, this means that equality-focused measures, such as anti-discrimination legislation, must be complemented by the promotion of equality within all policy fields, even where these might, at first glance, not seem to be especially relevant. For example, it might be assumed that enterprise policy is not particularly relevant to promoting ethnic equality. Yet entrepreneurs from ethnic minority communities can face greater difficulties in raising investment capital,[1] whilst self-employment remains a crucial avenue for circumventing obstacles experienced by ethnic minority communities within the labour market.[2]

This basic understanding of what mainstreaming means has been gradually absorbed within policy processes at the national, European, and international levels. Nevertheless, the precise manifestations of mainstreaming vary greatly and closer scrutiny often suggests a lack of consensus on what this approach actually entails. Comparative studies of different forms of mainstreaming risk descending into a confusing morass of specific policy initiatives with little common thread. Writing in 2000, Beveridge, Nott, and Stephen noted that there had been:

> little attempt to develop a general theory of mainstreaming which transcends the diversity of state practice in order to provide a universal frame of reference, or set of criteria, by which mainstreaming may be understood . . .[3]

This chapter explores in greater depth what is meant by mainstreaming. It will consider first its background and the reasons underpinning its emergence. It then turns to examine the different forms that mainstreaming can take, both at the

[1] Centre for Enterprise and Economic Development Research, 'Young entrepreneurs, women entrepreneurs, co-entrepreneurs and ethnic minority entrepreneurs in the European Union and Central and Eastern Europe' (Brussels: Commission, 2000).

[2] T Modood, 'Ethnic diversity and racial disadvantage in employment' in T Blackstone, B Parekh, and P Sanders (eds), *Race Relations in Britain—A Developing Agenda* (London: Routledge, 1998) 53, 57.

[3] F Beveridge, S Nott, and K Stephen, 'Mainstreaming and the engendering of policy-making: a means to an end?' (2000) 7 JEPP 385, 388.

strategic level and in the tools for its implementation. There is no doubt that mainstreaming has more frequently been applied in relation to gender equality. Consequently, a central objective of this chapter is to consider how mainstreaming can be applied in the context of promoting ethnic equality. To this end, reference will be made to some examples from national law and policy, including, in particular, the British duty on public authorities to promote race equality.[4] This is the most elaborate mainstreaming scheme in the EU in relation to combating racism, so it warrants special consideration.

A. The Emergence of Mainstreaming

There is no single original source of mainstreaming; however, many commentators highlight its evolution within the work of international institutions.[5] International development policy was the site of concerted efforts to incorporate a gender equality perspective. These can be traced backed to the 1970s and the rise of 'Women in Development' and later 'Gender and Development' policies.[6] Early examples of mainstreaming can also be found in national initiatives during the 1970s. For example, the Netherlands created the 'facet' policy whereby gender was to be treated as a facet of all areas of public policy.[7] In Norway, gender equality was designated a responsibility of all government ministries in 1977.[8] There is even evidence of attempts to mainstream ethnic equality; in Britain, section 71 of the Race Relations Act (RRA) 1976 placed all local authorities under a duty 'to promote equality of opportunity, and good relations, between persons of different racial groups'. It is possible retrospectively to apply the label of mainstreaming to such initiatives. Certainly, they reflect the sense that equality needs to be pursued across a range of policy areas. In practice, though, their implementation was often very weak.[9]

[4] Although this book generally uses the term 'ethnic equality', 'race equality' is the normal way of referring to this law in Britain.

[5] eg C McCrudden, 'Equality' in C Harvey (ed), *Human Rights, Equality and Democratic Renewal in Northern Ireland* (Oxford: Hart Publishing, 2001) 75, 76; C Booth and C Bennett, 'Gender mainstreaming in the European Union: towards a new conception and practice of equal opportunities?' (2002) 9 *European Journal of Women's Studies* 430, 438.

[6] R Jahan, *The Elusive Agenda—Mainstreaming Women in Development* (London: Zed Books, 1995) 10.

[7] M Verloo, 'Making women count in the Netherlands' in F Beveridge, S Nott, and K Stephen (eds), *Making Women Count—Integrating Gender into Law and Policy-making* (Aldershot: Ashgate, 2000) 49, 56.

[8] M Verloo, 'Gender mainstreaming: practice and prospects' Report EG (1999) 13 (Strasbourg: Council of Europe, 1999).

[9] On the RRA, see: D Strazzardi, 'Nuove strategie di lotta alla discriminazione razziale nell'UE e in Gran Bretagna: il cosidetto principio di *mainstreaming* e il parternatario sociale. Verso un diverso approccio della legislazione antidiscriminatoria?' [2002] *Diritto pubblico comparato ed europeo* Part 1: 161, 167.

Contemporary mainstreaming policies are often linked to the 1995 UN Beijing Conference on Women.[10] Its Platform for Action contained a commitment that governments would:

> facilitate the formulation and implementation of government policies on equality between women and men, develop appropriate strategies and methodologies, and promote coordination and cooperation within the central government in order to ensure mainstreaming of a gender perspective in all policy-making processes.[11]

Although the mainstreaming approach was already starting to feature within EU gender equality policy,[12] the Beijing Conference provided an added impetus to make gender mainstreaming an explicit commitment.[13] From this point onwards, mainstreaming was rapidly diffused beyond gender and incorporated into other aspects of EU equality policy. In 1996, the Commission adopted a mainstreaming strategy in respect of disability[14] and in 1998 this approach was extended to combating racism.[15] Whilst it is clear that the vogue for mainstreaming had taken hold by the late 1990s, further consideration is needed of the reasons explaining the desire to pursue this strategy.

B. Explaining the Rise of Mainstreaming

The recourse to mainstreaming can be primarily diagnosed as a response to perceived weaknesses within the existing arsenal of equality law. In addition, mainstreaming chimes a chord with broader trends in EU governance. Both of these factors are examined further below.

Weaknesses in existing equality law instruments

Although there was no EC legislation on racial discrimination prior to 2000, most of the then 15 Member States already had some legislative provisions in this area. For the most part, national legislation prior to 2000 relied upon litigation as the main lever for combating discrimination. Whilst some states had complemented the right to individual legal redress with other instruments, such as

[10] F Beveridge and J Shaw, 'Introduction: mainstreaming gender in European public policy' (2002) 10 FLS 209; D Izzi, *Eguaglianza e differenze nei rapporti di lavoro—il diritto antidiscriminatorio tra genere e fattori di rischio emergenti* (Naples: Casa Editrice Jovene, 2005) 364.

[11] para 205(a), Platform for Action: <http://www.un.org/esa/gopher-data/conf/fwcw/off/a—20.en> accessed 18 June 2008.

[12] T Rees, *Mainstreaming Equality in the European Union—Education, Training and Labour Market Policies* (London: Routledge, 1999) 62.

[13] Commission, 'Incorporating equal opportunities for women and men into all Community policies and activities' COM (1996) 67, 2.

[14] Commission, 'Equality of opportunity for people with disabilities—a new European Community Disability Strategy' COM (1996) 406-1.

[15] Commission, 'An action plan against racism' COM (1998) 183.

national equality bodies, the majority had not yet taken this step.[16] The right of individuals to seek redress when they have experienced discrimination is evidently a cornerstone of any legal strategy to combat racism. The notion that individuals should be able to challenge the discriminatory denial of a job or an apartment accords with a popular sense of justice. More broadly, individual cases can be strategically valuable in allowing courts to elaborate how bare statutory provisions should be applied to real life situations. They can raise awareness through media coverage and encourage employers and service providers to modify their behaviour in order to avoid such litigation.

Notwithstanding these salutary qualities, individual litigation encounters certain constraints. First, individual dispute resolution tends to be retrospective in nature, revolving around the attribution of responsibility.[17] Success for the individual depends upon the identification of sufficient evidence to demonstrate fault on the part of the respondent. This typically gives rise to an adversarial process where cases become focused on questions such as who did what, when, and why. In order to pursue complaints through a judicial process, individuals will frequently need professional legal representation, with the financial costs that this entails. Such barriers suggest that successful litigants are more likely to be well-resourced individuals[18] or those able to draw on organizational support, such as trade union representation.

Linked to these types of difficulties, a second barrier is the emotional cost which litigation can impose upon individuals. Research into claimants under the British Race Relations Act 1976 found that many experienced stress and associated health problems, such as depression, anxiety, and sleep problems.[19] Most litigants were unable to continue working for the employer against which their case was brought, either because they had been dismissed or they felt compelled to resign. Indeed, 16% were unemployed after the conclusion of their case. Overall, 87% of the claimants said that the case had a negative effect on them.[20]

By the late 1990s, it was increasingly evident that providing individuals with legal avenues for challenging discrimination was not, by itself, sufficient to eradicate ethnic inequalities. On the one hand, in many Member States litigation on racial discrimination remained uncommon. On the other, those states which did have higher levels of litigation, such as the UK or the Netherlands, continued to experience substantial inequalities for ethnic minorities in socio-economic

[16] M Bell, *Anti-discrimination Law and the European Union* (Oxford: OUP, 2002) ch 6.

[17] S Fredman, *Discrimination Law* (Oxford: OUP, 2002) 177.

[18] S Fredman, 'The age of equality' in S Fredman and S Spencer (eds), *Age as an Equality Issue* (Oxford: Hart Publishing, 2003) 21, 53.

[19] J Aston, D Hill, and N D Tackey, 'The experience of claimants in race discrimination Employment Tribunal cases' Employment Relations Research Series No 55 (London: Department of Trade and Industry, 2006) 104.

[20] M Peters, K Seeds, and C Harding, 'Findings from the survey of claimants in race discrimination Employment Tribunal cases' Employment Relations Research Series No 54 (London: Department of Trade and Industry, 2006) xxi.

outcomes. Against this backdrop, there was an understandable interest in alternative strategies for promoting ethnic equality. This trajectory was most pronounced in Britain. As mentioned in Chapter 1, the Stephen Lawrence Inquiry gave high profile recognition to the concept of institutional racism. In response, the Race Relations (Amendment) Act 2000 marked a clear departure from the traditional focus on individual litigation. Instead, new provisions were introduced which placed most public authorities under a legally enforceable duty to 'have due regard to the need (a) to eliminate unlawful racial discrimination; and (b) to promote equality of opportunity and good relations between persons of different racial groups'.[21] The clear direction of this type of reform was to encourage public authorities to mainstream ethnic equality issues into all aspects of policy-making.

At EU level, the rationale for promoting gender mainstreaming was very similar. Although legislation prohibiting sex discrimination in employment had been in place since the 1970s, marked inequalities remained between the situation of women and men in the labour market. A prime example is remuneration, where women's average hourly pay continues to be 15% less than that of men.[22] The rise of gender mainstreaming within EU policy discourse can therefore be partly explained by its ability to offer an alternative recipe to the litigation model.[23] It shifts the focus away from the retrospective resolution of individual disputes and towards an anticipatory, preventative strategy.[24] In relation to ethnic equality, it is less easy to explain the European Commission's recourse to mainstreaming as a reaction to disillusionment with the litigation model. When the Commission first committed itself to using mainstreaming as part of anti-racism policy,[25] the Racial Equality Directive had not yet been adopted. This provides a peculiar example of mainstreaming *preceding* individual litigation rights. The application of mainstreaming to anti-racism seems best described as cross-fertilization within equality policy.[26] The lessons about the limitations of individual litigation in tackling gender inequalities were being incorporated from the outset in anti-racism policy.

[21] s 71(1) RRA 1976 (as amended).

[22] Commission, 'Report on equality between women and men 2008' (Luxembourg: OOPEC, 2008) 29.

[23] Izzi (n 10 above) 362.

[24] S Nott, 'Accentuating the positive: alternative strategies for promoting gender equality' in F Beveridge, S Nott, and K Stephen (eds), *Making Women Count—Integrating Gender into Law and Policy-making* (Aldershot: Ashgate, 2000) 247, 262; C McCrudden, 'Theorizing European equality law' in C Costello and E Barry (eds), *Equality in Diversity—The New Equality Directives* (Dublin: Irish Centre for European Law, 2003) 1, 37.

[25] Commission, 'An action plan against racism' COM (1998) 183.

[26] S Parmar, 'The European Court of Justice and anti-discrimination law: some reflections on the experience of gender equality jurisprudence for the future interpretation of the Racial Equality Directive' in J Niessen and I Chopin (eds), *The Development of Legal Instruments to Combat Racism in a Diverse Europe* (Leiden: Martinus Nijhoff, 2004) 131, 135.

Mainstreaming and EU governance

A second factor which helps to explain the rise of mainstreaming within EU policy-making circles is its comfortable fit with wider trends in EU governance since the mid-1990s. Traditional regulatory methods have been complemented (or replaced) by 'new' methods of governance. Beginning with the former, EU governance was traditionally associated with achieving change through the adoption of binding legal instruments. EC legislation would establish obligations for the Member States which were then expected dutifully to ensure implementation within the national legal system. This model of regulation can clearly be characterized as 'top-down' and it implicitly relies on the ability of legal institutions, principally courts, to secure compliance.[27] Anti-discrimination legislation typifies this approach; EC legislation pronounced an objective (the prohibition of sex discrimination) and relied upon adequate enforcement of the legislation for its achievement.

EU law and policy have never been exclusively based around traditional regulation in the form of binding legislation (hard law). Social policy, to provide one example, has always involved a blend of hard law alongside funding programmes and non-binding policy recommendations (soft law).[28] The debate around the balance between traditional regulation and other approaches sharpened during the 1990s. In part, this can be attributed to high-level political challenges for the EU. The expanding membership of the Union, coupled with evidence of public alienation in at least some Member States, posed questions over the extent to which further harmonization of legal rules was feasible or desirable.[29] Alternative approaches to regulation have been gathered under the label of 'new governance', or sometimes 'experimental governance'.[30] New governance often provides a foil to the dominant characteristics of traditional 'command and control' regulation.[31] The top-down use of hard law as a method of directing change is replaced by an emphasis on flexibility and fluidity.[32] Legal requirements which are binding and rigid are not favoured. Emphasis is instead placed on identifying common policy objectives with discretion left to national authorities as to how these objectives are pursued. Reference to experimental governance conveys the

[27] J Scott and D Trubek, 'Mind the gap: law and new approaches to governance in the European Union' (2002) 8 ELJ 1.

[28] C Kilpatrick, 'New EU employment governance and constitutionalism' in G de Búrca and J Scott (eds), *Law and New Governance in the EU and the US* (Oxford: Hart Publishing, 2006) 129; S Sciarra, 'Social values and the multiple sources of European social law' (1995) 1 ELJ 60, 81.

[29] G de Búrca, 'The constitutional challenge of new governance in the European Union' (2003) 28 ELR 814, 820.

[30] E Szyszczak, 'Experimental governance: the open method of coordination' (2006) 12 ELJ 486.

[31] Kilpatrick (n 28 above) 124.

[32] G de Búrca, 'New modes of governance and the protection of human rights' in P Alston and O de Schutter (eds), *Monitoring Fundamental Rights in the EU—The Contribution of the Fundamental Rights Agency* (Oxford: Hart Publishing, 2005) 25, 26.

importance attached to the idea of mutual learning.[33] This starts from the premise that, despite having shared policy objectives, neither the EU, nor its individual Member States, have a monopoly over how best to achieve these objectives. Member States are encouraged to experiment with different policy approaches.[34] The added value of EU level cooperation becomes the possibility to pool experience and to learn from each other. New governance is, therefore, a slippery concept where the notion of 'enforcement' is hard to pin down. The flexibility of new governance implies that individuals are not conferred with rights which can be enforced by courts. At the same time, new governance is more than simply an 'anything goes' approach to European integration.

In order to appreciate how new governance techniques can be applied in practice, the classic illustration within the European Union has been the 'open method of coordination' (OMC). This method has been applied to a range of EU economic and social policies largely under the aegis of the 'Lisbon strategy'.[35] One of the hallmarks of the OMC processes is a departure from the traditional legal instruments used for policy implementation. Instead, the emphasis has been upon the agreement of common policy objectives at EU level combined with flexibility for Member States in their pursuit of these objectives. Judicial avenues of enforcement have been displaced by procedures for monitoring progress.[36] These concentrate on reporting obligations for Member States, followed by peer review, external evaluation of performance, and the benchmarking of good practices.[37]

Given that mainstreaming shares certain characteristics of new governance,[38] it is not surprising to find their parallel development during the 1990s. Like new governance, mainstreaming represents a departure from traditional hard law instruments and the reliance on judicial enforcement strategies. Mainstreaming also focuses on identifying a common objective (promoting equality) and then permitting diversity in how this is to be pursued. Moreover, the tools of mainstreaming, such as performance monitoring and target-setting, are consistent with the techniques found within the OMC processes. It seems no coincidence that the archetype OMC process, the European Employment Strategy, included a

[33] G de Búrca and J Scott, 'New governance, law and constitutionalism' in G de Búrca and J Scott (eds), *Law and New Governance in the EU and the US* (Oxford: Hart Publishing, 2006) 1, 3.

[34] M Barbera, 'I problemi teorici e pratici posti dal metodo di coordinamento aperto delle politiche sociali' in M Barbera (ed), *Nuove forme di regolazione: il metodo aperto di coordinamento delle politiche sociali* (Milan: Giuffrè, 2006) 1, 13.

[35] See further: <http://europa.eu.int/growthandjobs/index_en.htm> accessed 18 June 2008.

[36] Scott and Trubek (n 27 above) 8.

[37] E Szyszczak, 'The evolving European Employment Strategy' in J Shaw (ed), *Social Law and Policy in an Evolving Union* (Oxford: Hart Publishing, 2000) 197, 213; D Ashiagbor, *The European Employment Strategy—Labour Market Regulation and New Governance* (Oxford: OUP, 2005) 200.

[38] D Schiek, 'Broadening the scope and the norms of EU gender equality law: towards a multidimensional conception of equality law' (2005) 12 MJ 427, 442.

specific commitment to gender mainstreaming.[39] De Búrca argues that another feature of new governance is 'policy linkage',[40] that is, trying to coordinate policy initiatives across different fields, as witnessed in the comprehensive view of economic and social reform found within the Lisbon Strategy. Again, there is a strong resonance with mainstreaming, which is premised on the need for equality matters to be incorporated across all areas of law and policy.

The general turn of the EU towards new governance in the 1990s, coupled with the search for alternatives to the litigation model within equality policy, provided a ripe environment within which mainstreaming could flourish. Having now considered the background to mainstreaming and the factors supporting its evolution, it is necessary to examine further what is meant by mainstreaming. The following section considers the various models of mainstreaming that can be found as well as the instruments deployed for its implementation.

C. Models of Mainstreaming

Defining mainstreaming remains a challenge. Beveridge and Nott have commented that 'everyone understands the general idea but no one is sure what it requires in practice'.[41] Perhaps the most commonly cited definition is that provided by the Council of Europe's Group of Specialists on Mainstreaming:

> Gender mainstreaming is the (re)organisation, improvement, development and evaluation of policy processes, so that a gender equality perspective is incorporated in all policies at all levels and at all stages, by the actors normally involved in policy-making.[42]

The emphasis on *policy processes* helps to distinguish mainstreaming from specific laws and policies on equality. The latter are measures which have equality as their central, if not exclusive, objective. Anti-discrimination legislation is a prime example or alternatively policy initiatives, such as a public awareness campaign against racist behaviour in football stadiums. Mainstreaming differs from specific laws and policies on equality because it seeks to weave the objective of promoting equality into laws and policies which are primarily designed with a different objective in mind. An anti-smoking campaign is designed to promote public health, but mainstreaming would prompt health policy-makers to consider whether the campaign is likely to be equally effective for all ethnic groups.[43]

[39] J Rubery, 'Gender mainstreaming and gender equality in the EU: the impact of the EU employment strategy' (2002) 33 IRJ 500.

[40] de Búrca (n 32 above) 30.

[41] F Beveridge and S Nott, 'Mainstreaming: a case for optimism and cynicism' (2002) 10 FLS 299.

[42] Group of Specialists on Mainstreaming, 'Gender Mainstreaming—conceptual framework, methodology and presentation of good practice. Final report of activities of the Group of Specialists on Mainstreaming (EG-S-MS)' (Strasbourg: Council of Europe, 1998) 19.

[43] Some ethnic groups may have different patterns of tobacco consumption, such as chewing tobacco, which suggests a need for public health messages that go beyond giving up cigarettes.

In seeking to make equality an integral concern of all policy-making processes, mainstreaming attempts to alter the range of issues typically regarded as relevant considerations. In other words, it aims to place equality on the agenda and to move beyond taken-for-granted assumptions that a given issue has no relevance to equality.[44] In so doing, there are clear parallels between mainstreaming and institutional racism, both of which shine a spotlight on hidden or unintended causes of inequality.

Although all forms of mainstreaming broadly pursue the objective of promoting equality across law and policy, the way in which this has been implemented in practice differs greatly. The remainder of this section examines three dimensions to mainstreaming: goals, methods, and instruments.

The goals of mainstreaming

As well as separating mainstreaming from specific equality law and policy, it is necessary to disentangle its goals from its methods. One of the risks within a mainstreaming strategy is that a focus on the reorganization of policy processes loses sight of the underlying objectives. It may become bogged down in bureaucracy, becoming simply another box to be ticked before decisions are taken. Various authors argue that the way in which these goals are understood reflects different models of mainstreaming. Jahan distinguishes 'integrationist' and 'agenda-setting' mainstreaming.[45] Other writers have referred to 'transformative'[46] or even 'revolutionary'[47] mainstreaming. Fundamentally, these categorizations are concerned with the type or extent of change that mainstreaming is seeking to achieve.

At one end of the spectrum, the 'integrationist' model of mainstreaming is perhaps best translated as 'taking equality into account'. Here, there is a recognition that equality issues have been overlooked in the past and that mechanisms need to be established in order to ensure that they are considered by policy-makers in the future. Whilst policies might be adapted in order to avoid obvious forms of unlawful discrimination, the basic institutional structures are not brought into question. This model fits well with ideas of joined-up governance; equality is just one of many issues that need to be given greater consideration across all public policies. It is primarily seeking to bring about equal treatment within the boundaries of the pre-existing policy framework. This approach, which implies minimal change, seems more inclined towards the objective of formal equality, as discussed in Chapter 2.

[44] S Mazey, 'Integrating gender—intellectual and "real world" mainstreaming' (2000) 7 JEPP 333, 336.

[45] Jahan (n 6 above) 13.

[46] Rees (n 12 above) 46.

[47] L Mósesdottir, 'Moving Europe towards the dual-breadwinner model' in D Foden and L Magnussen (eds), *Five Years' Experience of the Luxembourg Employment Strategy* (Brussels: European Trade Union Institute, 2003) 183, 192.

The 'transformative' model of mainstreaming seeks a more radical and searching review of policy processes. It questions the assumed neutrality of norms and practices, requiring fundamental policy reconstruction in order to reflect diversity. Equality issues are not being 'fitted in' around the existing structures; instead, the active promotion of equality becomes central. Rees argues:

> Mainstreaming policies are those which respect and respond to differences, rather than seeking to assist women to fit into male institutions and cultures . . . the task is to challenge and change the male-streamism of organisations.[48]

Transformative mainstreaming is consequently better equipped to tackle institutional racism and to pursue substantive equality. It recognizes that equality does not automatically flow from ensuring the same treatment of all persons. Instead, eradicating group inequalities can demand accommodation of diversity and positive action.

Understandably, the choice between these two theoretical models may be less stark in the everyday application of mainstreaming. Nevertheless, it is important to recognize the different questions being asked. Consider, for instance, the impact of each model on public transport policy. An integrationist approach to mainstreaming ethnic equality would seek to prevent discrimination in the use of public transport. This might mean cultural awareness training for staff, taking measures against customers who harass staff and other travellers, or even using public transport as a venue for information campaigns against racism. Transformative mainstreaming probes deeper and, in line with institutional racism, it will be concerned with ensuring equal outcomes as an indicator of equality. It is likely to ask more searching questions about the way in which the transport system is organized; is the infrastructure equally efficient in areas of the city with a high ethnic minority population?

Methods of mainstreaming

The goals selected for mainstreaming are closely linked to the methods chosen for its implementation. In practice, mainstreaming will not be expressly labelled as 'integrationist' or 'transformative'; however, this may flow from the selected methods. Beveridge and Nott distinguish between *expert-bureaucratic* methods on the one hand, and *participatory-democratic* methods on the other.[49]

Expert-bureaucratic methods

The expert-bureaucratic model relies on the existing circle of decision-makers, but it seeks to incorporate equality expertise in order to change the content of

[48] Rees (n 12 above) 40.

[49] Beveridge and Nott (n 41 above) 301.

decisions. A good example was a scheme in Sweden to employ 'flying gender experts' who would spend a period of time working with a government department in order to raise its awareness about gender mainstreaming and how it could incorporate a gender perspective into its work.[50] This methodology relies heavily on the capacity of high-level expertise to diagnose problems and to locate the correct solutions. Its strengths lie in its capacity to go with the grain of existing governance processes and to embed itself within top-level decision-makers.[51] To date, expert-bureaucratic methods have dominated within the EU institutions.[52] This is most pronounced in relation to gender where there are well-established institutional structures, such as High Level Groups on gender mainstreaming.[53] The institutional apparatus is weaker in relation to mainstreaming ethnic equality. As discussed further in Chapter 4, there are 'inter-service groups' which bring together officials from various Directorates-General (DGs) on the topics of racism and Roma. Whether weak or strong, these structures are primarily based on mainstreaming via internal expertise with little emphasis on dialogue with 'outsiders' during this process. The insularity of the expert-bureaucratic method is perhaps the greatest brake on its capacity to effect change. Squires argues that this method will be suitable for achieving the 'integrationist' model of mainstreaming.[54] It is well adapted for ensuring that equality issues are taken into account, but it will not pose fundamental questions about organizational culture and practice. Moreover, as a concept of equality, there seems very little emphasis on equal participation by all ethnic groups. Given that elite decision-makers within the Union are far from a mirror of Europe's social diversity, their capacity for autonomous understanding of equality issues can be queried.

Participatory-democratic methods

In contrast, the participatory-democratic method demands the active involvement of the communities affected by discrimination in putting mainstreaming into practice. Decision-makers are required to establish a dialogue, opening themselves to new voices. In this respect, the participatory model is much more ambitious in its objectives; indeed, it seeks to transform the very style of governance.[55] Mainstreaming in Northern Ireland provides a good example

[50] Group of Specialists on Mainstreaming (n 42 above) 68.

[51] J Squires, 'Is mainstreaming transformative? Theorizing mainstreaming in the context of diversity and deliberation' (2005) 12 *Social Politics* 366, 374.

[52] S Mazey, 'Gender mainstreaming strategies in the EU: delivering on an agenda?' (2002) 10 FLS 227, 232; F Beveridge, 'Building against the past: the impact of mainstreaming on EU gender law and policy' (2007) 32 ELR 193, 211.

[53] Beveridge, ibid 198.

[54] Squires (n 51 above) 373; S Fredman, *Human Rights Transformed—Positive Rights and Positive Duties* (Oxford: OUP, 2008) 200.

[55] J Edwards, 'Mainstreaming equality in Wales: the case of the National Assembly building' (2004) 32 *Policy & Politics* 33, 46.

of this approach. Section 75 of the Northern Ireland Act 1998 created the following duty:

'A public authority shall in carrying out its functions relating to Northern Ireland have due regard to the need to promote equality of opportunity—

(a) Between persons of different religious belief, political opinion, racial group, age, marital status, sexual orientation;
(b) Between men and women generally;
(c) Between persons with a disability and those without; and
(d) Between persons with dependants and those without.'

Schedule 9 of the Act further specifies that all public authorities are required to prepare an 'equality scheme'. In essence, this is a structured plan for practical compliance with the section 75 duty. Importantly, the Act builds a participatory approach into the fabric of all equality schemes. Each authority is required to explain its arrangements for consultation on policies that have already been adopted and those which will be proposed in the future. Alongside this principle of participation, there is a requirement for transparency. Equality schemes must describe how each authority will publish the results of its consultations and policy assessments.[56] In practice, the implementation of section 75 seems to have generated a higher engagement of civil society organizations in the policy-making process.[57] Unlike the expert-bureaucratic method, there is a reliance on *external* expertise on equality issues.

There are, though, a number of drawbacks to this approach. NGOs take on a central role as a conduit for reaching affected communities. Consequently, it is necessary to consider whether NGOs enjoy sufficient capacity to assume this role. This emerged as a flaw within the Northern Ireland mainstreaming model. Equality NGOs were expected to involve themselves in the many new opportunities to influence policy-making, but they often lacked the necessary resources and 'consultation-fatigue' emerged.[58] Within the NGO community, there is also a risk that dialogue becomes skewed towards established, well-resourced organizations with the consequent marginalization of looser, grassroots associations.[59] This is a relevant consideration at EU level, where lobbying for ethnic equality is heavily dependent on those organizations which receive most of their funding from the Commission.[60] In addition, EU level civil society is predominantly

[56] Sch 9, s 4(2).

[57] T Barnett Donaghy, 'Mainstreaming: Northern Ireland's participative-democratic approach' (2004) 32 *Policy & Politics* 49, 56.

[58] B Hinds, 'Mainstreaming equality in Northern Ireland' in A Dobrowolsky and V Hart (eds), *Women Making Constitutions—New Politics and Comparative Perspectives* (Houndmills: Palgrave Macmillan, 2003) 185, 197; Barnett Donaghy, ibid 57.

[59] C Lloyd, 'Anti-racist responses to European integration' in R Koopmans and P Satham (eds), *Challenging Immigration and Ethnic Relations Politics* (Oxford: OUP, 2000) 389, 400–1; Fredman (n 54 above) 201.

[60] See Ch 4.

organized around specific grounds of discrimination. This poses the risk that intersectional perspectives will not be given sufficient attention, such as those of ethnic minority women.[61]

The instruments of mainstreaming

The choices made regarding the basic goals and methods of mainstreaming will influence the specific instruments employed for putting mainstreaming into practice. Whilst many different techniques for implementing mainstreaming exist, this section examines three central options: how to define the mainstreaming duty, impact assessment, and arrangements for measuring progress.

Defining the duty

Mainstreaming is founded on the idea that decision-makers are under an obligation to promote equality throughout their activities. A core choice regards the *status* of any mainstreaming duties. Some are essentially political commitments or statements of intent. This seems an apt description of the Commission's 1998 'Action Plan Against Racism'.[62] Although it was a public promise to follow the mainstreaming approach, it was not underpinned by any legal obligations. Non-legal or soft law techniques remain vulnerable to changes in political will.[63] Implementation is often criticized for its patchy nature and the apparent absence of sanctions for non-compliance.[64] More recently, this dissatisfaction appears to have inspired greater interest in the potential role for law in mainstreaming.

Law holds the perceived advantage of transforming rather woolly and well-meaning intentions into binding obligations. These duties can be given teeth through provisions for compulsory enforcement and/or sanctions for non-compliance. The mere fact that duties are legal in nature does not automatically translate into greater effectiveness. Indeed, some legal duties can remain highly ambiguous regarding their scope for enforcement. For example, EC Treaty, Article 3(2) states 'the Community shall aim to eliminate inequalities, and to promote equality, between women and men'. There is no further indication on how this general duty should be put into effect or the possible sanctions for its neglect.[65] A similar observation could be made regarding the Treaty on the Functioning of the European Union (TFEU), Article 10, which states:

[61] Fredman (n 54 above) 202. [62] COM (1998) 183; see Ch 4.

[63] F Beveridge, S Nott, and K Stephen, 'Setting the scene: the why, what and how of promoting equality between the sexes' in F Beveridge, S Nott, and K Stephen (eds), *Making Women Count—Integrating Gender into Law and Policy-making* (Aldershot: Ashgate, 2000) 1, 21.

[64] J Squires and M Wickham-Jones, 'New Labour, gender mainstreaming and the Women and Equality Unit' (2004) 6 *British Journal of Politics and International Relations* 81, 95.

[65] Beveridge suggests that 'the duty might be better regarded as a political rather than legal obligation' (n 52 above) 208.

In defining and implementing its policies and activities, the Union shall aim to combat discrimination based on sex, racial or ethnic origin, religion or belief, disability, age or sexual orientation.[66]

The strength of this provision may lie in its constitutional characteristics, in the sense that a mandate for mainstreaming will be included amongst the basic rules of the Union. At the same time, to be effective in practice further measures are needed to put flesh on the bones of this general commitment.

At national level, there are examples of more detailed legal frameworks for mainstreaming ethnic equality. In Finland, the Non-Discrimination Act 2004 places a wide-ranging duty on public authorities in relation to ethnic equality: 'in all they do, the authorities shall seek purposefully and methodically to foster equality'.[67] To this end, public authorities are required to draw up 'equality plans' on how they will comply with the duty to foster ethnic equality.[68] Similarly, the British RRA 1976 couples a general duty to promote equality of opportunity with more prescriptive requirements on public authorities set out in secondary legislation.[69] Whilst the procedure for enforcing the Finnish duty is unclear,[70] there have already been several examples in Britain of individuals or organizations successfully challenging the actions of public authorities based on their failure to comply with the duty to promote race equality.[71]

Impact assessment

Whether or not the duty to undertake mainstreaming is legally binding, a common element of mainstreaming schemes is 'impact assessment'. In short, this requires decision-makers to evaluate the likely effects of a proposed law or policy in advance of its adoption. A soft form of impact assessment is the issuing of guidance for decision-makers; this may be little more than a recommendation on issues to 'keep in mind' during policy formulation. More intense forms of impact assessment typically require policy-makers to prepare written reports setting out a detailed (quantitative and/or qualitative) analysis of the effects of the proposed course of action, possibly including an analysis of why the current proposal is more effective than alternative measures. The approach to impact assessment tends to reflect the overall model of mainstreaming. An elite-bureaucratic model fits with a closed system of impact assessment based on analysis by the existing decision-makers, possibly with the contribution of expert advisors. In contrast, a participatory model would open the impact assessment process to external

[66] Consolidated version of the TFEU [2008] OJ C115/53. This will enter into force only if the Treaty of Lisbon is ratified.

[67] s 4(1), Non-Discrimination Act, 21/2004.

[68] T Makkonen, 'Report on measures to combat discrimination: Directive 2000/43/EC and 2000/78/EC: Finland' (Brussels: European Commission, 2007) 41.

[69] RRA 1976 (Statutory Duties) Order, SI 2001/3458.

[70] Makkonen (n 68 above).

[71] *R (Elias) v Secretary of State for Defence* [2006] 1 WLR 3213, CA; *R (on the application of Eisai Ltd) v National Institute for Health and Clinical Excellence* [2007] EWHC 1941 (Admin), QB.

contributions. The British public sector duty to promote race equality constructs impact assessment as an open and interactive process. Many public authorities are placed under a duty to prepare 'race equality schemes' and these require the authority to specify the arrangements for 'assessing and consulting on the likely impact of its proposed policies on the promotion of race equality'.[72] Closely linked to participation is the question of transparency.[73] The degree of public participation will be in part dependent on the openness of the process. Even within a closed, elite-driven process, it may be possible to draw selectively on external expertise. Here, participation is by invitation and revocable. In contrast, a participatory process of impact assessment will be open at the stage of consultation, but also in reporting any subsequent results and determinations.

Impact assessment is a familiar tool within EU policy-making. It is perhaps most associated with environmental policy, where the idea of assessing environmental impact across a range of policy fields originated in the early 1980s.[74] This approach was subsequently mirrored in enterprise policy. In 1992, the Council requested that the Commission conduct impact assessments for proposals that could have a substantial effect on small and medium-sized enterprises.[75] These techniques were then imported into gender mainstreaming during the 1990s.[76] In 2002, the Commission announced its intention to establish a comprehensive impact assessment scheme which would be applied to all legislative and policy proposals with 'a potential economic, social and/or environmental impact and/or require some regulatory measure for their implementation'.[77] Those proposals likely to have a 'substantial' impact, or constituting 'a major policy reform', would be subject to 'extended impact assessment'.[78] This is presumed to require some measure of public consultation, thereby introducing a participatory element into the process. In practice, extended impact assessment means that legislative or policy proposals are now accompanied by a detailed report. This considers the various regulatory options that were available to the Commission and explains why it has concluded that the proposal being presented is the most appropriate course of action. In so doing, there is consideration of issues such as economic costs linked to the proposal, as well as its social consequences. Although the impact assessment scheme was not specifically created as a vehicle for mainstreaming, its analysis of 'social impacts'

72 Art 2(2)(b)(i), RRA 1976 (Statutory Duties) Order, SI 2001/3458.

73 Fredman (n 54 above) 199.

74 A Lenschow, 'New regulatory approaches in "greening" EU policies' (2002) 8 ELJ 19, 22.

75 F Beveridge and S Nott, 'Gender auditing—making the Community work for women' in T Hervey and D O'Keeffe (eds), *Sex Equality Law in the European Union* (Chichester: John Wiley & Sons, 1996) 383, 395.

76 M Pollack and E Hafner-Burton, 'Mainstreaming gender in the European Union' (2000) 7 JEPP 432, 436.

77 Commission, 'Communication on impact assessment' COM (2002) 276, 5.

78 ibid 7; O de Schutter, 'Mainstreaming human rights in the European Union' in P Alston and O de Schutter (eds), *Monitoring Fundamental Rights in the EU—The Contribution of the Fundamental Rights Agency* (Oxford: Hart Publishing, 2005) 37, 53.

includes 'changes affecting gender equality'.[79] In 2005, the Commission augmented the category of social impacts by introducing a specific sub-heading of fundamental rights.[80] Even if no specific reference to issues of racism yet exists within the impact assessment scheme, such matters presumably could be raised under the fundamental rights category.

Measuring progress

The final dimension to be considered in this section is arrangements for measuring progress. In other words, having put in place a mainstreaming scheme, are there any mechanisms for reviewing how it works in practice? Whilst this may seem obvious, gender mainstreaming literature contains examples of national schemes which have foundered due to the very weak procedures for evaluation.[81] Indeed, Woodward argues that one of the main risks for mainstreaming is the 'issue-attention cycle'.[82] It may, for a moment, become the new kid on the block, but unless there is a mechanism for follow-up and reviewing progress, then the initial momentum can quickly dissipate. In considering evaluation mechanisms, two common themes emerge: data collection and institutional accountability.

In relation to gender mainstreaming, the production of data disaggregated by gender has been a key tool.[83] The compilation of statistics can be a first step in gaining a more accurate picture of the current state of play. Rees argues that gender data can uncover the extent of inequality, thereby challenging the assumed neutrality of existing institutional practices.[84] At the same time, such information acts as a benchmark for measuring progress in the future and setting timetabled targets for achieving change. Data collection has been a central element of the British duty to promote race equality, where public authorities have been required to collect data on the ethnic origin of their employees.[85] Some public bodies must go further; universities must monitor the ethnic origin of students in relation to recruitment and academic performance.[86] Although

[79] Commission (n 77 above) 15.

[80] Commission, 'Compliance with the Charter of Fundamental Rights in Commission legislative proposals—methodology for systematic and rigorous monitoring' COM (2005) 172, 5; H Toner, 'Impact assessments and fundamental rights protection in EU law' (2006) 31 ELR 316.

[81] Verloo (n 7 above) 74; K Stephen, 'Catalysts for change? The effectiveness of state agencies in promoting equality' in F Beveridge, S Nott, and K Stephen (eds), *Making Women Count—Integrating Gender into Law and Policy-making* (Aldershot: Ashgate, 2000) 223, 228.

[82] A Woodward, 'Too late for mainstreaming?: dealing with difference in Brussels', European Consortium of Political Research Joint Sessions, Granada, 14–19 April 2005; S Kingsley, 'Creating the climate for diversity and race equality in health care' (2001) 6 *Ethnicity & Health* 255, 261.

[83] This was one of the most common responses to gender mainstreaming within the EU Employment Strategy: U Behning and A Serrano Pascual, 'Comparison of the adaptation of gender mainstreaming in national employment strategies' in U Behning and A Serrano Pascual (eds), *Gender Mainstreaming in the European Employment Strategy* (Brussels: European Trade Union Institute, 2001) 321, 329.

[84] Rees (n 12 above) 43.

[85] Art 5, RRA 1976 (Statutory Duties) Order, SI 2001/3458.

[86] ibid Art 3(4)(b).

compliance with the data collection requirement is not universally respected,[87] the data which have been accumulated have sharply exposed inequalities. The university data, for instance, reveal that white undergraduate students are over four times more likely to graduate with a first class degree than black Caribbean students.[88]

In relation to ethnic equality, data collection faces considerable obstacles within Europe. As discussed in more depth in Chapter 2, few European states have a tradition of collecting data by reference to ethnic origin. There remains considerable opposition linked to issues such as data protection and the basic notion of categorizing people according to ethnic origin. At least in the short run, this implies that quantitative data collection is likely to be a weaker element of ethnic equality mainstreaming in comparison to gender mainstreaming. As a consequence, it is necessary to consider other methods for overseeing implementation.

A common response in gender mainstreaming has been to establish institutional bodies with a specific mandate to monitor mainstreaming.[89] This technique can also be witnessed in relation to ethnic equality. The British Equality and Human Rights Commission enjoys powers to investigate and compel public authorities to comply with the duty to promote race equality.[90] A key distinction is whether such bodies can be characterized as 'insiders' or 'outsiders'. Insider agencies are typically located within the administration, staffed by civil servants, and ultimately subject to political (ministerial) control. Agencies in this mould fit comfortably with the elite-bureaucratic model of mainstreaming. For example, the European Commission has established an Impact Assessment Board to oversee its impact assessment process.[91] This currently consists of five high-level officials who selectively review impact assessment reports. The Board issues comments on the quality of impact assessment reports and recommendations for how the analysis could be improved.

A different approach is to entrust an outsider agency with monitoring mainstreaming. This strategy has been pursued in the UK, where pre-existing equality bodies have been given a specific mainstreaming mandate. This is most pronounced in the case of the Equality Commission for Northern Ireland. Each public authority submits an annual report to the Equality Commission on the

[87] eg a survey in 2006 by the Equal Opportunities Review of 109 public bodies found that whilst 94% were collecting some data relating to employees' ethnic origin, only 16% were collecting data for all the categories required by the legislation: K Godwin, 'Race equality: an ongoing obligation' (2006) 154 *Equal Opportunities Review* 13, 15.

[88] The Equalities Review, 'Fairness and freedom: the final report of the Equalities Review' (London: Cabinet Office, 2007) 61.

[89] eg Squires and Wickham-Jones (n 64 above); M Gillberg, 'Making women count in Sweden' in F Beveridge, S Nott, and K Stephen (eds), *Making Women Count—Integrating Gender into Law and Policy-making* (Aldershot: Ashgate, 2000) 131, 155.

[90] ss 31–32 Equality Act 2006.

[91] See: <http://ec.europa.eu/governance/impact/iab_en.htm> accessed 18 June 2008.

operation of its equality scheme. The principal promise of external agencies is more objectivity and greater political independence. By possessing greater distance from the body being regulated, external agencies may have a greater capacity to challenge the traditional organizational culture and thereby tackle institutional racism. Yet, as outsiders these agencies are vulnerable to certain weaknesses. Fundamentally, their capacity to oversee mainstreaming across all government activities must be questioned. The scale of the mandate creates doubts; in Britain, the government estimates that the race equality duty applies to around 43,000 organizations.[92]

D. Conclusions

This chapter has examined what is meant by the concept of mainstreaming, with specific reference to its application to ethnic equality. The basic premise of mainstreaming is that equality is relevant to all areas of law and policy. Consequently, it rejects the assumption that certain fields are neutral or irrelevant to equality. This outlook fits closely with the concept of institutional racism, discussed in Chapter 1. Like mainstreaming, it also challenges 'taken-for-granted' aspects of organizational culture, using outcomes for different ethnic groups as a key indicator of whether equality is being secured in practice. Closer scrutiny of mainstreaming revealed that there were various ways in which this could be implemented in practice. At one end of the spectrum, the 'integrationist' model demands least change to decision-making processes or policies. It is based around the existing decision-makers and simply seeks to stimulate them to take equality matters into account during policy formulation and evaluation. Insofar as it implies relatively limited change to current practices, this model seems apt for preventing overt or obvious forms of discrimination. As such, it resonates more closely with the formal concept of equality discussed in Chapter 2, or the scientific and cultural concepts of racism discussed in Chapter 1.

At the other end of the spectrum, there is the 'transformative' model. This seeks to change the existing method of decision-making in order to usher in a 'participatory-democratic' approach. Policy-making should be more transparent and based around the involvement of all groups affected by policies, for example, through dialogue between government and civil society organizations. The mainstreaming duties in this model are designed to mobilize all areas of law and policy for the promotion of equality, a more ambitious outlook than merely taking equality into account. Given the more far-reaching objective, stronger methods for monitoring enforcement will normally be required. This approach

[92] Department of Work and Pensions, 'Delivering equality for disabled people—a consultation on the extension of the Disability Discrimination Act to functions of public authorities, and the introduction of a duty to promote equality for disabled persons' (London: The Stationery Office, 2004) 19.

Table 3.1 Models of mainstreaming

Model	Integrationist	Transformative
Goals	Taking equality into account	Promoting equality
Methods	Elite-bureaucratic	Participatory-democratic
Duties	Soft, flexible	Precise, enforceable
Measuring progress	Internal audit	External review
Concept of racism	Scientific/cultural	Institutional
Concept of equality	Formal	Substantive

Data from: J Squires, 'Is mainstreaming transformative? Theorizing mainstreaming in the context of diversity and deliberation' (2005) 12 *Social Politics* 366, 372–3.

seems closely connected to the concepts of substantive equality and institutional racism examined in previous chapters. In everyday practice, mainstreaming schemes will often fall somewhere between these two poles or might combine elements of both. Nevertheless, the models provide a template against which mainstreaming schemes can be analyzed. An overview of the two models of mainstreaming is given in Table 3.1.

Many of the points made above, and throughout this chapter, are not specifically confined to mainstreaming ethnic equality. Most of the empirical experience with mainstreaming in Europe concerns gender equality. There are, though, some examples of this technique being applied to ethnic equality. Unlike gender, there are few instances of ethnic equality mainstreaming which do not, in some fashion, bring in other equality grounds. In Finland, the duty to promote ethnic equality followed a separate obligation in relation to gender equality.[93] In Britain, the original duty to promote race equality has since been mirrored with separate duties for disability and gender.[94] This pattern is also evident within the EU. Gender mainstreaming is well established; it is underpinned by EC Treaty, Article 3(2), and implemented through specific committees and bodies. In contrast, the initial evidence of arrangements for mainstreaming ethnic equality suggests a mixed bag of ground-specific measures (such as the 1998 Action Plan Against Racism) and more general measures, such as fundamental rights impact assessment. If the TFEU, Article 10, comes into effect, this would underscore the assumption that mainstreaming ethnic equality is interlinked with other equality grounds. This offers potential benefits, especially in relation to tackling intersections of inequality, such as ethnicity and gender. At the same time, Verloo

[93] Centre for Strategy and Evaluation Services, 'Non-discrimination mainstreaming—instruments, case studies and way forwards' (Brussels: Commission, 2007) 43.

[94] C O'Cinnéide, 'A new generation of equality legislation? Positive duties and disability rights' in A Lawson and C Gooding (eds), *Disability Rights in Europe—From Theory to Practice* (Oxford: Hart Publishing, 2005) 237; C O'Cinnéide, 'Positive duties and gender equality' (2005) 8 *International Journal of Discrimination and the Law* 91.

cautions against a 'one size fits all' approach.[95] This chapter suggested that, in some respects, the techniques applied to gender mainstreaming may not always be easily transferred to ethnic equality. The most notable example is data collection, which has been central to gender mainstreaming, but remains more contested in relation to ethnicity. Furthermore, the participatory model presupposes the existence of well-developed civil society organizations capable of contributing to consultations. In contrast, ethnic minority mobilization at European level has been relatively limited, a point explored further in Chapter 4.

At the outset, this chapter explained that mainstreaming was not an alternative to those areas of law and policy which make equality their primary objective, such as anti-discrimination legislation. Instead, mainstreaming is designed to be complementary.[96] In order to understand the legal and policy context of mainstreaming within the European Union, it is thus necessary to consider also those measures which are specifically designed to combat racism and promote equality. This is the topic of the next chapter which examines anti-discrimination law and policy.

[95] M Verloo, 'Multiple inequalities, intersectionality and the European Union' (2006) 13 *European Journal of Women's Studies* 211, 223.

[96] L Waddington, 'The expanding role of the equality principle in European Union law' Policy Papers (Series on Constitutional Reform of the EU) 2003/04 (Florence: European University Institute, 2003) 17; Izzi (n 10 above) 369.

4

Racism and Anti-Discrimination

Adopting a strategy of mainstreaming does not imply the abandonment of specialized law and policy on equality. As discussed in the previous chapter, mainstreaming is only one element of a twin-track policy. On the one hand, there should be measures which have as their main focus combating racism and promoting equality; on the other, mainstreaming seeks to ensure that other areas of law and policy also incorporate these objectives. A helpful way to imagine this duality is to visualize mainstreaming as horizontal in nature (cutting across every area of law and policy), whilst the specialized measures represent a vertical strand. In order to make sense of the EU's approach to mainstreaming, it is necessary to begin by analyzing the vertical strand: anti-discrimination law and policy. This field provides the first evidence of the conceptual framework which underpins EU measures to combat racism and promote equality. Anti-discrimination law and policy do not, of course, only concern issues relating to racism. At EU level, the principal grounds of discrimination addressed are nationality, sex, racial or ethnic origin, religion or belief, disability, age, and sexual orientation.[1] Consequently, it will also be relevant in this chapter to consider the position of racism within anti-discrimination law and policy (that is, vis-à-vis the other discrimination grounds).

This chapter is divided into two main sections. The first part focuses on how matters relating to racism are addressed within the anti-discrimination *legislation* of the EU. This is complemented by the second part of the chapter which examines *policy* interventions, namely, non-legal instruments.

A. Racism and Anti-Discrimination Legislation

From the perspective of combating racism, legal interventions by the EU can be divided into two periods, pre- and post-1999. Prior to 1999, there was no specific reference to racism and/or racial discrimination in the EC or EU Treaties. In contrast, there was an express commitment to equal pay for women and men in the former EEC Treaty, Article 119.[2] Accordingly, when EC anti-discrimination legislation first emerged in the 1970s, this was confined to gender

[1] EC Treaty, Art 12 and 13.

[2] On its origins, see C Barnard, *EC Employment Law* (3rd edn, Oxford: OUP, 2006) 298.

discrimination. During the 1990s, pressure grew from the European Parliament and NGOs for legal measures against other forms of discrimination.[3] This agenda encountered both political and legal obstacles. On one side, not all Member States were favourable to such an expansion of EU activity and, on the other, the silence of the Treaties provoked debate over the precise scope of the Union's competence to legislate beyond gender discrimination.[4] A gradual shift in the political support for an EU role amongst the Member States culminated in an agreement to amend the EC Treaty via the 1999 Treaty of Amsterdam.[5] This inserted Article 13, which explicitly conferred competence to 'take appropriate action to combat discrimination based on sex, racial or ethnic origin, religion or belief, disability, age or sexual orientation'.

In the period post-1999, the EU's legal framework on anti-discrimination has been transformed. Three main steps can be identified. First, in June 2000, a Directive prohibiting discrimination on grounds of racial or ethnic origin was adopted, hereafter referred to as the Racial Equality Directive.[6] Second, in November 2000, a Directive was adopted prohibiting discrimination in employment and vocational training on grounds of religion of belief, disability, age, and sexual orientation (the Employment Equality Directive).[7] Third, there was a lengthy process between 2002 and 2006 of revising and consolidating the original legislation on sex discrimination in employment,[8] as well as introducing new legislation on sex discrimination in the provision of goods and services.[9] Furthermore, in 2008, the Commission proposed a Directive prohibiting discrimination in areas outside employment, in relation to the grounds

[3] E Bleich and M C Feldmann, 'The rise of race? Europeanization and antiracist policymaking in the EU'. Paper presented at the conference 'The impact of Europeanization on politics and policy in Europe: trends and trajectories', University of Toronto, 7–9 May 2004.

[4] D Curtin and M Geurts, 'Race discrimination and the European Union Anno 1996: from rhetoric to legal remedy?' (1996) 14 *Netherlands Quarterly of Human Rights* 147.

[5] For a detailed account of the factors and events leading up to this decision, see L Flynn, 'The implications of Article 13 EC—after Amsterdam, will some forms of discrimination be more equal than others?' (1999) 36 CML Rev 1127; L Waddington, 'Testing the limits of the EC Treaty Article on non-discrimination' (1999) 28 ILJ 133.

[6] Council Directive (EC) 2000/43 implementing the principle of equal treatment between persons irrespective of racial or ethnic origin [2000] OJ L180/22.

[7] Council Directive (EC) 2000/78 establishing a general framework for equal treatment in employment and occupation [2000] OJ L303/16.

[8] EP and Council Directive (EC) 2002/73 amending Council Directive (EEC) 76/207 on the implementation of the principle of equal treatment for men and women as regards access to employment, vocational training and promotion, and working conditions [2002] OJ L269/15; EP and Council Directive (EC) 2006/54 on the implementation of the principle of equal opportunities and equal treatment of men and women in matters of employment and occupation (recast) [2006] OJ L204/23.

[9] Council Directive (EC) 2004/113 implementing the principle of equal treatment between men and women in the access to and supply of goods and services [2004] OJ L373/37 (the 'Gender Goods and Services Directive').

of religion or belief, disability, age, and sexual orientation.[10] Amongst the existing legislation, it is self-evident that the Racial Equality Directive constitutes the primary expression of the Union's legal response to racism.[11] Therefore, the remainder of this section will concentrate on this instrument.

The main elements of the Racial Equality Directive

An extensive body of academic literature has accumulated since 1999 on Article 13 and the subsequent Directives.[12] This includes detailed analysis of the provisions of the Racial Equality Directive.[13] This section provides a résumé of the Directive's key features, before proceeding to an analysis of what this reveals about the EU's conception of racism and equality.

Article 1 defines the purpose of the Directive as to 'lay down a framework for combating discrimination on grounds of racial or ethnic origin'. 'Discrimination' is then broken down into four separate unlawful acts. First, direct discrimination occurs where a person is 'treated less favourably than another is, has been or would be treated in a comparable situation on grounds of racial or ethnic origin'.[14] Second, indirect discrimination covers situations 'where an apparently neutral provision, criterion or practice would put persons of a racial or ethnic origin at a particular disadvantage compared with other persons, unless that provision, criterion or practice is objectively justified by a legitimate aim and the means of achieving that aim are appropriate and necessary'.[15] Third, harassment is treated as discrimination where 'an unwanted conduct related to racial or ethnic origin takes place with the purpose or effect of violating the dignity of a person and of creating an intimidating, hostile, degrading, humiliating or offensive

[10] Commission, 'Proposal for a Council Directive on implementing the principle of equal treatment between persons irrespective of religion or belief, disability, age or sexual orientation' COM (2008) 426.

[11] Legal measures against racist crimes adopted under the EU Treaty will be examined separately in Chapter 8 on criminal law.

[12] For a detailed, multi-lingual bibliography of this literature, see Focus Consultancy, 'Critical review of academic literature relating to the EU Directives to combat discrimination' (Brussels: Commission, 2004).

[13] eg E Guild, 'The EC Directive on race discrimination: surprises, possibilities and limitations' (2000) 29 ILJ 416; S McInerney, 'Equal treatment between persons irrespective of racial or ethnic origin: a comment' (2000) 25 ELR 317; A Tyson, 'The negotiation of the European Community Directive on Racial Discrimination' (2001) 3 EJML 199; C Brown, 'The Race Directive: towards equality for *all* the peoples of Europe?' (2002) 21 YEL 195; G Toggenburg, 'The Race Directive: a new dimension in the fight against ethnic discrimination in Europe' (2001/2) 1 *European Yearbook of Minority Issues* 231; E Ellis, 'The principle of non-discrimination in the post-Nice era' in A Arnull and D Wincott (eds), *Accountability and Legitimacy in the European Union* (Oxford: OUP, 2002) 291; T Jones, 'The Race Directive: redefining protection from discrimination in EU law' [2003] EHRLR 515; E Howard, 'Anti race discrimination measures in Europe: an attack on two fronts' (2005) 11 ELJ 468; E Ellis, *EU Anti-Discrimination Law* (Oxford: OUP, 2006).

[14] Art 2(2)(a). [15] Art 2(2)(b).

environment'.[16] Finally, an instruction to discriminate on grounds of racial or ethnic origin shall also be treated as unlawful discrimination.[17]

The four-fold definition of discrimination described above is now also found (in very similar language) within the other EC anti-discrimination Directives. Hence, the first distinguishing aspect of the Racial Equality Directive is its material scope. It applies to employment, vocational training, social protection (including social security and healthcare), social advantages, education, and access to goods and services which are available to the public (including housing).[18] In this respect, protection against discrimination based on racial or ethnic origin surpasses that available for all the other Article 13 discrimination grounds. The Employment Equality Directive is limited to matters relating to employment and vocational training and even the combined body of gender equality legislation does not include education.[19]

Another notable aspect of the Directive is the relatively narrow scope for justifying discrimination. In common with all the other anti-discrimination Directives, exceptions are provided for genuine occupational requirements[20] and positive action.[21] Beyond this, the only express exception is difference of treatment linked to nationality.[22] Whilst the latter is undoubtedly a rather significant lacuna, the Directive is otherwise more rigorous than the Employment Equality Directive or the Gender Goods and Services Directive, both of which include several open-ended exceptions.[23]

All of the post-1999 Directives anticipate the barriers to enforcement of the legislation faced by individual litigants.[24] To this end, they include measures to protect individuals involved in discrimination proceedings from victimization[25] and require a shift in the burden of proof from the complainant to the respondent once 'facts from which it may be presumed that there has been direct or indirect discrimination' have been established.[26] In addition, 'effective, proportionate and dissuasive' sanctions must be available where unlawful discrimination has occurred[27] and organizations with a legitimate interest in the promotion of equal treatment are to have legal standing to 'engage' in legal proceedings 'either on behalf or in support of the complainant'.[28] The Racial Equality Directive also obliges Member States to designate 'a body or bodies for the promotion of equal treatment'.[29] This body's core functions must include

[16] Art 2(3).
[17] Art 2(4). eg an order to an employee working at the entrance of a bar not to let in any Roma.
[18] Art 3(1). [19] Art 3(3), Dir (EC) 2004/113.
[20] Art 4. This applies in very limited circumstances where ethnic origin is relevant to the person's ability to perform a job, eg where a firm requires a woman of African or Caribbean origin in order to model products designed for such women's hair.
[21] Art 5. [22] Art 3(2).
[23] eg Art 6, Dir 2000/78 on age discrimination and Art 4(5), Dir 2004/113 on services provided primarily or exclusively to members of one sex.
[24] For a discussion of the difficulties encountered with individual litigation, see Ch 3.
[25] eg Art 9, Dir 2000/43. [26] ibid Art 8(1). [27] ibid Art 15.
[28] ibid Art 7(2). [29] Art 13(1).

assisting victims of discrimination, conducting independent surveys and publishing reports or making recommendations on racial or ethnic discrimination.[30] A similar duty can be found within the gender equality Directives,[31] but not in the Employment Equality Directive.

Racism and the Racial Equality Directive

Having summarized the key provisions in the Directive, it is now appropriate to consider what it communicates about the Union's concept of racism. Chapter 1 has already touched on this theme, noting two aspects. First, the preamble of the Directive denies the existence of separate human races,[32] thereby rejecting a basic tenet of scientific racism (the view that humanity can be divided into 'races' and that some of these are biologically superior). Second, by excluding nationality and (implicitly) religious discrimination,[33] the Directive fails to recognize the relevance of these characteristics when considering ethnic discrimination.[34] Cultural racism, that is, racism based around hostility to cultural difference, is closely intertwined with opposition to 'otherness'.[35] Often the markers of cultural 'otherness' will be different religious practices or national traditions, such as dress. By not including religion and nationality within a shared legal framework, the Racial Equality Directive may be limited in its capacity to tackle all aspects of cultural racism. Similarly, it is difficult to trace any influence of the concept of institutional racism on the Directive. As discussed in the next section, its perspective is based around individual litigation, with little attention to ensuring equal outcomes for all ethnic groups.

The Directive prohibits discrimination on grounds of racial or ethnic origin in respect of all persons, so in principle it applies universally. Nevertheless, it is clear that certain target groups were in the mind of the legislator at the time of its negotiation. A hint is provided in Recital 8 which refers to the need to foster an inclusive labour market by combating discrimination against 'groups such as ethnic minorities'. This terminology is also evident in the Commission's proposal for the Directive, which mentions 'the marginalization of individuals from ethnic minority and immigrant backgrounds'.[36] Notably, there was no express reference to Roma at this time, nor was there any attempt to address segregation within the

[30] Art 13(2). [31] eg Art 20, Dir 2006/54. [32] Recital 6.

[33] This is separately prohibited under the Employment Equality Directive.

[34] E Howard, 'The road to equality—developing the protection against discrimination on racial or ethnic grounds within the European Union' Ph.D. thesis, Queen Mary, University of London, February 2007, ch 5.

[35] S Fredman, 'Combating racism with human rights: the right to equality' in S Fredman (ed), *Discrimination and Human Rights: The Case of Racism* (Oxford: OUP, 2001) 9, 10.

[36] Commission, 'Proposal for a Council Directive implementing the principle of equal treatment between persons irrespective of racial or ethnic origin' COM (1999) 566, 5.

Directive's concept of discrimination.[37] A similar framing of racism as an issue primarily affecting ethnic (immigrant) minorities can be found in the policy documentation of the Starting Line Group.[38] This Group published in 1998 a draft Directive which appears to have significantly influenced the content of the subsequent Commission proposal.[39] It is telling that the Group's proposal was for a package of measures addressing racial and religious discrimination on the one hand, and the rights of third country nationals on the other.[40] A picture emerges of a Directive largely framed by an immigration policy context. The social context in which the Directive operates has since altered, especially in light of the Union's eastward enlargement. This is acknowledged in the Commission's 2006 evaluation of the Racial Equality Directive, which expressly refers to both national minorities[41] and Roma,[42] thereby recognizing the broader range of social groups in Europe affected by discrimination based on ethnic origin.

Equality and the Racial Equality Directive

On first impressions, the Directive seems to provide a framework within which both formal and substantive equality can be pursued.[43] The prohibition of direct discrimination clearly accords with formal equality's demand for the equal treatment of similarly situated persons. The influence of substantive equality can be traced in the concept of indirect discrimination, which acknowledges that the application of identical rules will not always result in equality in practice.[44] Nonetheless, the overall balance of the Directive ultimately seems tilted in favour of a formal equality concept.[45] Two features in particular support this conclusion.

[37] O de Schutter and A Verstichel, 'Integrating the Roma into European society: time for a new initiative' in European Centre for Minority Issues (eds), *European Yearbook of Minority Issues. Vol 4, 2004/05* (Leiden: Koninklijke Brill, 2006) 429, 432.

[38] The Starting Line Group campaigned from 1991 for a Directive on racial discrimination and an amendment to the EC Treaty to create a specific competence for the Community in this field. Its proposals were prepared by a legal working group and received the backing of almost 300 non-governmental and quasi-governmental organizations, as well as the EP: I Chopin, 'The Starting Line Group: A harmonised approach to fight racism and to promote equal treatment' (1999) 1 EJML 111. The author of this book was a member of the legal working group which drafted the Starting Line Group's 1998 draft Directive.

[39] Tyson (above n 13) 200; A Geddes and V Guiraudon, 'Britain, France and EU anti-discrimination policy: the emergence of an EU policy paradigm' (2004) 27 *West European Politics* 334, 349.

[40] I Chopin and J Niessen (eds), 'Proposals for legislative measures to combat racism and to promote equal rights in the European Union' (London: CRE, 1998).

[41] Commission, 'The application of Directive 2000/43/EC of 29 June 2000 implementing the principle of equal treatment between persons irrespective of racial or ethnic origin' COM (2006) 643, 3.

[42] ibid 8.

[43] On formal and substantive equality, see Ch 2.

[44] D Schiek, 'A new framework on equal treatment of persons in EC law?' (2002) 8 ELJ 290, 305.

[45] B Hepple, 'Race and law in Fortress Europe' (2004) 67 MLR 1, 12.

First, the Directive remains relatively agnostic with regard to positive action. Article 5 states:

> With a view to ensuring full equality in practice, the principle of equal treatment shall not prevent any Member State from maintaining or adopting specific measures to prevent or compensate for disadvantages linked to racial or ethnic origin.

An expansive reading of this provision could emphasize that it legitimizes positive action measures and rejects a very strict application of the formal equality concept. Yet, the issue has been delegated to the Member States and consequently national law is free to exclude the possibility of positive action. Most states have included provisions in national law providing space for positive action linked to racial or ethnic origin, but, as mentioned in Chapter 2, there are some exceptions.[46] Although states thus enjoy the discretion to restrict positive action at national level, paradoxically it is the Directive which acts as a major constraint for any state wishing to pursue strong forms of positive action, such as preferential treatment schemes. The assumption of the Commission[47] and many commentators[48] is that the Court of Justice will interpret the Racial Equality Directive in a manner similar to the gender equality legislation, where it has rebuked measures that automatically confer preferential treatment on under-represented groups (women) at the point of employment selection. Whilst the Court may yet confound this analysis, one impact of the Directive is to rein in the range of tools available to Member States in the area of positive action.

The second aspect of the Directive which pulls in the direction of formal equality is its focus on the protection of individuals. This is most evident in Article 7(2) on legal standing for associations; there is no possibility for associations to bring cases in the absence of an identifiable individual litigant. Individual cases can, of course, be used to advance substantive equality and this is most likely in the context of indirect discrimination claims. Individual cases seem less equipped to tackle subtle organizational practices which can be the source of group inequality. This lies at the heart of the concept of institutional racism. McCrudden provides the example of employers who recruit through informal methods, relying on personal contacts or the friends and family of existing workers.[49] Such practices are very likely to reproduce the existing ethnic profile of the workforce and exclude those who are outside established social networks, such as recent migrants. At the same time, there may be no identifiable act of discrimination against any specific individual, thus hindering a legal challenge.

[46] eg Slovakia: O de Schutter, 'Positive action' in D Schiek, L Waddington, and M Bell (eds), *Cases, Materials and Text on National, Supranational and International Non-discrimination Law* (Oxford: Hart Publishing, 2007) 757, 830.

[47] Commission (n 41 above) 7.

[48] eg C Kimber, 'Recent developments in EC equality law' in M Lucey and C Keville (eds), *Irish Perspectives on EC Law* (Dublin: Round Hall Ltd, 2003) 291, 311; Brown (n 13 above) 217; Tyson (n 13 above) 211.

[49] C McCrudden, 'Institutional discrimination' (1982) 2 OJLS 303, 314.

This dilemma is exposed by the case of *Firma Feryn*.[50] Here, an employer publicly announced that he did not recruit 'Moroccans', supposedly due to his customers' opinions. In its opinion, the Court of Justice acknowledges that the practical effect of this statement would be to deter such applicants, thereby reducing the prospect of legal challenge by an identifiable individual victim.[51]

Alongside the overall emphasis on formal equality, it can also be noted that the Directive provides little space for either mainstreaming or engagement with intersectionality. Beginning with the former, in recent years EC gender equality Directives have begun to build mainstreaming obligations into the legal framework. The Gender Employment (Recast) Directive includes a duty on Member States to 'actively take into account the objective of equality between men and women' when formulating and implementing laws and policies in the fields covered by the Directive.[52] The Racial Equality Directive, in contrast, has no express provisions on mainstreaming ethnic equality.[53] The closest the Directive comes to a mainstreaming approach lies in the duty to create a body or bodies for the promotion of equal treatment. This is accompanied by duties on the Member States to promote social dialogue 'with a view to fostering equal treatment' and to 'encourage dialogue with appropriate non-governmental organisations'.[54] The Directive anticipates, therefore, a deliberative dimension which accords with the participatory-democratic model of mainstreaming discussed in Chapter 3. Whilst not a duty to pursue mainstreaming per se, this could be characterized as creating a framework within which mainstreaming might take place.

With regard to intersectionality, it has already been noted that the Directive unhelpfully stratifies closely related forms of discrimination, such as that based on nationality or religion. Individuals experiencing discrimination on a combination of grounds, such as gender and ethnic origin, may encounter legislative gaps. If one considers discrimination against Roma girls in education,[55] EC legislation provides remedies in relation to ethnic discrimination in education, but not in relation to that based on sex. The preamble to the Racial Equality Directive did anticipate the relevance of an intersectionality perspective. Recital 14 states:

> In implementing the principle of equal treatment irrespective of racial or ethnic origin, the Community should, in accordance with Article 3(2) of the EC Treaty, aim to eliminate inequalities, and to promote equality between men and women, especially since women are often the victims of multiple discrimination.

[50] Case C-54/07 *Centrum voor gelijkheid van kansen en voor racismebestrijding v NV Firma Feryn*, judgment of 10 July 2008.

[51] ibid para 25. The case was brought by the Belgian Centre for Equal Opportunities which enjoyed autonomous legal standing under national law.

[52] Art 29, Dir 2006/54 (n 8 above).

[53] There is, however, reference to gender mainstreaming within the Directive (Recital 14 and Art 17(2)).

[54] Arts 11 and 12 respectively.

[55] C Fagan, P Urwin, and K Melling, 'Gender inequalities in the risks of poverty and social exclusion for disadvantaged groups in thirty European countries' (Luxembourg: OOPEC, 2006) 108.

Yet, the Commission's 2006 evaluation of the Directive concluded that the problem of multiple discrimination remained 'largely untackled', with few states submitting any evidence of how they had taken into account gender during the transposition process.[56]

Combating racism enjoys a strong foothold within EC anti-discrimination legislation. Since the adoption of the Racial Equality Directive, racial discrimination has often been viewed as enjoying 'pole position'[57] within the EU's equality law hierarchy. Whilst the strength of the Directive relative to the legislation applying to other discrimination grounds is manifest, it is not a framework without internal flaws. Its disposition seems most apt for tackling scientific racism and some forms of cultural racism, but not adequate to tackle effectively institutional racism. This reflects the tendency of the Directive to lean towards an individualistic, formal concept of equality. These shortcomings have been increasingly illuminated in recent years by trends in EU anti-discrimination *policy*, to which the next section now turns.

B. Racism and Anti-Discrimination Policy

Non-legal interventions in this field both pre-date and post-date the adoption of the Racial Equality Directive. Whilst there is no definitive turning point in policy evolution, the place of racism within anti-discrimination policy has unequivocally altered during the past decade. This section will begin by identifying the primary facets of anti-racism policy prior to Article 13, before turning to consider the post-Article 13 picture.

Pre-Article 13

This section does not aim to provide a complete chronology of the myriad initiatives that were adopted over the years as anti-racism policy gradually expanded.[58] Instead, it seeks to identify a number of key dimensions: target groups, key actors, and policy orientations.

Target groups

As already mentioned, anti-racism policy in this period was heavily shaped by an immigration policy frame. In policy discourse, the term racism was normally used in conjunction with *xenophobia*, literally defined as fear of foreigners.[59]

[56] para 3.5, Commission (n 41 above). [57] Brown (n 13 above) 222.

[58] For a detailed account, see M Bell, *Anti-Discrimination Law and the European Union* (Oxford: OUP, 2002) 59–72.

[59] eg Council Resolution on the response of educational systems to the problems of racism and xenophobia [1995] OJ C312/1; EP Resolution on racism and xenophobia [1993] OJ C342/19.

An analysis of the 176 projects funded by the European Year Against Racism (1997) reveals an overwhelming emphasis on immigrant-related racism; only five projects appear to have specifically addressed Roma.[60] Moreover, an immigration policy frame is also implied by the policy imagery; the Year's logo was a silhouette of two people of contrasting colours.[61]

Aside from discrimination against migrants, the other main target group of policy in this period was the Jewish community. Frequently, the spur which placed racism on the EU's political agenda was electoral success by extreme right-wing political parties, combined with violent acts of racism and anti-Semitism.[62] It was common in this period to find express reference to anti-Semitism in the title of policy documentation[63] and several projects funded during the European Year Against Racism were focused on anti-Semitism and Holocaust denial.[64] Indeed, in 1996, when the Council adopted its first legislative instrument on racist criminal offences, this included reference to Holocaust denial.[65]

Key actors

As an emerging field, the main actors pushing for policy expansion were initially the European Parliament and NGOs. Within the Parliament, issues of racism were principally dealt with by the Civil Liberties Committee which produced a steady stream of reports and resolutions from the late 1980s onwards.[66] One of its many recommendations was the creation of an EU-level forum for dialogue with civil society on combating racism.[67] This was taken up by the Commission and in 1991 the European Union Migrants' Forum (EUMF) was established. This body was mainly composed of representatives of migrants' organizations, but only those representing third country migrants rather than intra-EU migrants. Neveu points out that this created tensions from the outset; it assumed that EU citizens did not encounter discrimination based on ethnic origin when

60 Commission, 'European Year Against Racism—Directory of Projects' (Luxembourg: OOPEC, 1998).

61 <http://ec.europa.eu/employment_social/fundamental_rights/public/arcreyar_en.htm> accessed 18 June 2008.

62 eg two weeks after the desecration of Jewish graves in Carpentras (France) in May 1990, the Council adopted its first Resolution dedicated to racism and xenophobia: [1990] OJ C157/1.

63 eg Commission, 'Communication on racism, xenophobia and anti-Semitism' COM (95) 653; Commission, 'Countering racism, xenophobia and anti-Semitism in the candidate countries' COM (1999) 256.

64 Commission (n 60 above) 29, 90.

65 Joint Action (EU) 96/443 concerning action to combat racism and xenophobia [1996] OJ L185/5. This is discussed in more detail in Ch 8 on criminal law.

66 T Hervey, 'Putting Europe's house in order: racism, race discrimination and xenophobia after the Treaty of Amsterdam' in D O'Keeffe and P Twomey (eds), *Legal Issues of the Amsterdam Treaty* (Oxford: Hart, 1999) 329, 346.

67 EP, 'Report of the Committee of Inquiry on Racism and Xenophobia' (Luxembourg: OOPEC, 1991) 103.

moving within the Union and excluded ethnic minority EU citizens.[68] The EUMF never became a major voice in anti-racism policy[69] and in 2001 its funding was discontinued over concerns about financial irregularities.[70]

The NGO which appears to have had most influence in this period was the Starting Line Group. This can be likened to a hybrid model of civil society engagement. It stemmed from an informal coalition in the early 1990s of NGOs (such as the Churches Commission on Migrants in Europe) and quasi-governmental bodies (such as the British Commission for Racial Equality). It was not grassroots ethnic mobilization,[71] but by focusing on a precise agenda of key legal reforms (principally the Racial Equality Directive), it built up a wide-ranging coalition of support.[72] This was an effective model of issue-specific lobbying, but it did not provide a permanent framework for ongoing dialogue between the EU institutions and communities affected by racism.

At the end of this period, the Union took the first steps to increase its institutional capacity on combating racism; in 1997, the Council approved the creation of the EU Monitoring Centre on Racism and Xenophobia (EUMC).[73] The idea for a specialized agency emerged from the work of an ad hoc group of Member States' representatives, which was charged by the European Council with reviewing the scope for EU anti-racism policy in the mid-1990s.[74] Its establishment dovetailed with the 1997 European Year Against Racism and it provided a symbolic indicator of the degree to which anti-racism policy was becoming entrenched within EU institutional frameworks.

Policy orientations

Much of the focus in this early period of anti-racism policy was on jurisdictional issues rather than substantive policy content; in other words, the debate centred more on *whether* the EU should intervene rather than *how* to tackle racism. Nevertheless, it is possible to trace some loose threads which connect initiatives at this time. First, it is noticeable that anti-racism was typically conceived as a

[68] An exception was made for British representatives in the Forum who were permitted to come from organizations representing ethnic minorities in general, rather than just migrants: C Neveu, 'Is "black" an exportable category to mainland Europe? Race and citizenship in a European context' in J Rex and B Drury (eds), *Ethnic Mobilization in a Multi-cultural Europe* (Aldershot: Averbury, 1994) 97, 102.

[69] A Geddes, 'Lobbying for migrant inclusion in the European Union: new opportunities for transnational advocacy?' (2000) 7 JEPP 632, 639.

[70] The termination of financial support was later upheld by the Court of First Instance: Case T-217/01 *Forum des migrants de l'Union européenne v Commission* [2003] ECR II-1563.

[71] V Guiraudon, 'Anti-discrimination policy' in P Graziano and M Vink (eds), *Europeanization—New Research Agendas* (Houndmills, Palgrave Macmillan, 2007) 295, 301.

[72] See n 38 above.

[73] Council Regulation (EC) 1035/97 establishing a European Monitoring Centre for Racism and Xenophobia [1997] OJ L151/1.

[74] Consultative Commission on Racism and Xenophobia, 'Final Report' Ref 6906/1/95 Rev 1 Limite RAXEN 24 (Brussels: General Secretariat of the Council of the European Union, 1995).

free-standing issue with low emphasis on the links to other discrimination grounds. There are many examples of specific measures taken that concentrated only on racism, ranging from the European Year Against Racism to the creation of the EUMC. Correspondingly, there is little evidence that intersectionality issues were taken into account. Second, there was a clear priority attached to tackling racism through legal instruments. Although the insertion of Article 13 had the secondary effect of creating a firmer platform for non-legal measures, the underlying rationale was to open the door to legislation. A third strand to policy, which emerges towards the end of this period, witnesses a move beyond a purely legal approach. In 1998, the Commission published an 'Action Plan Against Racism'.[75] This promised to 'actively develop a mainstreaming approach to combating racism',[76] listing a range of policy fields, such as employment, education, youth, and research, where anti-racism objectives would be integrated. It announced the creation of an inter-service group within the Commission to coordinate anti-racism measures across the different Directorates-General (DGs).[77] As discussed in Chapter 3, this was part of a wider turn towards mainstreaming, evident first in gender equality policy, but also in relation to disability.[78] The foray into mainstreaming chimes with another theme emerging within anti-racism policy at this time: data collection. The need for better data was anticipated through the creation of the EUMC, whose 'prime objective' was:

> to provide the Community and its Member States . . . with objective, reliable and comparable data at European level on the phenomena of racism, xenophobia and anti-Semitism in order to help them when they take measures or formulate courses of action within their respective spheres of competence.[79]

In summary, by the time that Article 13 was introduced, EU anti-racism policy had already assumed several clear dimensions. It was largely autonomous from other parts of anti-discrimination policy and it focused on discrimination faced by ethnic (immigrant) minorities. The civil society capacity (at EU level) remained fragile, but institutional mechanisms were being created in order to bolster policy expertise via data collection and to emulate existing gender equality strategies through mainstreaming.

Post-Article 13

In retrospect, the adoption of a separate Directive on racial discrimination appears to have been a high watermark for the idea of a stand-alone EU anti-racism policy.

[75] Commission, 'Action Plan Against Racism' COM (1998) 183.
[76] ibid 3. [77] ibid 16.
[78] L Waddington, 'The expanding role of the equality principle in European Union law' Policy Papers (Series on Constitutional Reform of the EU) 2003/04 (Florence: European University Institute, 2003) 17.
[79] Art 2(1), Reg 1035/97.

Since then, there has been a steady repositioning of racism within anti-discrimination policy. This has gone in two directions which, on the surface, are contradictory. First, the concept of racism has diversified, with greater policy recognition of differences between groups affected by racism. This process of breaking down a monolithic notion of racism has, though, gone hand-in-hand with increasing assimilation of racism into broader anti-discrimination policy.

These changes in policy trajectory primarily took place under the aegis of the Community Action Programme to Combat Discrimination (2001–2006).[80] The Action Programme was established as part of a package of measures adopted in 2000, complementing the Racial Equality and Employment Equality Directives. Its general goal was to combat discrimination on the grounds of racial or ethnic origin, religion or belief, disability, age, and sexual orientation; a separate Action Programme was created in respect of gender.[81] A budget of €98.4 million was allocated with three core objectives:

- Strand 1: analysis and evaluation (research);
- Strand 2: capacity building (transnational projects and funding EU-level NGOs);
- Strand 3: awareness-raising (conferences, programme website, media campaign).[82]

Although the Action Programme has since finished, it has been reincarnated within the umbrella social policy programme called 'Progress' (2007–2013).[83] This has a strand devoted to 'anti-discrimination and diversity' which has similar objectives to the Action Programme and a budget of €151 million. The remainder of this section draws on the Action Programme to examine post-Article 13 policy developments according to the themes of target groups, key actors, and policy orientations.

Target groups

Distinct changes can be identified in the perceived target groups of anti-racism policy. Whilst immigrant communities remain a prime concern, there has been growing recognition of other affected groups, principally Roma.[84] The catalyst for this change was the enlargement of the EU to include new members from central, eastern, and southern Europe. The political criteria for accession (the

[80] Council Decision (EC) 2000/750 establishing a Community action programme to combat discrimination (2001 to 2006) [2000] OJ L303/23.

[81] Council Decision (EC) 2001/51 establishing a programme relating to the Community framework strategy on gender equality (2001–2005) [2001] OJ L17/22.

[82] For a more detailed analysis, see G de Búrca, 'EU race discrimination law: a hybrid model?' in G de Búrca and J Scott (eds), *Law and New Governance in the EU and the US* (Oxford: Hart Publishing, 2006) 97.

[83] EP and Council Decision (EC) 1672/2006 establishing a Community programme for employment and social solidarity—Progress [2006] OJ L315/1.

[84] L Waddington, 'Taking stock and looking forward: the Commission Green Paper on equality and non-discrimination in an enlarged European Union' (2004) 33 ILJ 367.

1993 'Copenhagen criteria') included 'respect for and protection of minorities'.[85] The process of monitoring the applicant states drew the EU institutions into closer scrutiny of their prevailing social situation. Problems of inter-ethnic inequalities featured within the Commission's annual monitoring reports[86] and in 1999 the Commission published a specific report on 'countering racism, xenophobia and anti-Semitism in the candidate countries'.[87]

With regard to Roma, a crescendo of research uncovered severe evidence of socio-economic disadvantage including practices such as segregation of school-children and coerced sterilization of Roma women.[88] The EUMC's annual reports began to flag up Roma as the most disadvantaged group amongst those vulnerable to racism[89] and in 2004 the Commission published a comprehensive study entitled 'The situation of Roma in an enlarged European Union'.[90] In response, policy has gradually oriented towards more Roma-specific measures. The 2004 Green Paper on Equality described the Roma as the 'largest ethnic minority group in the enlarged EU'[91] and in the same year the Commission created its own inter-service group on Roma, in order to coordinate Roma-related initiatives across 14 different departments.[92] A specific focus on Roma continues to be a feature of present-day policy. In 2008, the Commission published a detailed overview of how a range of EU policies is being deployed to promote Roma inclusion.[93] This was followed up with an 'EU Roma Summit', reporting to the European Council.[94]

The 1999 Commission report on racism in the candidate countries placed as much emphasis on the situation of national minorities as it did on Roma. Nevertheless, there is relatively little evidence that EU anti-racism policy has since engaged with national minorities. In 2006, the Commission established a High Level Advisory Group on the social integration of ethnic minorities and its remit included 'recent migrants, established ethnic minorities, *national minorities*,

[85] Commission (1999) (n 63 above) 2.

[86] For an overview, see EP, 'Report on the communication from the Commission on countering racism, xenophobia and anti-Semitism in the candidate countries' [Ludford] A5-55/2000, PE 232.460, 15–17.

[87] COM (1999) 256.

[88] eg the Open Society Institute produced a series of reports on minority protection in the candidate countries, many of which focused on the Roma: <http://www.eumap.org> accessed 18 June 2008. The European Roma Rights Centre has also pursued an active research agenda since its creation in 1996: <http://www.errc.org> accessed 18 June 2008.

[89] EUMC, 'Racism and xenophobia in the EU Member States: trends, developments and good practice. Annual report 2003/2004—Part 2' (Vienna: EUMC, 2004) 3.

[90] (Luxembourg: OOPEC, 2004).

[91] Commission, 'Equality and non-discrimination in an enlarged European Union' COM (2004) 379, 20.

[92] E Sobotka, 'Targeting and mainstreaming the integration of Roma at the EU and European level' (2005) 16 *Equal Voices* 4.

[93] Commission, 'Community instruments and policies for Roma inclusion' Commission Staff Working Paper, 2 July 2008.

[94] Commission, 'Non-discrimination and equal opportunities: a renewed commitment' COM (2008) 420/3, 10.

the Roma and stateless persons'.[95] It concluded that there was little evidence that national minorities experienced significant inequalities in socio-economic outcomes, such as labour market participation.[96] This finding is not beyond criticism. For example, research in Estonia has uncovered significant labour market disparities between ethnic Estonians and non-Estonians (predominantly Russian minorities).[97] Nonetheless, the perception that national minorities are not subject to substantial inequalities, alongside the political sensitivities surrounding their recognition,[98] helps explain why Roma rather than national minorities became a greater focus of anti-racism policy.

Other trends can also be identified within the target groups of anti-racism policy. As mentioned earlier, anti-Semitism was a distinct strand of anti-racism policy initiatives pre-Article 13. The visibility of this issue has greatly diminished in the post-Article 13 period and it is rarely mentioned nowadays in the discourse of anti-discrimination policy. One explanation for this change is the dominant manifestations of anti-Semitism. Bleich draws a distinction between *access* racism and *physical* or *expressive* racism.[99] EU anti-discrimination law and policy have oriented towards access racism, that is, tackling discrimination in access to socio-economic spheres, such as the labour market or services. In contrast, anti-Semitism is more closely connected to physical racism (violent acts) and expressive racism (propaganda and Holocaust denial).[100] The latter issues have been addressed by the EU, but not under the policy frame of 'anti-discrimination'. Such issues tend to be characterized as criminal law matters. They fall within the remit of DG Justice, Freedom and Security and under the legal provisions of the EU Treaty (Title VI on 'police and judicial cooperation in criminal matters').[101] In addition, it may be that the geopolitical sensitivities surrounding anti-Semitism discourage greater EU intervention. This was graphically illustrated by an international political storm which embroiled the EUMC's research strategy on anti-Semitism. In 2003, the Centre decided not to publish a report it had commissioned on anti-Semitism, citing concerns about the methodological approach of the authors.[102] Some Jewish organizations argued, however, that the

[95] Emphasis added, Art 2, Commission Dec (EC) 2006/33 establishing a high level advisory group on social integration of ethnic minorities and their full participation in the labour market [2006] OJ L21/20.

[96] High Level Advisory Group of Experts on the social integration of ethnic minorities and their full participation in the labour market, 'Ethnic minorities in the labour market—an urgent call for social inclusion' (Brussels: European Commission, 2007) 29.

[97] K Kasesaru and A Trumm, 'The socio-economic situation of non-Estonians' in M Heidmets (ed), *Estonian Human Development Report 2007* (Tallinn: Eesti Koostöö Kogu, 2008) 46, 53. Thanks to Vadim Poleshchuk for drawing my attention to this source.

[98] G Sasse, 'EU conditionality and minority rights: translating the Copenhagen criterion into policy' EUI Working Papers, RSCAS No 2005/16 (Florence: European University Institute, 2005).

[99] E Bleich, *Race Politics in Britain and France—Ideas and Policymaking Since the 1960s* (Cambridge: Cambridge University Press, 2003) 170.

[100] ibid 181. [101] See further Ch 8.

[102] See answer to written question P-3693/2003, [2004] OJ C78E/313.

EUMC was trying to suppress evidence that contemporary anti-Semitism was less exclusively linked to the far right and instead increasingly stemmed from Muslim communities.[103] Such controversies indicate the potential conflicts that may arise between different groups affected by racism.

Key actors

Civil society

The most significant development in the period since Article 13 has been the establishment of the European Network Against Racism (ENAR). Although effective lobbying had previously taken place through the Starting Line Group, this was an issue-specific campaign and the Group ceased its work following the adoption of the Racial Equality Directive. By this stage, steps had been taken to create a permanent structure for representing anti-racism organizations at European level. During the course of the 1997 European Year Against Racism, a conference of anti-racism organizations agreed to open a discussion on creating an EU network[104] and, following a series of national consultations, ENAR was established in October 1998.[105] ENAR is a Brussels-based organization, with about seven staff and an annual budget of just under €1 million.[106] From its inception, its main source of funding has been the Commission, which also financed the preparatory activities leading to ENAR's creation.[107] In the financial years 2004–2006, for example, around 88% of ENAR's funding was derived from the Commission, under Strand 2 of the Action Programme.[108] Accordingly, ENAR is almost exclusively focused on lobbying the EU institutions. It functions through national coordinating networks in each of the 27 Member States, bringing together around 600 NGOs.[109]

There is no doubt that ENAR is an obvious reference point for anti-racist civil society at EU level. It provides the EU institutions with an interlocutor which, given its extensive national network, can claim to represent at least a significant strand of the anti-racism movement in Europe. Naturally, it is vulnerable to the critique that its financial reliance on the Commission calls into question its

[103] eg the Canadian Jewish Congress protested to the EU ambassador to Canada (5 December 2003), see <http://www.cjc.ca/template.php?action=briefs&item=58> accessed 18 June 2008.

[104] Commission, '1997 European Year Against Racism—closing conference report' (Luxembourg: OOPEC, 1998) 21.

[105] D Bouget and L Prouteau, 'National and supranational government–NGO relations: anti-discrimination policy formation in the European Union' (2002) 22 *Public Administration and Development* 31, 35.

[106] ENAR, '2006 Annual report' (Brussels: ENAR, 2007) 12.

[107] Joint answer to written questions E-2072/00, E-2073/00, E-2074/00 and E-2075/00 [2001] OJ C81E/139.

[108] A grant of €767,834 was received for 2004–2005 (ENAR, '2005 Annual report' (Brussels: ENAR, 2006) 11) and €816,210 in 2005–2006 (ENAR n 106 above, 12).

[109] ENAR, 'The voice of the anti-racist movement in Europe', 6 (Brussels: ENAR, undated).

political autonomy.[110] This is a dilemma which confronts many EU NGOs, where the model of substantial Commission funding is rather typical. Geddes argues that it would be wrong to depict such organizations as surrogate spokespersons for the EU; however, the underlying constraint lies in the direction of their work.[111] An organization such as ENAR would risk losing its funding were it to depart from an EU-focused agenda (for example, if it were to shift focus towards the Council of Europe).

Questions can be raised about the choice to fund only one anti-racism organization under the Action Programme. This has the appeal of administrative simplicity, but it tends to downplay the diverse forms that racism can take. In contrast, disability funding has supported one umbrella network and five smaller organizations dealing with specific disabilities.[112] The growing sensitivity to diversity within the concept of racism is illustrated by the subsequent decision in 2005 to issue a tender to fund a specific European-level organization on Roma.[113] The Commission has since agreed a three-year partnership agreement with the European Roma Information Office, whilst in 2008 a network of European NGOs formed the 'Roma Policy Coalition'.[114] The Commission has also announced its intention to fund 'smaller networks of NGOs representing intersectional groups'.[115]

Institutional actors

Prior to Article 13, the Parliament was one of the main motors for the expansion of anti-racism policy. This commitment has continued through the familiar techniques of reports and resolutions. In addition, the Parliament now has an Intergroup on Race and Diversity. Perhaps the most significant change, though, has been in the expansion of Commission-related policy actors.

Beginning with the Commission itself, a dedicated anti-discrimination unit was created within DG Employment and Social Affairs following Article 13. This had a remit for all Article 13 grounds other than sex, which continued to be dealt with by a separate unit. This unit has since been reorganized to divide policy from legal affairs; the policy unit continues to oversee all Article 13 grounds with the exception of sex. There has also been a significant growth in external structures which contribute to the Commission's capacity for legal and policy analysis. Initially, the primary forum for such expertise was anticipated to be the

[110] A Lentin, *Racism and Anti-racism in Europe* (London: Pluto Press, 2004) 289; C Lloyd, 'Anti-racist responses to European integration' in R Koopmans and P Statham (eds), *Challenging Immigration and Ethnic Relations Politics* (Oxford: OUP, 2000) 397.

[111] A Geddes, 'Integrating immigrants and minorities in a wider and deeper Europe' in W Spohn and A Triandafyllidou (eds), *Europeanisation, National Identities and Migration—Changes in Boundary Constructions between Western and Eastern Europe* (London: Routledge, 2003) 83, 88.

[112] Ernst & Young, 'Évaluation du programme d'action communautaire de lutte contre la discrimination (2001–2006)—bilan final 2006' (Brussels: Commission, 2006) 18.

[113] ibid 19.

[114] Commission (n 93 above) 28–9.

[115] Commission (n 94 above) 9.

EUMC. Its institutional history turned out to be rather turbulent, ending in February 2007.[116] The EUMC's difficulties were both functional and scientific in nature. On the functional side, its practical establishment had a slow gestation, substantially under-spending its budget in 1998 and 1999. On the scientific side, the EUMC's core goal was the provision of 'objective, reliable and comparable data at European level on the phenomena of racism, xenophobia and anti-Semitism'.[117] Initially, the Centre was criticized for embarking on a rather general research programme, which was not sufficiently focused on the achievement of this mission.[118] More fundamentally, questions were raised over the extent to which the EUMC could actually fulfil this mandate. On the one hand, it was charged with producing comparable data; on the other, it lacked any powers to direct national data collection systems. The Commission's 2003 review of the EUMC concluded that 'ultimately the Monitoring Centre's remit is unachievable unless national authorities adopt compatible if not common classification systems'.[119] The tarnished image of the Centre left it politically vulnerable and in December 2003 the European Council took the unexpected decision to change its mandate into that of a Fundamental Rights Agency (FRA).[120]

From the perspective of anti-racism, this shift from a specialist agency to one with a much broader remit carries the risk that work on racism will be diminished or sidelined. A particularly unfavourable contrast arose from the contiguous decision to create an Institute for Gender Equality.[121] The FRA commenced its work on 1 March 2007, so it is too early to tell how it will compare to its predecessor. Its core task is expressed in looser terms than that of the EUMC; it is to provide 'assistance and expertise relating to fundamental rights' for the EU institutions and Member States (when the latter are implementing EC law).[122] Significantly, 'the fight against racism, xenophobia and related intolerance' is a

[116] See further de Búrca (n 82 above) 113–16; M Bell, 'EU anti-racism policy: the leader of the pack?' in H Meenan (ed), *Equality Law in an Enlarged Europe* (Cambridge: Cambridge University Press, 2007) 178, 193.

[117] Art 2(1), Reg 1035/97.

[118] In 2002, an external evaluation reached the conclusion that 'the EUMC cannot be said to have demonstrated value for money for the €13 million it has committed': Centre for Strategy and Evaluation Services, 'Evaluation of the European Monitoring Centre on Racism and Xenophobia' (Brussels: Commission, 2002) 79.

[119] Commission, 'Communication on the activities of the European Monitoring Centre on Racism and Xenophobia, together with proposals to recast Council Regulation (EC) 1035/97' COM (2003) 483, 5.

[120] Council, 'Brussels European Council: 12 and 13 December 2003. Presidency Conclusions' POLGEN 2, 5 February 2004, 27.

[121] EP and Council Regulation (EC) 1922/2006 on establishing a European Institute for Gender Equality [2006] OJ L403/9.

[122] Art 2, Council Regulation (EC) 168/2007 establishing a European Union Agency for Fundamental Rights [2007] OJ L53/1.

mandatory element of the FRA's five-year thematic work programmes,[123] which should guarantee some degree of continuity with the work of the EUMC.

Aside from the travails of the EUMC, the Commission has made strategic use of the Action Programme as a means to build up multiple sources of legal and policy analysis. First, a series of legal networks was created, primarily to compile reports on national implementation of the Directives. As yet another indicator of the shift away from specialist anti-racism initiatives, the Commission decided in 2004 to replace the separate networks on race, disability, and sexual orientation with a general non-discrimination legal network.[124] In addition, the transnational projects element of the Action Programme was used to fund a European network of national equality bodies.[125] de Búrca draws attention to the impact over time of such networks:

> A whole array of other actors is drawn into the process of elaboration and enforcement of the Directive both by the terms of the legislation itself as well as by the gradual evolution of the action programme and its funding priorities.[126]

Certainly, a comparison with the period pre-Article 13 reveals a much richer variety of key actors in anti-racism policy. It is clear that many lawyers, activists, and policy-makers in this field now have more regular engagement with their European counterparts and EU law/policy has become established as a point of reference. In this respect, a subtle process has been under way of 'Europeanizing' of anti-racism policy.

Finally, it is important to note those actors whose presence remains less visible. This is certainly true of the Court of Justice. Whilst several (uncomplicated) infringement proceedings were successfully brought by the Commission against Member States,[127] the Court has lacked opportunities to provide a substantive interpretation of the Racial Equality Directive.[128] On the surface, the role of the Council also appears limited to occasional, but vital, strategic decisions, such as the adoption of the Directive or the creation of the FRA. Nevertheless, the Member States undoubtedly exercise a more ongoing 'behind the scenes' influence, for example, through the committee of national representatives which monitored the Action Programme. More recently, a 'non-discrimination governmental expert group' has been established by the Commission with a view to benchmarking good practice in national and EU policy.[129]

[123] ibid Art 5(2)(b). [124] Ernst & Young (n 112 above) 12.

[125] Equinet: <http://www.equineteurope.org/> accessed 18 June 2008.

[126] de Búrca (n 82 above) 119.

[127] Case C-327/04 *Commission v Finland* [2005] OJ C239/3; Case C-320/04 *Commission v Luxembourg* [2005] OJ C93/2; Case C-329/04 *Commission v Germany* [2005] OJ C143/13; Case C-335/04 *Commission v Austria* [2005] OJ C171/5.

[128] Aside from Case C-54/07 *Firma Feryn* [2007] OJ C82/21, the only other preliminary reference under Dir 2000/43 was rejected as inadmissible: Case C-328/04 *Attila Vajnai* [2005] ECR I-8577.

[129] Commission (n 94 above) 9.

Policy orientations

The final part of this chapter turns to consider the main shifts in the substantive content of anti-racism policy post-Article 13. Three themes, some of which have already emerged, can be highlighted.

Moving from anti-racism to anti-discrimination

The first discernible change in policy direction is the move away from specific policy initiatives related to racism and towards integrated measures that cover several discrimination grounds. This was signalled from the outset of the Action Programme; during the first round of transnational projects, 24 of the 27 funded projects concerned more than one discrimination ground.[130] Moreover, the discourse of the Action Programme's awareness-raising campaign was couched in broad terms of 'diversity' and 'difference'.[131] This trend was also evident in actions such as the change in the EUMC's mandate or the combination of the legal expert networks.

Connected to this shift, a growing attention to intersectionality can be traced. The Action Programme expressly included 'multiple discrimination' within its work programme[132] and, accordingly, some of the transnational projects focused on this perspective.[133] More recently, raising awareness of multiple discrimination was identified as a key objective in the Decision establishing 2007 as European Year of Equal Opportunities for All.[134] As yet, it would be an exaggeration to suggest that the EU has developed a clear policy response to intersectionality; it has, though, sought to raise the visibility of this issue through projects and research.[135]

Recognizing the limits of individual litigation

A second thematic trend which has emerged since Article 13 is a growing recognition that legal protection for individuals will not, by itself, be a sufficient mechanism for eliminating inequalities.[136] As discussed earlier, the Racial Equality Directive primarily allows enforcement by individual litigants. In particular, the situation of Roma has underscored the need for complementary strategies. Whilst litigation has been an important tool for advancing Roma

[130] Commission, 'Compendium: Transnational actions for the exchange of information and good practice' (Brussels: Commission, 2002) 3.

[131] <http://www.stop-discrimination.info> accessed 18 June 2008.

[132] para 1(e), Annex (n 80 above).

[133] eg the TRIANGLE project on double discrimination on grounds of racial or ethnic origin and sexual orientation: Commission (n 130 above) 8.

[134] Art 2(a), EP and Council Decision (EC) 771/2006 establishing the European Year of Equal Opportunities for All (2007)—towards a just society [2006] OJ L146/1.

[135] eg Commission, 'Tackling multiple discrimination—practices, policies and laws' (Luxembourg: OOPEC, 2007). See also, Commission (n 94 above) 9.

[136] E Howard, 'The European Year of Equal Opportunities for All—2007: is the EU moving away from a formal idea of equality?' (2008) 14 ELJ 168, 183.

rights,[137] O'Cinnéide points out that litigation processes are 'problematic for disenfranchised groups that face cultural, language, poverty or educational barriers to participation in formal public enforcement mechanisms'.[138] In 2005, the Commission published a 'Framework Strategy' which shifted away from the earlier emphasis on individual legal remedies:

> It is clear that implementation and enforcement of anti-discrimination legislation on an individual level is not enough to tackle the multifaceted and deep-rooted patterns of inequality experienced by some groups.[139]

Instead, the 'positive and active promotion of non-discrimination and equal opportunities for all' is identified as the core objective.[140] This new direction was part of the stimulus for the 2007 European Year of Equal Opportunities for All, as well as initiatives which have promoted exchange of experience on the use of positive action.[141] Moreover, it linked into work that the Commission had already initiated on mainstreaming and data collection.

Mainstreaming and data collection

The final theme in current anti-discrimination policy is mainstreaming. At first glance, this might seem evidence of continuity. The Commission's 1998 Action Plan Against Racism was built around the mainstreaming approach. Yet, this initial commitment to the mainstreaming approach quickly withered away. A follow-up report was published in 2000,[142] but the associated inter-service group subsequently disintegrated.[143] Indeed, the Action Plan Against Racism seems to have been largely forgotten in the subsequent years.

Mainstreaming has returned to the foreground of anti-discrimination policy in the period since 2004. Following the political controversy in autumn 2004 surrounding the (failed) nomination to the Commission of Rocco Buttiglione, the incoming President, José Manuel Barroso, established a Group of Commissioners on Fundamental Rights, Anti-Discrimination and Equal Opportunities. The Group is composed of eight Commissioners and meets 3–4 times per year.[144]

[137] The European Roma Rights Centre has pursued an active litigation strategy in national and European courts.

[138] C O'Cinnéide, 'Making use of positive equality duties: the UK experience' in C Costello and E Barry (eds), *Equality in Diversity—The New Equality Directives* (Dublin: Irish Centre for European Law, 2003) 75, 79.

[139] Commission, 'Non-discrimination and equal opportunities for all—a framework strategy' COM (2005) 224, 2.

[140] ibid 12.

[141] <http://ec.europa.eu/employment_social/fundamental_rights/spot/may07_en.htm> accessed 18 June 2008.

[142] Commission, 'Report on the implementation of the action plan against racism—mainstreaming the fight against racism' (Brussels: Commission, 2000).

[143] J Shaw, 'Mainstreaming equality in European Union law and policymaking' (Brussels: ENAR, 2004) 23.

[144] Commission, 'A roadmap for equality between women and men, 2006–2010' (Luxembourg: OOPEC, 2006) 34.

As discussed in Chapter 3, the Commission subsequently decided to incorporate compliance with fundamental rights into its impact assessment procedure, which applies to all new proposals for legislation or major policy changes. This process is subject to an overarching review by the aforesaid Group of Commissioners.[145] These are general initiatives that could be vehicles for mainstreaming ethnic equality, although this is not their explicit objective. More concrete structures for mainstreaming can be found in two inter-service groups within the Commission: one on Roma issues and another on anti-racism. The latter group was revived in 2005 and it reports to the Group of Commissioners mentioned above.[146] It meets several times each year and contains representatives of eight DGs, dealing with issues such as education, employment, justice, and external relations. It primarily provides a venue for sharing information and it is not linked to the impact assessment process. Although both inter-service groups are essentially internal bureaucratic bodies, outsiders are occasionally invited to participate in their meetings, such as ENAR or the Fundamental Rights Agency. The European Roma Information Office has criticized the quality of these engagements, concluding that 'there is no real input from the Roma in the process of policy design'.[147]

Unlike the initial attempts at mainstreaming in the late 1990s, currently, there appears to be a more sustained commitment. The Decision establishing the Progress programme states that the main goal of the anti-discrimination and diversity strand is to 'support the effective implementation of the principle of non-discrimination and promote its mainstreaming in all Community policies'.[148] Furthermore, in December 2007, the Council called on the Commission to ensure mainstreaming 'of non-discrimination and equality issues' in various sectors, including the Guidelines for Growth and Jobs and the Objectives for Social Inclusion and Social Protection.[149]

Allied to mainstreaming is the question of data collection. The Commission incrementally pushed forward this agenda under the aegis of the Action Programme. A working group on data collection was established in 2003.[150] This gave rise to an international conference on the topic, alongside a series of comparative research publications.[151] As with the expert networks, the gradual

[145] ibid 7. [146] Interview: Commission official, Brussels, 12 December 2007.

[147] I Ivanov, 'Mainstreaming of Roma in European policy', 2: <http://www.erionet.org/files/Mainstreaming_Romain_Eu_Policy.pdf> accessed 18 June 2008.

[148] Art 7, Dec 1672/2006.

[149] Council Resolution on the follow-up of the European Year of Equal Opportunities for All [2007] OJ C308/1. In response, the Commission restated its commitment to apply mainstreaming to all discrimination grounds found in EC Treaty, Article 13: Commission (n 94 above) 6.

[150] T Makkonen, *European Handbook on Equality Data* (Luxembourg: OOPEC, 2006) 100.

[151] Commission, 'Comparative study on the collection of data to measure the extent and impact of discrimination within the United States, Canada, Australia, the United Kingdom and the Netherlands' (Luxembourg: OOPEC, 2004); N Reuter, T Makkonen, and O Oosi, 'Study on data collection to measure the extent and impact of discrimination in Europe' (Brussels: Commission, 2004); E Olli and B Kofod Olsen, 'Towards common measures for discrimination: exploring possibilities for combining existing data for measuring ethnic discrimination' (Copenhagen: Centre for Combating Ethnic Discrimination and the Danish Institute of Human Rights, 2005).

impact of the Working Group seems to be the Europeanization of this issue. The various studies undertaken emphasize the plurality of data collection mechanisms which exists and seek to move the debate beyond a narrow focus on the relative merits of ethnic classifications. There is some evidence that these initiatives have managed to promote a degree of policy convergence. In December 2007, the Council requested the Commission and the Member States:

> to gather statistical data, whenever possible disaggregated by sex and, if necessary, on an anonymous basis, as an essential tool for improving the design and monitoring of policies and programmes aiming at providing equal opportunities for all and at tackling multiple discrimination . . .[152]

C. Conclusions

This chapter set out to map the way in which issues relating to racism have been addressed within anti-discrimination law and policy. This forms the backdrop to the EU's efforts to mainstream ethnic equality, so it is a crucial source in beginning to explore how the Union conceptualizes racism and equality. Considering the concepts of racism introduced in Chapter 1, both law and policy seem more geared towards tackling scientific and cultural racism than institutional racism. The Racial Equality Directive is primarily equipped to tackle individual cases of discrimination through litigation. Much of the work of the Action Programme has been directed towards supporting the (legal) implementation of the Directive.[153] As time has progressed, the limitations of the Directive have become more evident and, consequently, there have been attempts to reposition policy with a greater emphasis on substantive equality, as seen in the trend towards positive action, mainstreaming, and data collection. This trajectory indicates a de facto recognition of institutional racism, even if this term is rarely used in EU policy discourse. A connection can be made here with the relatively rapid growth in awareness of the situation of Roma. Although Roma communities experience inequality in both western and eastern Europe, the accession process lifted the lid on the severity of this disadvantage. This strengthened the rationale for positive action, but it also drew attention to the complex manifestations of ethnic inequality across Europe. The immigration policy paradigm, which was the dominant influence shaping anti-racism policy in the 1990s, has given way to an enhanced appreciation of the differences that exist between those vulnerable to racism. This is particularly evident in relation to Roma where there is a discernible shift towards Roma-specific initiatives.

[152] Council (n 149 above). On the Commission's specific plans for enhanced data collection, see: Commission (n 94 above) 7.

[153] para 3.1, Ernst & Young, '2005 evaluation of the Community action programme to combat discrimination—executive summary' (Brussels: Commission, 2005).

Anti-racism law and policy have established relatively firm roots in the past decade. The Action Programme has been used to populate the surrounding policy space, both through support for civil society organizations (notably ENAR) and also through the growth in networks of national policy-makers and legal experts. Anti-racism is often perceived as a privileged category within EC anti-discrimination legislation. This flows from the relative strength of the Directive, but also its high political profile. For example, opposition to racism and xenophobia was explicitly mentioned in the European Council Declaration on the 50th anniversary of signing the EEC Treaty.[154] Nonetheless, anti-racism has been steadily realigned. Bleich and Feldmann argue that it is increasingly assimilated under a general policy frame of 'anti-discrimination' and also 'human rights'.[155] This is not an entirely negative development. Closer integration of racism and other forms of discrimination should facilitate better responses to intersectionality. Yet, the decline in specialist anti-racism policy carries with it the risk of dilution and reduced priority.[156] Moreover, any benefits in responding to intersectionality are tempered by the ongoing separation of both law and policy relating to gender equality from that applying to the other discrimination grounds.[157] In essence, the challenge lies in negotiating the appropriate policy mix between separate and integrated measures. An over-emphasis on measures that relate to all grounds will neglect the distinctive features of individual grounds. It seems that policy is pulling in two different directions at once; there is increasing recognition of diverse forms of racism and at the same time greater assimilation of racism to other discrimination grounds.

One area where there has been a marked shift from anti-racism to anti-discrimination is mainstreaming. Having committed itself to an energetic programme of mainstreaming anti-racism in 1998, the Commission subsequently wavered in its attachment to this goal. The current embodiment of mainstreaming is based on a loose framework of structures specific to racism (the inter-service groups), as well as more general initiatives, such as fundamental rights impact assessment and the Group of Commissioners. It might be a stretch to describe this as a conscious strategy for mainstreaming ethnic equality, although it holds the potential to have this effect. Considering the models of mainstreaming discussed in Chapter 3, the loose nature of the existing processes inclines towards the integrationist model, predominantly reliant on elite-bureaucratic methods.

154 <http://www.eu2007.de/de/News/download_docs/Maerz/0324-RAA/English.pdf> accessed 18 June 2008.

155 Bleich and Feldmann (n 3 above).

156 J Shaw, 'Mainstreaming equality and diversity in European Union law and policy' in J Holder and C O'Cinnéide (eds), *Current Legal Problems 2005, Vol 58* (Oxford: OUP, 2006) 255, 263.

157 The European Year of Equal Opportunities for All marked a departure from this approach as it combined all Article 13 grounds in the same initiative.

The remainder of this book turns to consider four specific areas of law and policy in order to assess the extent to which the objectives of combating racism and promoting equality have been mainstreamed in practice. This provides an opportunity to consider both the processes through which mainstreaming occurs and the results it has delivered.

5

Employment

The next four chapters each examine a specific area of EU law and policy in order to assess the extent to which the objectives of combating racism and promoting equality have been mainstreamed. The first example to consider is employment law and policy. There are several reasons which render this an apt point of departure. Historically, participation in the labour market has been the focus of EU social policy, rather than other issues such as health, education, and housing.[1] Although the Racial Equality Directive applies beyond the sphere of employment, it has the hallmarks of a labour law template[2] and one of its express aims is 'to foster conditions for a socially inclusive labour market'.[3] From a bureaucratic perspective, Directorate-General Employment, Social Affairs and Equal Opportunities deals with both employment and anti-discrimination. Therefore, if mainstreaming functions effectively, it would be reasonable to expect to find evidence that it takes place within this administrative unit, before looking to see if it has permeated into other DGs. Finally, there is considerable experience with gender mainstreaming in EU employment policy,[4] so it is logical to explore whether this work has been extended to ethnic equality issues.

More generally, it is incontestable that employment is a key area in promoting equality. If equal participation in the labour market is not secured, then this will have negative consequences in terms of economic inequality and social isolation. There is already a large body of research which indicates that ethnic inequalities are prevalent throughout European labour markets. Third country nationals frequently experience higher unemployment rates and lower employment rates.[5] They are over-represented in unskilled sectors of the labour market, such as construction, catering, and household services.[6] This phenomenon has been

[1] T Hervey, *European Social Law and Policy* (London: Longman, 1998) 4.

[2] eg Art 11 on social dialogue; Council Directive (EC) 2000/43 implementing the principle of equal treatment between persons irrespective of racial or ethnic origin [2000] OJ L180/22.

[3] Recital 8.

[4] J Rubery, 'Gender mainstreaming and gender equality in the EU: the impact of the EU employment strategy' (2002) 33 IRJ 500.

[5] M Ambrosini and C Barone, 'Employment and working conditions of migrant workers' (Dublin: European Foundation for the Improvement of Living and Working Conditions, 2007) 39.

[6] ibid 28.

referred to as 'the so-called "3D jobs"—dirty, dangerous and demanding'.[7] Indeed, where data exist, these tend to reveal a higher rate of workplace accidents and fatalities amongst third country nationals compared to EU nationals.[8] Although a picture of labour market disadvantage emerges, it is equally important to recognize diversity within this broad canvas. In some countries, especially eastern European and southern Mediterranean states, third country nationals have higher economic activity rates than EU nationals: see Table 5.1. Differences also emerge between ethnic groups; for example, in Finland, the unemployment rate for Iraqis is over 55%, in contrast to a rate of 35% for those from Bosnia.[9] Another key variable is gender. Third country national women typically have higher unemployment rates and lower economic activity rates than EU nationals (male or female). This is not, however, true in all states.[10] Moreover, there are marked differences within the generic category of 'migrant women'. The economic activity rate of women from south-east Europe (Croatia, Bosnia, Albania) is two or three times higher than that of women from north Africa (Morocco, Algeria).[11]

Whilst the employment rate of third country nationals often exceeds that of domestic nationals in central and eastern European states, in these states severe disparities in labour market performance can be found in relation to Roma communities. In some states, such as Slovakia and the Czech Republic, Roma unemployment rates are estimated to be as high as 80%.[12] Fagan et al. report that this picture is combined with gender equalities, citing the example of Bulgaria where it is estimated that 66% of Roma women have never had a paid job.[13] The weak position of Roma in the labour market is undoubtedly linked to a legacy of educational disadvantage, but research for the European Roma Rights Centre (ERRC) also revealed substantial evidence of discrimination. In interviews with 402 Roma persons, 64% claimed to have experienced discrimination in employment and 49% said they had been openly told that this was because they were Roma.[14]

Within the confines of a single chapter, it is clearly not possible to provide a comprehensive analysis of all aspects of EU employment law and policy. Kilpatrick has identified three core strands to what she terms the 'EU employment

[7] M Jandl, A Kraler, and A Stepien, 'Migrants, minorities and employment—exclusion, discrimination and anti-discrimination in 15 Member States of the European Union' (Luxembourg: OOPEC, 2003) v.

[8] Ambrosini and Barone (n 5 above) 37. [9] ibid 17.

[10] ibid 18–19. In several states (Austria, Germany, Sweden, the UK) migrant women have a lower unemployment rate than migrant men.

[11] Commission, 'Employment in Europe 2003' (Luxembourg: OOPEC, 2003) 198; C Fagan, P Urwin, and K Melling, 'Gender inequalities in the risks of poverty and social exclusion for disadvantaged groups in thirty European countries' (Luxembourg: OOPEC, 2006) 123.

[12] Fagan et al., ibid 109–10. [13] ibid.

[14] ERRC, 'The glass box: exclusion of Roma from employment' (Budapest: ERRC, 2007) 9.

Table 5.1 Employment rate of persons born in the country and those born outside the European Union, 2006

Member State	Born in the country	Born outside the EU
Austria	71.6	61.6
Belgium	62.7	45.2
Cyprus	69.3	75.3
Czech Republic	65.4	65.2
Denmark	78.4	61.5
Estonia	67.4	72.6
Finland	69.7	53.7
France	64	52.8
Hungary	57.3	62.4
Germany	69.1	48.1
Greece	60.5	68.8
Ireland[a]	66.9	59.3
Italy	57.9	66.4
Latvia	65.7	72.7
Lithuania	63.3	69.7
Luxembourg	60	55.3
Malta	54.8	54.9
Netherlands	76.2	59.5
Poland	54.6	35
Portugal	67.6	72.9
Spain	63.8	71.6
Slovakia	59.5	57.5
Slovenia	66.6	68.4
Sweden	75.1	56.9
UK	72.2	63.1
EU25	65	60.2

[a] The data for Ireland relate to 2005 and are taken from Commission, 'Joint report on social protection and social inclusion—supporting document' SEC (2007) 329, 164.

Notes: The data are based on 25 EU Member States excluding Bulgaria and Romania which were not members in 2006. They concern the employment rates of persons aged 15–64. In relation to Germany, country of birth data did not exist, so the figures are based on nationality.

Adapted from: Commission, 'Overarching Indicators': <http://ec.europa.eu/employment_social/spsi/docs/social_inclusion/data_overarching_en.xls> accessed 10 April 2008.

governance regime'.[15] These are employment legislation, the European Employment Strategy, and the European Social Fund. This is a helpful framework, which will be adopted for the remainder of this chapter. Each strand will be considered for evidence of mainstreaming ethnic equality, looking both at

[15] C Kilpatrick, 'New EU employment governance and constitutionalism' in G de Búrca and J Scott (eds), *Law and New Governance in the EU and the US* (Oxford: Hart Publishing, 2006) 129.

substantive results, and also the procedural arrangements through which mainstreaming could take place.

A. Employment Legislation

It is difficult to find a neat explanation for the rather uneven pattern of EC employment legislation. Whilst it stretches across both individual and collective aspects of the employment relationship, significant omissions remain, such as the lack of protection from unjust dismissal or the absence of provisions on freedom of association.[16] Regarding those elements of employment law regulated by the Union, much is potentially significant for ethnic minority workers. For example, there is an extensive body of EC legislation relating to health and safety at work and, as mentioned above, there are (some) data suggesting that migrant workers have a higher risk of encountering an accident at work. If mainstreaming were in place, it could be expected that such data would prompt specific measures to improve the safety of migrant workers, such as ensuring safety instructions were available in a language understood by the worker. Even though it is relatively easy to identify points of connection between EC employment law and ethnic equality issues, very little evidence could be uncovered which showed that such mainstreaming had occurred in practice. As illustrated below, where there is some indication of mainstreaming, this tends to be highly general with no consideration of the specific situation of ethnic minorities.

During the mid-1990s, there was an initial attempt to introduce some (weak) mainstreaming within various employment Directives. This consisted of either the Commission or Parliament inserting anti-discrimination clauses to the effect that there should be no discrimination on grounds such as race or nationality in the implementation of that Directive.[17] Given that such proposals pre-dated the extension of the EC Treaty legal competence via Article 13, there was some reluctance within the Council to accept this approach. Consequently, the most that was achieved was a rather bland reference to non-discrimination in the preamble of several Directives.[18]

In the same period, concrete opportunities for more substantive mainstreaming were arguably missed. A good example is the range of legislation relating to worker participation. EC legislation requires procedures to exist for the information and consultation of employees, both within national-level

[16] For a comprehensive overview, see C Barnard, *EC Employment Law* (3rd edn, Oxford: OUP, 2006); J Kenner, *EU Employment Law: from Rome to Amsterdam and beyond* (Oxford: Hart, 2003).

[17] eg Art 2(3), Commission, 'Proposal for a Council Directive on the framework agreement on parental leave concluded by UNICE, CEEP, and the ETUC' COM (96) 26.

[18] See further, M Bell, *Anti-discrimination Law* (Oxford: OUP, 2001) 97.

enterprises[19] and within transnational undertakings.[20] One of the characteristics of these Directives is a degree of flexibility in the manner of their implementation; however, both contain fall-back minimum standards. These requirements include a specification of the topics where information and consultation are required;[21] equality is not included in this list. This omission might be understandable in relation to the 1994 European Works Council Directive, which preceded the active pursuit of mainstreaming by the Commission. It is less explicable as regards Directive 2002/14 on national-level information and consultation. At one stage, the Parliament specifically amended this Directive in order to add 'equal opportunities' to the list of topics where information and consultation were required.[22] This idea was not taken up by the Commission or the Council. Considering that Directive 2002/14 was adopted almost two years after the Racial Equality Directive, this seems a clear example of a lack of mainstreaming. Article 11 in the Racial Equality Directive identifies a specific role for social dialogue in furthering the objectives of the Directive:

> 1. Member States shall, in accordance with national traditions and practice, take adequate measures to promote the social dialogue between the two sides of industry with a view to fostering equal treatment, including through the monitoring of workplace practices, collective agreements, codes of conduct, research or exchange of experiences and good practices.

Making equality a core agenda item in the information and consultation of employees would seem a very practical contribution to furthering the types of actions encouraged in the Racial Equality Directive. This would also fit with the emphasis on participatory strategies which is a central element of the transformative model of mainstreaming, discussed in Chapter 3. In recent years, the Commission has been reviewing the European Works Council Directive and it noted that equal opportunities are increasingly the subject of workplace consultation.[23] Accordingly, the ETUC recommended adding this to the list of subsidiary requirements (the fall-back provisions).[24] In 2008, the Commission proposed a series of amendments to the Directive, including a revision of the

[19] EP and Council Directive (EC) 2002/14 establishing a general framework for informing and consulting employees in the European Community [2002] OJ L80/29.

[20] Council Directive (EC) 94/45 on the establishment of a European Works Council or a procedure in Community-scale undertakings and Community-scale groups of undertakings for the purposes of informing and consulting employees [1994] OJ L254/64. There are several other Directives also relevant to worker participation: see Barnard (n 16 above) ch 15.

[21] Annex, para 2, Dir 94/45; Art 4, Dir 2002/14.

[22] Amendment 23, Legislative Resolution embodying Parliament's opinion on the proposal for a Council Directive establishing a general framework for informing and consulting employees in the European Community [1999] OJ C219/228.

[23] para 3.2, Commission, 'European Works Councils: fully realising their potential for employee involvement for the benefit of enterprises and their employees' (1994): <http://ec.europa.eu/employment_social/news/2004/apr/ewc_consultation_en.pdf> accessed 18 June 2008.

[24] para 20, ETUC, 'ETUC strategy in view of the revision of the European Works Councils Directive' (2003): <http://www.etuc.org/a/578> accessed 18 June 2008.

subsidiary requirements.[25] Despite the ETUC's recommendation, the Commission has not proposed adding equality to this part of the Directive. The accompanying impact assessment noted that 50% of European Works Councils already included equality within their remit and reasoned that adding this to the legislation would have only an 'indirect impact'.[26]

The lack of evidence of mainstreaming in EC employment legislation can perhaps be attributed to the fact that anti-discrimination legislation has placed considerable focus on the labour market. There is an impression that other employment legislation is viewed as neutral or not particularly relevant to equality issues. This obviously runs counter to the ethos of mainstreaming and, in places, leads to potentially significant equality issues being overlooked. A good recent example is the Green Paper on Labour Law.[27] This examines the changing nature of the individual contract of employment, highlighting factors such as fixed-term contracts, agency work, and the fuzzy distinction between employment and self-employment. Surprisingly, there is no reference to ethnic minority or migrant workers, despite research which suggests that they are over-represented in some of these categories.[28] Whilst reference is made to the gender and age-related issues arising in respect of non-standard employment relationships, migrant workers remain invisible.[29] This example exposes a weakness in the Commission's internal procedures for mainstreaming. In relation to employment legislation, the only vehicle for mainstreaming is the impact assessment procedure.[30] Yet this is not comprehensive in its scope. In relation to worker participation, it was not triggered by the consultation of the social partners, even though this could result in legislation. Similarly, the Green Paper was not subject to impact assessment because it was only a consultative document.

B. The European Employment Strategy

As discussed in Chapter 3, the growing attention to mainstreaming during the second half of the 1990s corresponded with the rise of 'new governance'

[25] Commission, 'Proposal for a EP and Council Directive on the establishment of a European Works Council or a procedure in Community-scale undertakings and Community-scale groups of undertakings for the purposes of informing and consulting employees (recast)' COM (2008) 419.

[26] Commission, 'Proposal for a EP and Council Directive on the establishment of a European Works Council or a procedure in Community-scale undertakings and Community-scale groups of undertakings for the purposes of informing and consulting employees (recast)—impact assessment' SEC (2008) 2166, 50.

[27] Commission, 'Green paper: modernising labour law to meet the challenges of the 21st century' COM (2006) 708.

[28] Ambrosini and Barone (n 5 above) 32–3. Data from Spain indicate that 57% of Roma were employed on fixed-term contracts, almost 20 percentage points higher than the national average: I Begg and E Marlier, '"Feeding in" and "feeding out", and integrating immigrants and ethnic minorities' (Brussels: Commission, 2007) 27.

[29] Footnote 7 baldly states that 'the Green Paper does not address economic immigration, which is dealt with under the common immigration policy'.

[30] See further Ch 3.

methods. Although these are heterogeneous, they are characterized by a departure from the 'command-and-control' methods of traditional regulatory governance.[31] In the field of law, this has implied a reduction in the emphasis on instruments often described as 'hard law', Regulations and Directives. Instead, new governance reflects an ethos of experimentalism, flexibility, and diversity.[32] Rigid legal prescriptions are declined in favour of discretion for states to adopt the measures most suitable to their own circumstances, combined with mechanisms to promote transnational policy learning.

Employment law and policy have been key sites for the application of new governance techniques. The role for the EU in labour market regulation has long been troubled with boundary disputes centring on the possibilities and limitations of the competence conferred by the relevant EC Treaty provisions.[33] As with other areas of EU law and policy, tension arose between a reluctance from some states to cede authority to the EU institutions, yet an increasing reality that labour market performance was affected by transnational factors (such as business relocation) both inside the internal market and more generally in the globalized economy.[34] New governance methods have attempted to find a way through these conflicting claims by pursuing common policy objectives, but with much greater space for diverse national approaches. This direction has been epitomized in the European Employment Strategy (EES), which marked a shift towards a structured and self-conscious approach to new governance.[35]

The structure of the Employment Strategy

The EES was institutionalized in 1999 through amendments to the EC Treaty by the Treaty of Amsterdam. This inserted Title VIII which mandated 'a coordinated strategy for employment'.[36] The strategy rested on a cyclical procedure set out in EC Treaty, Article 128. Each year, the Council would adopt a set of guidelines on employment policy. Member States would report annually on the measures taken domestically 'in the light of' these guidelines.[37] In response, the Council could adopt recommendations to Member States and there would be an annual joint report from the Commission and the Council on the employment situation. Based on this joint report, a new set of employment guidelines would be adopted and the annual cycle would recommence.

[31] G de Búrca and J Scott, 'New governance, law and constitutionalism' in G de Búrca and J Scott (eds), *Law and New Governance in the EU and the US* (Oxford: Hart Publishing, 2006) 1.

[32] E Szyszczak, 'Experimental governance: the open method of coordination' (2006) 12 ELJ 486.

[33] eg Case C-84/94 *UK v Council (Working Time)* [1996] ECR I-5793.

[34] G de Búrca, 'The constitutional challenge of new governance in the European Union' (2003) 28 ELR 814, 827.

[35] On the background to the EES, see D Ashiagbor, *The European Employment Strategy—labour market regulation and new governance* (Oxford: OUP, 2005).

[36] Art 125. [37] Art 128(3).

This structure remains intact, but it has undergone several mutations since its inauguration in 1997. Initially, the employment guidelines were built around four pillars: employability, entrepreneurship, adaptability, and equal opportunities.[38] In the early years, there was quite a lot of tinkering with the detailed content of the guidelines. Following a review in 2002, a simplified framework was introduced based on three 'overarching and interrelated objectives of full employment, quality and productivity at work, and social cohesion and inclusion'.[39] This was intended to provide stability for the subsequent three-year period; however, a second wave of reform occurred in 2005. The new governance approach characterized by the EES had swiftly risen in popularity and it had been reproduced, in various forms, across a wide range of EU policies.[40] A signal moment in this trend was the European Council meeting in spring 2000, which ushered in the 'Lisbon Strategy'. This set a goal for the EU of becoming 'the most competitive and dynamic knowledge-based economy in the world capable of sustainable economic growth with more and better jobs and greater social cohesion'.[41] The dominant regulatory approach to achieve this goal would be the new governance style found in the EES, henceforth dubbed the 'open method of coordination' (OMC).

The subsequent proliferation of OMC processes was eventually reined in following a high-level review in 2004.[42] This resulted in a streamlined process, which integrated the annual economic and employment policy guidelines.[43] The integrated guidelines are designed to remain constant for three-year periods and, in tandem, states are required to develop three-year 'national reform programmes'. Whilst annual reporting still occurs, the bureaucratic burden on states has diminished and the triennial horizon is more significant. The first period under this new process was 2005–2008.[44]

Ethnic equality and the Employment Strategy

When the EES was launched, the 1998 Employment Guidelines were completely silent on the topic of ethnic equality. This might be explained away by the fact that the Commission's commitment to mainstreaming ethnic equality

[38] Council Resolution on the 1998 Employment Guidelines [1998] OJ C30/1.

[39] Council Decision (EC) 2003/578 on guidelines for the employment policies of the Member States [2003] OJ L197/13.

[40] Szyszczak (n 32 above) 494.

[41] para 7, European Council, 'Presidency Conclusions 23 and 24 March 2000'.

[42] Commission, 'Facing the challenge—the Lisbon strategy for growth and employment' (Luxembourg: OOPEC, 2004).

[43] C Chiattelli, 'The reform of the Lisbon Strategy's governance framework—is "new governance" the way forward?' (2006) 2 JCER 4, 6.

[44] For a more detailed picture of the new cyclical process, see Barnard (n 16 above) 159.

was only launched later in 1998[45] and this original omission was indeed subsequently addressed. In the 1999 Guidelines, Member States were asked to:

> give special attention to the needs of the disabled, ethnic minorities and other groups and individuals who may be disadvantaged, and develop appropriate forms of preventive and active policies to promote their integration into the labour market.[46]

It is notable that from the outset the situation of ethnic minorities was located not within the equal opportunities pillar of the guidelines, but within the employability pillar. The emphasis has consistently been on removing barriers to labour market participation and securing *access* to employment. There is much less focus on the treatment of those minorities already in work.

From 1999 onwards, the situation of ethnic minorities was expressly on the EES agenda, yet it remained a marginal concern.[47] The Commission noted that states were providing only limited data on this issue in their National Action Plans (NAPs).[48] It is a measure of the low political profile of ethnic equality that it was not until 2002 that any state was given a specific recommendation on the need to improve ethnic minority employment rates.[49] As a result, it is unsurprising that the Commission's 2002 review of the EES flagged up this area as one of considerable weakness.[50] In particular, it noted the absence of any apparent linkage between Member States' policies in response to the EES and the Directives adopted under EC Treaty, Article 13.[51] This message was reaffirmed by the 2003 report of the Employment Taskforce. This high-level group was created by the European Council to make a wide-ranging review of national employment policies. On 'minorities and immigrants', the report underlined the evidence of labour market disadvantage and drew specific attention to the low participation rates of migrant women.[52]

In the wake of these reports, the labour market situation of ethnic minorities began to assume a higher profile within the EES. The 2003 guidelines called for a 'significant reduction in each Member State in the unemployment gaps between

[45] Commission, 'An action plan against racism' COM (1998) 183.

[46] Guideline 9, Council Resolution on the 1999 Employment Guidelines [1999] OJ C69/2.

[47] For a more detailed examination of developments in this period, see M Bell, 'Combating racial discrimination through the European Employment Strategy' in J Bell and C Kilpatrick (eds), *The Cambridge Yearbook of European Legal Studies. Vol 6, 2003–2004* (Oxford: Hart Publishing, 2005) 55.

[48] Commission, 'Assessment of the implementation of the 2001 Employment Guidelines' SEC (2001) 1398, 62; Commission, 'Employment policies in the EU and in the Member States: Joint Employment Report 2002' (Luxembourg: OOPEC, 2003) 40.

[49] See recommendations to Denmark and Germany: Council Recommendation on the implementation of Member States' employment policies [2002] OJ L60/70.

[50] Commission, 'Impact evaluation of the EES. Background paper: social inclusion' (2002): <http://europa.eu.int/comm/employment_social/employment_strategy/eval/papers/inclusion_en.pdf> accessed 18 June 2008.

[51] ibid 6.

[52] Employment Taskforce, 'Jobs, jobs, jobs—creating more employment in Europe. Report of the Employment Taskforce chaired by Wim Kok' (Brussels: Commission, 2003) 45.

Table 5.2 Country-specific recommendations on employment policies relating to immigrants, Roma, or ethnic minorities, 2004

Member State	Groups mentioned	Action required
Austria	Immigrants	Better access to training
Belgium	Immigrants	Raise employment rates Improve response of public employment services
Cyprus	Immigrants	Improve rights
Czech Republic	Roma	Raise employment rate
Denmark	Immigrants	Improve integration
Estonia	Ethnic minorities	Improve employment situation
Finland	Immigrants	Improve integration
France	Immigrants	Raise employment rates Improve response of public employment services
Germany	Immigrants	Improve integration
Greece	Immigrants	Better access to training
Hungary	Roma	Raise employment rate
Latvia	Ethnic minorities	Improve employment situation
Netherlands	Immigrants	Raise employment rate Improve integration
Portugal	Immigrants	Improve integration
Slovakia	Roma	Raise employment rate
Spain	Immigrants	Active labour market policies
Sweden	Immigrants	Improve integration

Adapted from: Council Recommendation on the implementation of Member States' employment policies [2004] OJ L326/47.

non-EU and EU nationals, according to any national targets'.[53] The real signal of changed priorities lay in the recommendations to individual Member States. Within the new governance enforcement toolbox, recommendations are the strongest sanction available to the Union. By publicly 'naming and shaming' the weakest areas of domestic policy, the clear hope is that this will generate political pressure for reform. In 2004, most Member States received a recommendation relating to the position of ethnic minorities in the labour market: see Table 5.2. Change could also be detected in the NAPs from this period. In 2003, all states except Greece and Luxembourg addressed this issue in their NAP, albeit to varying extents.[54]

The positive trajectory developed during 2003–2004 was, though, interrupted by the wider reform of the Lisbon Strategy in 2005. As mentioned above, the specific employment guidelines were replaced with integrated economic and

[53] Guideline 7, Council Decision (EC) 2003/578 on guidelines for the employment policies of the Member States, [2003] OJ L197/13.

[54] For further analysis of the 2003 NAPs, see Bell (n 47 above).

employment policy guidelines, whilst the national action plans on employment policy were submerged within national reform programmes on economic and employment policy. This reform was explicitly designed to simplify the OMC processes and the reporting requirements they placed on Member States. As a consequence, there has been a general thinning in the content of the Employment Strategy. The attention devoted to ethnic inequalities in the labour market appears to have been one casualty of this reform.[55]

An initial indicator of change lay within the new Integrated Guidelines. For the first time since 1998, no guideline specifically mentioned ethnic minorities. Instead, Guideline 19 referred generally to 'inclusive labour markets... including disadvantaged people'.[56] The explanatory text attached declares 'integrating immigrants and minorities are particularly essential'.[57] By itself, this might simply be regarded as a technical matter of re-wording, but other evidence suggests a real decline in the priority attached to tackling ethnic inequalities. The Joint Employment Report of the Commission and Council (2004/05) painted a gloomy picture:

> Specific policies for the integration of migrants and minorities are being developed with a focus on assimilation and access to the labour market, including language training, literacy programmes or vocational guidance. The burden, however, is often placed on individuals to adapt. The Roma or migrants for example often seem to be portrayed [sic] largely responsible for their own situation.[58]

Despite this warning, momentum was further stalled by the policy of not making country-specific recommendations during the first years of the revised Lisbon Strategy.[59] Far from noting progress, the 2006/07 Joint Employment Report records evidence of a *deteriorating* situation for immigrants where the unemployment gap between EU and non-EU nationals was actually increasing.[60] Even so, the 2007 country-specific recommendations place much less priority on this theme than the previous set of recommendations in 2004.[61] The need to integrate immigrants is only mentioned in respect of three states (Ireland, Spain, Sweden) and there is a single reference to improving the situation of Roma

[55] Other commentators have observed a similar decline in the focus on gender issues: C Fagan, D Grimshaw, and J Rubery, 'The subordination of the gender equality objective: the National Reform Programmes and "making work pay" policies' (2006) 37 IRJ 571.

[56] Council Decision (EC) 2005/600 on guidelines for the employment policies of the Member States [2005] OJ L205/21. Guideline 19 has not been amended in the period since 2005.

[57] ibid.

[58] Council, 'Joint employment report 2004/2005' Ref 7010/05, SOC 102, ECOFIN 77, 9 March 2005, 16.

[59] Chiattelli (n 43 above) 11.

[60] Council, 'Joint Employment Report 2006/07' Ref 6706/07, SOC 74, ECOFIN 89, EDUC 39; 23 February 2007, 5.

[61] Council Recommendation on the 2007 update of the broad guidelines for the economic policies of the Member States and the Community and on the implementation of Member States' employment policies [2007] OJ L92/23.

addressed to Slovakia. Six other states have recommendations relating to 'vulnerable' or 'disadvantaged' groups[62] which might embrace ethnic minorities, but this is only implicit. A similar picture is found in the 2008 country-specific recommendations, where improving the integration of immigrants is a recommendation addressed to only four states (Denmark, Ireland, Spain, Sweden).[63]

The 2006 Implementation Reports on the National Reform Programmes paint a diverse picture.[64] On the one hand, most Member States include some reference to measures being taken in relation to ethnic disadvantage in the labour market.[65] Yet only a minority of states link this issue to discrimination. Measures to combat ethnic discrimination are mentioned in the Implementation Reports of Finland, France, Greece, Lithuania, the Netherlands, Sweden, and the UK. In the case of Greece, this is simply to note the adoption of a law transposing the Racial Equality Directive, whereas France, Sweden, and the UK have more elaborate information. Both Sweden and the UK, for example, mention steps to include non-discrimination norms within public procurement procedures. For most Member States, the accent is placed on integration policies, rather than combating discrimination. Several themes reoccur across the Implementation Reports:

- Integration programmes for immigrants: Austria, Czech Republic, Denmark, the Netherlands, Portugal, Spain;
- Language training: Austria, Belgium, Czech Republic, Denmark, Finland, Germany, the Netherlands, Italy;
- Reforms of immigration law: Austria, Cyprus, Czech Republic, Ireland, Italy, Malta, Portugal.

A similar pattern can also be found within the 2007 Implementation Reports.[66] Most Member States include some reference to the integration of immigrants or Roma in their reports, but it is quite rare to find any mention of discrimination as a factor contributing to their exclusion from the labour market.[67] There are also surprising omissions in the national reports: for example, the reports from Estonia and Latvia do not address the situation of Russian-speaking minorities. The fact that national policy responses vary is not unexpected; after all, the ethos of the EES is to permit diversity and to encourage experimentation. Nonetheless, the fairly infrequent reference to measures to combat racial discrimination suggests a disjuncture in many Member States between the steps taken in anti-discrimination law and the direction of labour market policy.

[62] Belgium, Czech Republic, Hungary, Netherlands, Austria, UK.

[63] Council, 'Country-specific integrated recommendations' Ref 6775/08, 26 February 2008.

[64] The 2006 Implementation Reports are available at: <http://ec.europa.eu/growthandjobs/key/nrp2006_en.htm> accessed 18 June 2008.

[65] There is almost no discussion of this issue in the NRPs of Estonia, Latvia, Luxembourg, and Poland.

[66] <http://ec.europa.eu/growthandjobs/national-dimension/member-states-autumn-2007-reports/index_en.htm> accessed 10 April 2008.

[67] Discrimination against immigrants or on grounds of ethnic origin is explicitly mentioned in the reports from France, Italy, Lithuania, and the Netherlands.

Mainstreaming ethnic equality into the Employment Strategy

Having considered the evidence of how issues relating to ethnic minorities have been dealt with in the EES, what observations can be made about the extent of mainstreaming? First, it is important to recognize the limits of the research method which has been applied. The documentary sources tell part of the story, but it may not be a complete or fully accurate picture. The manner in which national reports are drafted varies greatly, for example, with respect to the involvement of non-governmental actors.[68] There is clearly a risk that national reports engage in show-casing, giving a falsely optimistic impression of the situation.[69] Furthermore, cause and effect are difficult to determine. National employment policies respond to multiple stimuli and it is hard (if not impossible) to isolate the role played by the EES.[70] Despite these constraints, even the documentary sources reveal evidence of ostensible change, namely, the rise and fall in the prominence of ethnic minority issues.[71]

The first observation to make is the absence of any visible *process* through which mainstreaming ethnic equality takes place. This lack of structure helps explain why ethnic minorities were 'forgotten' at the outset of the EES, but also negatively affected by the 2005 Lisbon Strategy reform. If an effective process of mainstreaming was in place, then the impact of the 2005 reforms would have been assessed in advance and measures taken to mitigate any adverse effects. In respect of other issues, a mainstreaming process does exist. Gender mainstreaming was a commitment first inserted in the 1999 Employment Guidelines.[72] It has been kept under review by an independent group of experts[73] and underscored by the European Council's adoption of the 2006 European Pact for Gender Equality.[74] Whilst gender thus enjoys more precise mechanisms through which to advance mainstreaming, it must be acknowledged that concerns have been expressed about their effectiveness in practice. Indeed, eight years after gender mainstreaming was added to the guidelines, the 2006/07 Joint Employment Report concluded that 'the promotion of female employment and systematic gender mainstreaming of policies are rarely emphasised'.[75]

[68] C de la Porte and P Pochet, 'The European Employment Strategy: existing research and remaining questions' (2004) 14 JESP 71, 74.

[69] P Skidmore, 'The European Employment Strategy and labour law: a German case-study' (2004) 29 ELR 52, 72.

[70] M Barbera, 'I problemi teorici e pratici posti dal metodo di coordinamento aperto delle politiche sociali' in M Barbera (ed), *Nuove forme di regolazione: il metodo aperto di coordinamento delle politiche sociali* (Milan: Giuffrè, 2006) 1, 16.

[71] M Kate and J Niessen, 'Locating immigrant integration policy measures in the machinery of the European Commission' (Brussels: Migration Policy Group, 2007) 62.

[72] Rubery (n 4 above).

[73] The EC Gender and Employment Expert Group initially and now the Expert Group on Gender, Social Inclusion and Employment.

[74] This calls on Member States to incorporate a gender perspective into their NRPs: Council, 'Presidency Conclusions—23/24 March 2006' Ref 7775/06, Annex II, 27.

[75] Council (n 60 above) 4.

Aside from procedural issues, there are also problems with the *substance* of mainstreaming. Crucially, the EES lacks any well-defined concept of racism or racial discrimination. One manifestation of this is the persistent uncertainty surrounding the relevant target group. Already in 2000, the Joint Employment Report noted that some Member States focused measures on those of different ethnic origins, some on those of different nationality, and some on (historic) national minorities.[76] After 2000, the guidelines referred to both ethnic minorities and migrant workers in an attempt to be more inclusive; however, the 2004 country-specific recommendations follow a different approach. For most Member States, the focus is purely on 'immigrants', except for several central European states where Roma are highlighted and Estonia and Latvia, where reference is made to 'ethnic minorities'. In the latter cases, it is evident that 'ethnic minorities' is code for Russian minorities. More recent policy documentation is dominated by an immigrant policy frame.[77] The rather clumsy use of terminology reveals the unsophisticated analysis of racism within the EES. Notwithstanding the more elaborate commitment to gender mainstreaming, there is scant evidence of any engagement with intersectionality, such as the labour market situation of minority women.

More generally, it is notable that the terms 'racism' or 'discrimination' rarely feature in the EES discourse. To the extent that the labour market situation of ethnic minorities has been addressed, the EES has never placed great emphasis on combating discrimination as a means to promote employment participation. The policy recipe underpinning the EES has been described as 'supply-side';[78] in other words, it concentrates on removing barriers in access to the labour market. Over the years, there have been warnings to Member States that too much emphasis has been placed on integration into the labour market and not enough on combating discrimination.[79] The 'integration' paradigm tends to frame the 'problem' as residing within minorities, normally in terms of their skills.[80] For example, in considering the low employment participation rate of migrants, the Employment Taskforce concluded: 'the main causes of this situation are inappropriate or low levels of skills in general, as well as cultural or language barriers'.[81] Whilst the causes of labour market disadvantage are complex, the denial of the role of racial discrimination confounds theoretical and empirical studies. From a conceptual perspective, the emphasis on 'supply-side' factors

[76] para 3.1.5, Commission, 'Employment policies in the EU and in the Member States: Joint Employment Report 2000' (Luxembourg: OOPEC, 2001).

[77] eg Roma are not mentioned in the most recent Joint Report: Council, 'Joint Employment Report 2007/2008' Ref 7169/08 SOC 143 ECOFIN 95 EDUC 67, 3 March 2008.

[78] Barbera (n 70 above) 21.

[79] Commission (n 48 above); Commission, 'Taking stock of five years of the European Employment Strategy' COM (2002) 416, 12, Council (n 58 above) 16.

[80] EAPN, 'Strengthening the social dimension of the Lisbon Strategy' (Brussels: EAPN, 2007).

[81] Employment Taskforce (n 52 above) 44. See also the Joint Employment Report 2007/2008: Council (n 77 above).

runs contrary to the idea of institutional racism, which would interrogate the supposed neutrality of skills and language requirements. Empirical research also questions the heavy focus on skills factors. The ILO undertook a major research project into discrimination in job recruitment in several European states in the 1990s. By submitting job applications which were equivalent in terms of education, training, and language qualifications, but distinguished by reference to the nationality/ethnic origin of the job applicant, the project was able to uncover the extent to which ethnic minorities encountered disadvantage in the recruitment process which was not explicable by non-discriminatory factors. Across the states studied (which included Belgium, Germany, Italy, the Netherlands, and Spain) ethnic minority job applicants faced discrimination in 'more than every third application procedure'.[82]

Finally, one of the main instruments for mainstreaming remains missing from the EES toolbox: data collection. Overall, the EES attaches great weight to measuring progress through quantitative indicators. The most prominent targets have been those relating to employment participation rates (70% overall; 60% for women; 50% for older persons). There is though, a range of other 'targets and benchmarks' which has been in place since 2003 covering topics such as the early school leaving rate or the proportion of long-term unemployed persons participating in training programmes.[83] In contrast, no European targets have been set which relate to the labour market situation of national or ethnic minorities. Obviously, there are severe difficulties in data collection/target-setting where there is no settled definition of the object concerned–here, 'ethnic minorities'. This problem has been evident within the EES over several years, yet with no apparent action in response. Indeed, the Council did not adopt a proposal from the Commission to establish a target in relation to reducing the gap between EU/non-EU unemployment rates.[84] This failure to set any measurable benchmark for progress in tackling ethnic inequalities in the labour market provides a clear indicator of the relatively low priority attached to combating racism within the EES.

C. The European Social Fund

The EU promotes economic and social cohesion through its Structural Funds. This panoply of programmes includes initiatives which specifically focus on the labour market, gathered under the European Social Fund (ESF). The ESF has

[82] See the project summary: T Makkonen, 'European handbook for equality data' (Luxembourg: OOPEC, 2006) 77.

[83] See 2005 Employment Guidelines (n 56 above).

[84] Commission, 'Proposal for a Council Decision on guidelines for the employment policies of the Member States' COM (2003) 176, 13.

been operational since 1960[85] and its mission, as currently described in the EC Treaty, is to:

> render the employment of workers easier and to increase their geographical and occupational mobility within the Community, and to facilitate their adaptation to industrial changes and to changes in production systems, in particular through vocational training and retraining.[86]

Unlike the EES or EC employment legislation, the ESF deploys significant financial resources as a means to influence policy direction. This has risen over time to constitute more than 10% of the annual EC budget and more than €10 billion per year.[87] Over time, the ESF has gradually shifted towards greater emphasis on combating labour market exclusion.[88] This has gone hand-in-hand with its increasingly close connection to the objectives of the Employment Strategy, which is pronounced in the latest ESF round (2007–2013).[89] This section first considers the approach to mainstreaming under the ESF and then examines the use of the ESF to promote ethnic equality.

Mainstreaming and the European Social Fund

The access of different groups to ESF funding is not an especially new theme. Collins notes that there were tensions amongst the Member States in the 1970s over the extent to which ESF funds could be used in relation to third country nationals, with concerns that this encroached on (national) immigration policy.[90] The issue of mainstreaming came to the fore in the 1990s, initially via efforts to promote gender mainstreaming throughout the Structural Funds. Rees charts a shift in thinking during the 1990s in response to evidence that women were under-represented in EU funded programmes, including the ESF.[91] Beginning in 1993, this was reflected in the greater prominence for gender equality within the various regulations governing the Structural Funds and the ESF,[92] as well as practical guidance for fund recipients on how to implement gender mainstreaming. Significantly, a strong emphasis was placed on comprehensive data collection as a means to identifying any gender gaps, as well as ensuring the balanced participation of women and men in decision-making bodies administering the Funds.[93]

[85] J Brine, *The European Social Fund and the EU—flexibility, growth and stability* (London: Sheffield Academic Press, 2002) 11.

[86] Art 146.

[87] <http://ec.europa.eu/employment_social/esf/docs/esf_leaflet_en.pdf> accessed 18 June 2008.

[88] Brine (n 85 above) 12.

[89] eg Art 4(1), EP and Council Regulation (EC) 1081/2006 on the European Social Fund and repealing Regulation (EC) 1784/1999 [2006] OJ L210/12.

[90] D Collins, *The Operation of the European Social Fund* (London: Croom Helm, 1983) 33.

[91] T Rees, *Mainstreaming Equality in the European Union—education, training and labour market policies* (London: Routledge, 1999) ch 8.

[92] M Pollack and E Hafner-Burton, 'Mainstreaming gender in the European Union' (2000) 7 JEPP 432, 441.

[93] Commission, 'Mainstreaming equal opportunities in the Structural Funds' (Luxembourg: OOPEC, 2000).

The concentration on gender mainstreaming appears to have had beneficial spillover effects for other forms of inequality. One of the core objectives in the 1999 ESF Regulation was 'promoting equal opportunities for all in accessing the labour market'.[94] This is taken much further in the 2006 Regulations on the Structural Funds and the ESF. The umbrella Structural Funds Regulation states:

> The Member States and the Commission shall take appropriate steps to prevent any discrimination based on sex, racial or ethnic origin, religion or belief, disability, age or sexual orientation during the various stages of implementation of the Funds and, in particular, in the access to them.[95]

The accompanying ESF Regulation calls for 'specific action to increase the participation of migrants in employment'[96] and includes a duty on national authorities to include this topic in their implementation reports.[97] Those reports should also address measures taken to 'improve the social inclusion of minorities'.[98] For sure, the mechanisms for mainstreaming ethnic equality are not yet as sophisticated as those in place in respect of gender mainstreaming. Nevertheless, mainstreaming other grounds of discrimination has gradually worked its way onto the agenda.

Ethnic equality and the European Social Fund

The great majority of funds available through the ESF are directly disbursed to national authorities. In addition, there has been a practice of reserving some funds for 'Community Initiatives'. These programmes have a stronger input from the Commission and are geared towards influencing the direction of policy. The key ingredient of Community Initiatives under the ESF has been the search for *innovation*; funding is provided for exploratory projects with a view to identifying original and productive strategies. Having identified these bright ideas, then the aim is to share this knowledge across the EU, thereby enhancing policy expertise. This focus on experimentalism is a clear example of new governance approaches and resonates well with the ethos of the Employment Strategy.

Community Initiatives have been the most prominent vehicle through which racial discrimination has been tackled under the ESF. This occurred in two stages: the Integra programme and the Equal programme.

[94] Art 2(1)(b), EP and Council Regulation (EC) 1262/1999 on the European Social Fund [1999] OJ L161/53.

[95] Art 16, Council Regulation (EC) 1083/2006 laying down general provisions on the European Regional Development Fund, the European Social Fund and the Cohesion Fund and repealing Regulation (EC) 1260/1999 [2006] OJ L210/25.

[96] Art 3(1)(b)(iv), EP and Council Regulation (EC) 1081/2006 on the European Social Fund and repealing Regulation (EC) 1784/1999 [2006] OJ L210/12.

[97] ibid Art 10(b). [98] ibid Art 10(c).

The Integra programme 1997–1999

During the funding period 1994–1999, the ESF included a Community Initiative called 'Employment'. This umbrella programme aimed to promote access to the labour market for disadvantaged groups, such as women and disabled persons. In the second half of this funding period, the Commission introduced a specific strand called 'Integra':

> Integra offers a unique opportunity to experiment with new approaches which help those groups at most risk of exclusion to find their way towards employment—in particular, migrants, refugees and other similar groups which increasingly face negative discrimination, racism and xenophobia.[99]

The emphasis on combating racism was a new direction in the ESF and it reflected the rapid growth in the profile of anti-racism policy during the late 1990s.[100] A significant financial commitment was made; €418 million was spent on around 1,000 projects.[101] Whilst this is small in comparison to the overall scale of the Structural Funds, it is substantially larger than other equality policy initiatives. For example, the 2000–2006 Action Programme to Combat Discrimination had a total budget of €98 million.[102] The Commission's overview of projects funded under Integra reveals a clear emphasis on migrants and/or ethnic minorities, with few projects on groups such as Roma.[103] Although it is difficult to identify common themes amongst the rather disparate range of initiatives, a cultural concept of racism is frequently evident.[104] Various projects aimed to promote intercultural exchange or training courses on cultural diversity.[105] Notably, there is very little evidence of an intersectionality perspective; gender mainstreaming does not appear to have penetrated into this programme.

On the surface, Integra seems like healthy evidence of ethnic equality objectives being incorporated into the ESF. Yet its actual impact is questionable. It subsequently received a damning evaluation from the Court of Auditors.[106] The Court concluded that there were fundamental flaws in the design of Integra that undermined its capacity to achieve its objectives. Specifically, no indicators were identified at the outset of the programme which would allow for the measurement of its impact or the identification of good practice.[107] There was no effective strategy for the dissemination of results, therefore any opportunity for

[99] Commission, 'Towards employment for all—combating racism and promoting the integration of migrants' (Luxembourg: OOPEC, 2000) 40.

[100] See Ch 4.

[101] Court of Auditors, 'Special report No 3/2002 concerning the Community Initiative Employment—Integra' [2003] OJ C263/1, 4.

[102] Council Decision (EC) 2000/750 establishing a Community action programme to combat discrimination (2001 to 2006) [2000] OJ L303/23.

[103] Commission (n 99 above).

[104] For a discussion of this concept, see Ch 1.

[105] ibid 15–16, 19–21.

[106] Court of Auditors (n 101 above).

[107] ibid para 12.

transnational policy learning was lost. With regard to combating racism, the Court lamented the failure to define the target groups or to distinguish between the situations of sub-groups, such as refugees and migrant workers.[108] One of the most startling findings of the Court's investigation was the way in which the funds were actually distributed at national level:

> In none of the Member States visited did the selection procedures as implemented give particular emphasis to actions that focused on the special needs of migrants and refugees.[109]

The experience of the Integra programme underlines the difficulty of proceeding in the absence of reliable data. In its response to the Court's criticisms, the Commission argued that adequate indicators did not exist and that the diversity of the situation at national level called for broad discretion.[110]

The Equal programme 2000–2006

By the time that the Court of Auditors' critical assessment of Integra was published, the next round of ESF funding was already well developed. For the 2000–2006 round even greater focus on discrimination was brought by the Community Initiative 'Equal'. This programme also followed an experimentalist strategy. Its core aim was 'to promote new means of combating all forms of discrimination and inequalities in connection with the labour market, through transnational cooperation'.[111] It was explicitly aligned with the Employment Strategy, being structured around the four pillars (employability, entrepreneurship, adaptability, and equal opportunities) which initially were found in the Employment Guidelines. Under each pillar, two 'thematic fields' for Equal initiatives were identified; one of these, under the 'employability' pillar, was exclusively devoted to 'combating racism and xenophobia in relation to the labour market'.[112] The total budget allocated to Equal was €2,847 million almost 30 times the budget of the parallel Action Programme on Combating Discrimination.

Projects funded by Equal finish in 2008, so it is difficult to make a firm assessment at this stage of its longer term impact. There is no doubt that it has generated a lot of policy activity, but as with Integra questions surround its success in identifying (and transplanting) innovative practices. More effort was made to develop structures for such policy transfer. Each individual project is based on a national 'Development Partnership' (DP). Each DP is linked to DPs in other Member States in order to ensure transnational exchange between similar projects. 'National thematic networks' were created to identify good

108 ibid para 13. 109 ibid para 27. 110 ibid para V.

111 para 3, Commission, 'Communication establishing guidelines for the Community Initiative Equal concerning transnational cooperation to promote new means of combating all forms of discrimination and inequalities in connection with the labour market' [2000] OJ C127/2.

112 ibid, para 16.

practice amongst national projects, which then fed results upwards to 'European thematic networks'. Despite these mechanisms, in 2003, the Commission concluded that transnational cooperation 'is still producing limited added value and not contributing enough to innovation'.[113] This was echoed by the final report of the external evaluation of Equal: the 'impacts on policies are said by most evaluators to be limited ... impacts can be said to still be very much local in scope'.[114]

Looking specifically at the issue of racism, the approach under Equal is evidently more nuanced than that found in Integra. There is greater recognition of diversity in those affected by racism; a specific strand of activities was set aside for asylum-seekers. The second round of funding commenced in 2004 and a special focus was placed in this period on Roma,[115] which corresponds with the trend noted in Chapter 4 within anti-discrimination policy. Whilst it is possible to find examples of individual projects that recognize intersectionality,[116] both the Commission's mid-term report and the final evaluation of Equal recorded weak evidence of gender mainstreaming.[117] The types of activities funded vary widely. Some are directly concerned with discrimination, such as projects designed to reveal and combat discrimination in recruitment processes.[118] The final evaluation noted, though, 'the prevalence of a "supply side" approach to the detriment of initiatives addressing structural factors of discrimination on the demand side of the labour market'.[119] Given that this approach dominates within the Employment Strategy, it is not surprising to find that this has shaped Equal. This trend is also revealed by an analysis of how individual Member States funded projects across the different Equal themes. During the second round of Equal (2004–2006) 5.3% of Development Partnerships were located in the 'combating racism' theme. In contrast, the other element of the 'employability' pillar ('(re)integration to the labour market') received 32.5% of all funds. Indeed, 12 out of 25 states did not allocate any funds to the 'combating racism' theme.[120]

[113] Commission, 'Communication establishing the guidelines for the second round of the Community Initiative Equal concerning transnational cooperation to promote new means of combating all forms of discrimination and inequalities in the labour market—"free movement of ideas"' COM (2003) 840, 17.

[114] para 115, Bernard Brunhes International, 'EU-wide evaluation of the Community Initiative Equal 2000–2006. Final report—Vol 1' (Brussels: Commission, 2006).

[115] Commission (n 113 above) 12.

[116] eg projects on ethnic women entrepreneurs. See: <http://ec.europa.eu/employment_social/equal/news/200704-breaking_en.cfm> accessed 18 June 2008.

[117] Commission (n 113 above) 17; Bernard Brunhes (n 114 above) paras 82–90.

[118] 'Mainstreaming outcomes from Equal: combating discrimination against immigrants and ethnic minorities' (2007): <http://ec.europa.eu/employment_social/equal/news/200703-discrimmig_en.cfm> accessed 18 June 2008.

[119] para 30, Bernard Brunhes (n 114 above).

[120] <http://ec.europa.eu/employment_social/emplweb/empl_h/ecdb_reports/no_secured/n_101_en_rd2.htm> accessed 10 April 2008.

The European Social Fund, 2007–2013

The discussion above shows that some progress has been made in mainstreaming ethnic equality within the ESF. Through the Community Initiative programmes of Integra and Equal, a substantial increase in targeted funding occurred. The Community Initiatives represent, however, a minority of ESF spending. It is much harder to gain an impression of the extent to which national programmes for the use of ESF funds have incorporated ethnic equality objectives.[121] This is the challenge now being addressed through the latest round of ESF spending. The Equal programme was not continued beyond 2006. Instead, the Commission has sought to incorporate the policy lessons from Equal throughout all parts of the ESF. As mentioned earlier, combating discrimination and the integration of migrants have become core objectives in the ESF and national authorities are required to report on their implementation of these goals. Weaving such objectives throughout ESF spending is certainly consistent with the logic of mainstreaming. Yet, the simultaneous dissolution of any dedicated spending initiative carries considerable risk.[122] Moreover, unlike gender mainstreaming, the ESF has never possessed institutional structures devoted to mainstreaming other forms of discrimination.

D. Conclusions

This chapter has considered the extent to which the objectives of combating racism and promoting equality have been mainstreamed within EU employment law and policy. There are two facets to this inquiry; first, the process for mainstreaming and second, the outcome of mainstreaming in practice.

Regarding the process for mainstreaming, it was difficult to find any evidence of a concerted procedure in this field. There were signs that this was beginning to develop within the ESF, where combating racial discrimination has been woven into the ESF objectives and backed up with obligations for national authorities to report on how this objective was implemented. Nevertheless, the objectives and actions required are relatively limited; the approach to mainstreaming here seems to reflect the integrationist model discussed in Chapter 3. The lack of a systematic mainstreaming process may explain why (relatively obvious) opportunities for incorporating ethnic equality objectives have been missed, such as the absence of equality as a required topic in the information and consultation of workers or the initial failure to mention ethnic minorities in the Employment Guidelines.

[121] Examples of using the ESF to support projects on Roma inclusion are provided in Commission, 'Community instruments and policies for Roma inclusion' Commission Staff Working Paper, 2 July 2008, 13–24.

[122] J Shaw, 'Mainstreaming equality and diversity in European Union law and policy' in J Holder and C O'Cinnéide (eds), *Current Legal Problems 2005. Vol 58* (Oxford: OUP, 2006) 255, 262.

Turning to the outcome of mainstreaming in practice, there was evidence that issues relating to racism have filtered into EU employment policies, both within the EES and more visibly through the ESF. In both cases, the employment situation of ethnic minorities had risen in priority during the past decade. This manifested itself in specific responses, be it policy goals within the Employment Guidelines or the devotion of funding streams under the ESF. Yet, it is often difficult to decipher the underpinning concept of racism. The tendency to focus on 'supply-side' measures locates the causes of disadvantage within ethnic minority communities, for example, through an emphasis on skills shortages. This direction tends to assume that the labour market operates in a neutral fashion and that if minorities had the same skill-set as the majority ethnic population, then labour market disadvantage would wither away. This view conflicts with the concept of institutional racism which sees unequal outcomes as an indicator of the residual presence of discrimination.[123] Furthermore, the supply-side orientation of employment policy stands in tension with the EU's anti-discrimination policy.

The fuzziness around the concept of racism was also reflected in the understanding of the target groups. Although the EES began by referring to 'ethnic minorities' in the 1999 Employment Guidelines, it has slipped towards a discourse focused on 'immigrants'. There is only limited recognition of other groups, such as Roma. In contrast, the ESF, via the Equal programme, has engaged more directly with the differences between those vulnerable to racial discrimination. Ideally, there should be a symbiotic relationship between the EES and ESF; the policy lessons of one should feed into the other. In this field, however, it was hard to find evidence that the detailed policy experimentation within ESF programmes significantly informed the EES.[124]

It was particularly noticeable in the context of the EES that evidence of mainstreaming amounts to specific measures on 'ethnic minorities' or 'immigrants'. There was almost no evidence that ethnic inequalities had been mainstreamed *across* the EES policy objectives. For example, the promotion of small business and entrepreneurship has been a key strand from the outset of the EES and now within the Integrated Guidelines. If mainstreaming was functioning effectively, it would be reasonable to find evidence that these policies considered the situation of minority entrepreneurs. Indeed, there have been various projects on minority entrepreneurs under the auspices of DG Enterprise or funded through the ESF.[125] No substantive evidence could be found that such a perspective made its way onto the EES agenda.[126] The tendency to compartmentalize

[123] On the concept of institutional racism, see Ch 1.

[124] There are some Implementation Reports (on NRPs) where measures on ethnic minorities are linked to activities funded by the ESF (eg Sweden, UK). These examples of policy linkage were not reflected generally in the 2006 or 2007 Implementation Reports.

[125] Kate and Niessen (n 71 above) 67–70.

[126] EAPN, 'Social Inclusion Scoreboard' (Brussels: EAPN, 2008) 12.

'ethnic minority' initiatives also helps to explain the lack of engagement with intersectionality issues, such as minority women. This was also evident, albeit to a lesser extent, within the ESF.

Employment law and policy offers a contrast between traditional regulatory methods and the techniques of new governance. In Chapter 3, it was suggested that mainstreaming echoes some of the qualities of new governance insofar as it marks a shift away from the rights-based model found in anti-discrimination legislation.[127] This chapter provides evidence which suggests that new governance strategies may be more amenable to the application of mainstreaming. The hard and fixed nature of legislation, combined with the difficulty in reopening a legislative settlement, implies that opportunities for mainstreaming within employment legislation arise only during limited windows. In contrast, one aspect of the OMC is its 'openness' to renegotiation of the policy agenda and priorities. Even though ethnic minorities were left off the initial set of Employment Guidelines, change was relatively swift. Similarly, the rise of anti-racism policy in the 1990s was reflected in the quick decision to embark upon Integra as an experimental anti-racism programme under the ESF. With this openness comes fluidity. The 2005 reform of the Lisbon Strategy diminished the emphasis on ethnic inequalities in the labour market, whilst for the first time in 10 years there is no Community-level strand of the ESF with a specific focus on combating racism.

The influence of regulatory style on the functioning of mainstreaming is a theme which will be continued in the next chapter. This examines policies in the area of social inclusion and, in particular, the 'Social Inclusion Process' which was launched in 2000 as a counterpart to the EES.

[127] G de Búrca, 'EU race discrimination law: a hybrid model?' in G de Búrca and J Scott (eds), *Law and New Governance in the EU and the US* (Oxford: Hart Publishing, 2006) 97, 98.

6

Social Inclusion: Education, Health, and Housing

This chapter examines EU law and policy in the field of social inclusion in order to assess the extent to which the objectives of combating racism and promoting equality have been mainstreamed. There are several reasons which explain the choice of social inclusion as a case for analysis, most of which are similar to the justifications provided in Chapter 5 for scrutinizing employment law and policy. First, social inclusion embraces many key aspects of social policy which are also found within the material scope of the Racial Equality Directive. If there is to be a complementary relationship between specialized anti-racism policy (in the form of the Directive) and the Union's other policies, then it would be reasonable to expect to find evidence of mainstreaming within social inclusion policy. Amongst other areas, the Directive expressly covers education, health, and housing.[1] Second, social inclusion falls within the ambit of the Directorate-General Employment, Social Affairs and Equal Opportunities. In terms of administrative proximity, it is logical to consider whether mainstreaming has been achieved inside the DG with lead responsibility for combating discrimination. Third, social inclusion offers certain contrasts in relation to employment law and policy. This is an area where EC competence has been closely circumscribed and 'the classic Community method'[2] of binding legislation is less frequently used. Instead, social inclusion policy is dominated by new governance techniques, in particular, the open method of coordination (OMC). This case thus provides further insights into the potential application of mainstreaming within a field where 'hard' law is not central to the regulatory toolbox.

In considering the various dimensions to social inclusion, this chapter will focus on education, health, and housing, areas where ethnic inequalities are well documented. Looking first at education, research for the Organisation for Economic Cooperation and Development (OECD) concluded that 'despite strong learning dispositions, immigrant children often perform at significantly lower

[1] Art 3, Council Directive (EC) 2000/43 implementing the principle of equal treatment between persons irrespective of racial or ethnic origin [2000] OJ L180/22.

[2] T Hervey and L Trubek, 'Freedom to provide health care services within the EU: an opportunity for a transformative Directive' (2007) 13 CJEL 623, 624.

levels than their native peers in key school subjects'.[3] Whilst the reasons for unequal outcomes are complex, comparative research for the EU Monitoring Centre on Racism and Xenophobia (EUMC) found that:

> migrants and minorities tend to enrol in schools with lower academic demands. They are over-represented in vocationally oriented tracks and in special education. They finish school earlier and have higher dropout rates.[4]

This conclusion suggests that educational inequalities are partially linked to institutional factors which lead immigrants to be channelled into less favourable schools.[5]

At the same time, it is important to recognize diversity in the educational experience of those of different ethnic origins. The UK collects detailed statistics on ethnic origin and academic performance. Some ethnic groups, such as Chinese and Indian origin students, obtain results higher than the average for white students, while other groups experience poorer educational outcomes, in particular black Caribbean students.[6] Across Europe, the situation of Roma children in education is especially severe, sometimes as a result of segregation. For example, the Czech government estimated that around 75% of primary school age Roma children were educated in remedial special schools.[7] Serious problems of segregation have also been reported in countries such as Slovakia, Hungary, and Bulgaria.[8] In Hungary, only 2% of Roma children acquire the final school leaving qualification or graduate from university.[9]

The disadvantage confronted by Roma communities is not confined to education. Accommodation is a specific problem, which has been illustrated through a series of complaints brought by the European Roma Rights Centre (ERRC) under the European Social Charter of the Council of Europe.[10] The European Committee of Social Rights found various violations of housing rights by Greece, Italy, and Bulgaria in their treatment of Roma. In Greece, there was a lack of permanent dwellings of adequate quality within Roma settlements and

[3] OECD, 'Where immigrant students succeed—a comparative review of performance and engagement in PISA 2003' (Paris: OECD, 2006) 5; cited in L Bhandal and L Hopkins, 'Fighting racism and promoting equal rights in the field of education' (Brussels: ENAR, 2007) 5.

[4] M Luciak, 'Migrants, minorities and education—documenting discrimination and integration in 15 Member States of the European Union' (Luxembourg: OOPEC, 2004) v.

[5] R Alba, J Handl, and W Müller, 'Ethnic inequalities in the German school system' in P Schuck and R Munz (eds), *Paths to Inclusion—The Integration of Migrants in the United States and Germany* (Oxford: Berghahn Books, 1998) 115, 127.

[6] G Bhattacharyya, L Ison, and M Blair, 'Minority ethnic attainment and participation in education and training: the evidence' Research Topic Paper RTP01-03 (London: Department for Education and Skills, 2003) 12.

[7] Commission, 'The situation of Roma in an enlarged European Union' (Luxembourg: OOPEC, 2004) 18.

[8] ibid.

[9] Commission, 'Report on social inclusion in the 10 new Member States 2005' (Luxembourg: OOPEC, 2005) 82.

[10] European Social Charter (Turin, 18 October 1961; CETS 35) and the European Social Charter (Revised) (Strasbourg, 3 May 1996; CETS 163).

systematic evictions took place even where no alternative housing was available.[11] In Italy, the Committee found evidence that Roma had suffered 'unjustified violence' from law enforcement agencies during evictions (para 42), whilst there was indirect discrimination against Roma in the criteria used for access to social housing.[12] In Bulgaria, some of the practices uncovered included 'collective punishment', such as the disconnection of electricity supplies from entire settlements because certain households had unpaid bills.[13] These cases fit with general data on the detrimental housing situation of Roma. In Spain, around 80% of those living in shanty housing are Roma,[14] whilst in Slovakia around half of all Roma live in segregated settlements, some of which lack access to running water.[15]

Inequalities in housing are not, though, confined to Roma. A comparative study for the EUMC found sufficient evidence to conclude that:

> ethnic minorities are living in comparatively poor housing conditions which contribute to entrenched patterns of social and economic inequality. They are also subject to persistent, extensive and varied forms of ethnic, racist and national discrimination.[16]

Migrant workers are particularly vulnerable to low quality housing, with characteristics such as overcrowding and living in improvised places which lack adequate facilities.[17] Such phenomena contribute to urban segregation, where minority communities become spatially segregated. Multiple factors are at play here. On the one hand, minority communities may voluntarily choose to congregate in similar places in order to develop religious or cultural organizations as well as minority businesses, such as specialist food stores. On the other, these are often 'areas of poorest housing and environmental quality',[18] which cannot be attributed to a matter of personal preference. Other factors may be relevant, such as a concern to avoid harassment from the majority ethnic community or institutional discrimination in the housing market which steers minority communities towards certain districts.[19]

Turning finally to health, here the data available remain limited. Perhaps the clearest evidence of health inequalities relate to Roma. There is a legacy of severe discrimination in the health sector, most graphically illustrated by policies of

[11] *ERRC v Greece* (2005) 41 EHRR SE14.

[12] *ERRC v Italy* (2006) 43 EHRR SE7.

[13] *ERRC v Bulgaria* (2008) 46 EHRR SE10.

[14] Fundamental Rights Agency, 'Trends and developments 1997–2005—combating ethnic and racial discrimination and promoting equality in the European Union' (Hungary: Printer Elanders Hungary, 2007) 29.

[15] C Fagan, P Urwin, and K Melling, 'Gender inequalities in the risks of poverty and social exclusion for disadvantaged groups in thirty European countries' (Luxembourg: OOPEC, 2006) 106.

[16] M Harrison, I Law, and D Phillips, 'Migrants, minorities and housing: exclusion, discrimination and anti-discrimination in 15 Member States of the European Union' (Luxembourg: OOPEC, 2005) 6.

[17] Fundamental Rights Agency (n 14 above) 28.

[18] P Radcliffe, *'Race', Ethnicity and Difference—Imaging the Inclusive Society* (Maidenhead: Open University Press, 2004) 69.

[19] ibid 61.

forced sterilization of Roma women which only ceased in Slovakia and the Czech Republic in the early 1990s.[20] Yet, research by the ERRC indicates ongoing instances of discrimination, such as the segregation of Roma women within maternity wards.[21] Health outcomes for Roma reveal substantial disparities in comparison to the non-Roma population; for example, the Roma infant mortality rate in Romania is four times the national average.[22] There is also evidence that life expectancy rates are lower for Roma. In Slovenia, 1.7% of the Roma population are over 65, in contrast to 13% of the non-Roma population.[23] Similarly, in Ireland, only 3% of the Traveller community are over 65 compared to 11% of the general population.[24]

Regarding other national or ethnic minorities, there is little data available on overall health outcomes. The UK has engaged in more detailed ethnic monitoring than other states and this has revealed differences in the health status of minority communities. For example, death rates from strokes are higher than the national average in Bangladeshi, Pakistani, Irish, and Afro-Caribbean communities.[25] According to monitoring data, patients who defined themselves as black or having one black parent are three times more likely to be admitted to mental health facilities than the general population.[26] Across Europe, research suggests that health systems may be failing to respond to the specific needs of minority communities. ENAR has reported difficulties with language barriers in healthcare provision in Denmark, Estonia, Germany, Ireland, and Malta.[27] PRIAE[28] conducted EU-funded research into the situation of minority elderly care in ten European countries. It found that difficulties arose because services were designed around the standard needs of the majority ethnic population, which failed to acknowledge the different healthcare profile of minority communities.[29] This is a question of social needs (the manner of healthcare delivery), but also medical needs given the different incidence of health impairments across ethnic groups.

Even from a brief glance, it is clear that substantial issues relating to ethnic inequalities arise in the ambit of social inclusion policy. The chapter begins by providing a background to EU policy in this field and specifically the

[20] Fagan et al. (n 15 above) 107.

[21] ERRC, 'Ambulance not on the way—the disgrace of healthcare for Roma in Europe' (Budapest: ERRC, 2006) 56.

[22] Fagan et al. (n 15 above) 105.

[23] ibid 104.

[24] Based on data from 2002: C McCabe and F Keyes, 'A review of Travellers' health using primary care as a model of good practice' (Dublin: Pavee Point, 2005) 6.

[25] This information dates from the mid-1990s: The Runnymede Trust, *The Future of Multi-ethnic Britain—The Parekh Report* (London: Profile Books, 2002) 179.

[26] Commission for Racial Equality (CRE), 'A lot done, a lot to do—our vision of an integrated Britain' (London: CRE, 2007) 27.

[27] C Lynch, 'Racism in Europe—ENAR Shadow report 2005' (Brussels: ENAR, 2006) 21.

[28] Policy Research Institute on Ageing and Ethnicity.

[29] PRIAE Research Briefing, 'Minority elderly health and social care in Europe' (2004) 10: <http://www.priae.org/docs/MEC%20European%20Summary%20Findings2.pdf> accessed 10 April 2008.

construction of an OMC process devoted to social inclusion. The characteristics of the social inclusion OMC are discussed before turning to consider the extent to which it has addressed ethnic equality issues. Education and health are also the subject of separate EU policies which pre-date and now run in tandem with the social inclusion OMC. Consequently, the second half of the chapter looks beyond the formal horizons of the social inclusion OMC to consider whether evidence of mainstreaming can be found in other aspects of EU social policy.

A. From Combating Poverty to Promoting Social Inclusion

Some elements of European social policy can be traced back to the founding 1957 EEC Treaty, such as equal pay for women and men or the establishment of the European Social Fund. These initial interventions were, though, closely connected to the functioning of the labour market. Social policy, as typically conceived within the national context, stretches well beyond employment matters and encompasses the full spectrum of issues pertaining to human welfare. The 1974 Social Action Programme made some tentative steps in this direction by initiating an EC anti-poverty programme.[30] This was renewed on two further occasions but it ran into obstacles in the 1990s when agreement could not be reached amongst the Member States on a fourth anti-poverty programme.[31] During this period, a gradual shift took place moving the emphasis away from an exclusive focus on poverty and towards social exclusion.[32] Poverty has traditionally been linked to low income.[33] Although many different interpretations of social exclusion exist, it is generally regarded as a broader concept. Whilst a lack of material resources is one important factor which may contribute to social exclusion, attention is also paid to opportunities for participation in society.[34] The Commission has proposed the following definition:

> Social exclusion is a process whereby certain individuals are pushed to the edge of society and prevented from participating fully by virtue of their poverty, or lack of basic competencies and lifelong learning opportunities, or as a result of discrimination. This distances them from job, income and education opportunities as well as social and community networks and activities. They have little access to power and decision-making bodies and thus often feel powerless and unable to take control over the decisions that affect their day to day lives.[35]

[30] L Hantrais, *Social Policy in the European Union* (3rd edn, Houndmills: Palgrave Macmillan, 2007) 184.

[31] ibid 188.

[32] P Schoukens and L Carmichael, 'Social exclusion in Europe: testing the limits of European integration' in D Mayes, J Berghman, and R Salais (eds), *Social Exclusion and European Policy* (Cheltenham: Edward Elgar, 2001) 76.

[33] J Percy-Smith, 'The contours of social exclusion' in J Percy-Smith (ed), *Policy Responses to Social Exclusion—Towards Inclusion?* (Buckingham: Open University Press, 2000) 4.

[34] H Collins, 'Discrimination, equality and social inclusion' (2003) 66 MLR 16, 24.

[35] Commission, 'Joint report on social inclusion 2004' (Luxembourg: OOPEC, 2004) 10.

Promoting social *inclusion* hence requires more than attention to employment and income levels. Instead, there is a need to address participation in all aspects of economic, social, cultural, and political life.

The policy transition from combating poverty to promoting social inclusion occurred in the same period as the OMC emerged as an alternative to traditional forms of Community regulation. Whilst legal competence and subsidiarity arguments had stymied the fourth anti-poverty programme, a consensus was found to launch a new generation of 'social inclusion' policy via the OMC.

B. The Social Inclusion Process

In spring 2000, the European Council agreed to pursue a programme of economic and social reform termed 'the Lisbon Strategy'.[36] This capitalized upon the policy coordination processes which were already up and running on economic and employment policy. The Lisbon Strategy ostensibly sought to balance market-based objectives with a renewed social agenda. Indeed, the core goal was 'more and better jobs *and greater social cohesion*'.[37] The latter objective was given more precision when the European Council decided at Nice in December 2000 to establish an OMC process on social inclusion.[38] The basic framework of the 'Social Inclusion Process' was broadly comparable to the European Employment Strategy (EES). Member States were asked to prepare two-year National Action Plans (NAPs), which were then subject to review by the Commission and Council (through a Joint Report). This would in turn lead to a new round of national reporting and European-level review. The Social Inclusion Process can, though, be distinguished from the EES in several key aspects.

First of all, it was not grounded in the EC Treaty. This implies a more flexible legal foundation because the process has no fixed requirements regarding its cycle or structure. The only 'permanent' element is the Social Protection Committee, required by EC Treaty, Article 144.[39] Second, not all of the instruments available within the EES have been extended to social inclusion. The process commenced from a set of 'Common Objectives' defined by the Nice European Council (and since then periodically revised). Crucially, these loosely framed objectives were not accompanied by any European targets. Hence, there is nothing comparable to the EES goal of a 70% employment participation rate by 2010. Member States were encouraged from 2002 onwards to self-select domestic targets against

[36] See Ch 5.

[37] Emphasis added, para 7, European Council, 'Presidency Conclusions 23 and 24 March 2000'.

[38] For a detailed account, see M Ferrera, M Matsaganis, and S Sacchi, 'Open coordination against poverty: the new EU social inclusion process' (2002) 12 JESP 227; A Atkinson, 'Social inclusion and the European Union' (2002) 40 JCMS 625.

[39] This Committee, composed of Member State and Commission representatives, acts in an advisory capacity. It has a key role in managing the everyday mechanics of the process, such as agreeing the common indicators to be used.

which progress could be measured.[40] Furthermore, in the wake of the first set of national reports, the European Council approved a set of 'Common Indicators', such as the proportion of persons living in households with an income below 60% of national median income.[41] Member States were exhorted to include these statistical benchmarks within their national reports, thereby enhancing the possibility for comparing national performance.

Taking into account the above, a third observation is that the Social Inclusion Process is more open and less normative than the EES. The first Joint Report declared at the outset: 'this report does not evaluate the effectiveness of the systems already in place in different Member States'.[42] Similarly, it was argued that the Common Indicators were 'not a naming and shaming exercise'.[43] This is underscored by the absence of any power to issue Council Recommendations on individual state practice, as occurs within the EES. Nevertheless, the process is not simply a mere exchange of information between autonomous states. Ales notes that the trajectory over time has been to move from loose cooperation towards the promotion of convergence, for example, through the introduction of the Common Indicators.[44] Alternatively, Armstrong cites the 'Common Outline' (a template which the Social Protection Committee provides for how national reports should be structured) as one 'means of steering the substance of policy coordination'.[45]

As mentioned in Chapter 5, the proliferation of OMC processes following the Lisbon European Council in 2000 later encountered resistance from Member States. In the social sphere, the Social Inclusion Process was accompanied by a Social Protection OMC, which focused on making pension systems sustainable, as well as less structured policy cooperation relating to health and long-term care. In 2003, the Commission proposed to streamline these processes by combining the various reporting obligations.[46] Consequently, a new OMC on 'Social Protection and Social Inclusion' was launched in 2005.[47] This is founded on

[40] Commission (n 35 above) 42.

[41] A Atkinson, E Marlier, and B Nolan, 'Indicators and targets for social inclusion in the European Union' (2004) 42 JCMS 47, 53.

[42] Commission, 'Joint report on social inclusion' (Luxembourg: OOPEC, 2002) 9.

[43] F Vandenbrouke, 'Preface' in A Atkinson, B Cantillon, E Marlier, and B Nolan (eds), *The EU and Social Inclusion* (Oxford: OUP, 2002) v, viii.

[44] E Ales, 'La lotta all'esclusione sociale attraverso l'open method of co-ordination: prime riflessioni (2000–2002)' in M Barbera (ed), *Nuove forme di regolazione: il metodo aperto di coordinamento delle politiche sociali* (Milan: Giuffrè, 2006) 173, 186.

[45] K Armstrong, 'Tackling social exclusion through OMC: reshaping the boundaries of EU governance' in T Börzel and R Cichowski (eds), *State of the Union: Law, Politics and Society, Vol 6* (Oxford: OUP, 2003) 170.

[46] Commission, 'Strengthening the social dimension of the Lisbon Strategy: streamlining open coordination in the field of social protection' COM (2003) 261.

[47] Commission, 'Working together, working better: a new framework for the open method of coordination of social protection and inclusion policies in the European Union' COM (2005) 706. On the process of reform, see E Ales, 'Dalla politica sociale europea alla politica europea di coesione economica e sociale. Considerazioni critiche sugli sviluppi del modello sociale europeo nella stagione del metodo aperto di coordinamento' (2007) Working Paper 51/2007, Centro studi di diritto del lavoro europeo 'Massimo D'Antona', Università degli Studi di Catania.

'National Reports on Strategies for Social Protection and Inclusion' which are designed to run for three-year periods, with 'light touch' reporting in the intervening years. In response, the Commission and Council now adopt an annual Joint Report on Social Protection and Social Inclusion. Despite these reforms, the hallmarks of the initial Social Inclusion Process remain intact. It is still based around Common Objectives and Common Indicators, without the more rigorous targets and recommendations found within the EES.[48]

C. Promoting Ethnic Equality and the Social Inclusion Process

From invisibility to key objectives

The first concrete step in constructing the Social Inclusion Process was the adoption of the Common Objectives in December 2000.[49] The four objectives identified were:

- to facilitate participation in employment and access by all to resources, rights, goods, and services;
- to prevent the risks of exclusion;
- to help the most vulnerable;
- to mobilize all relevant bodies.

In principle, each of these objectives resonates well with promoting ethnic equality. The first clearly dovetails with the Racial Equality Directive. Even so, there was no express reference to racial discrimination or ethnic minorities in the document explaining the Common Objectives. There is an oblique reference to 'a group experiencing particular integration problems' under the third objective (helping the most vulnerable), as well as a passing mention that Member States may develop priority actions for specific target groups including 'minorities'.[50] In the same vein, the first set of Common Indicators contained no indicator addressing ethnic origin or nationality.[51] Whilst several indicators were to be disaggregated by gender and age, other dimensions to inequality remained invisible.

Despite this inauspicious start, the first Joint Report (in 2002) observed that the NAPs did frequently identify 'ethnic minorities and immigrants' as key groups experiencing social exclusion.[52] References are scattered throughout the

[48] The Commission has proposed reforms to strengthen the process, including the introduction of targets: Commission, 'A renewed commitment to social Europe: reinforcing the open method of coordination for social protection and social inclusion' COM (2008) 418.

[49] Objectives in the fight against poverty and social exclusion [2001] OJ C82/4.

[50] ibid.

[51] Council, 'Report on indicators in the field of poverty and social exclusion' Ref 13509/01 SOC 415, ECOFIN 310, EDUC 126, SAN 138, 5 November 2001.

[52] Commission (n 42 above) 26.

report, but immigrants/ethnic minorities are most frequently mentioned in connection with barriers to employment. In contrast, there is very little space devoted to this issue in the section on housing. The situation of Irish Travellers is briefly alluded to,[53] but there is no mention of Roma. The section of the report on 'justice' (dealing with access to rights) does focus on combating discrimination, albeit without mentioning the Article 13 Directives.[54] Unsurprisingly, the report concludes that there are 'big gaps' in the data available, inter alia, in relation to ethnic minorities.[55]

Whilst the lack of data is similar to the experience with the EES, the fact that many social inclusion NAPs identified ethnic minorities as a key group from the outset is rather different. Prior to 2003, few employment NAPs mentioned ethnic disadvantage in the labour market (see Chapter 5). Therefore, Member States were comparatively quicker to locate issues relating to ethnic inequality as germane to the Social Inclusion Process. Building on the evidence from the first round of NAPs, the Council agreed to revise the Common Objectives in 2002. In part, the revisions were designed to highlight social exclusion risks linked to immigration and, to this end, an express reference to 'immigrants' was inserted under the third objective of helping the most vulnerable.[56] This amendment had an impact; the 2004 Joint Report recorded much more attention in the NAPs to social exclusion risks linked to immigration/ethnic minorities.[57] Nevertheless, most of the focus continued to be on labour market exclusion, with less specific information on the situation of ethnic minorities as regards housing, and almost no discussion in relation to healthcare. Overall, the 2004 Joint Report remains sceptical on the real impact of the measures reported by Member States:

> Although the vulnerability of immigrants and ethnic minorities to poverty and social exclusion has been recognised by all Member States, in only a few cases specific targets and objectives have been set out.[58]

Many of the features of the 2004 Joint Report are echoed in the policy documentation produced since then. Issues relating to immigration/ethnic minorities are consistently acknowledged as a 'key priority' and, in the wake of EU enlargement, greater prominence has been given to the situation of Roma communities. In 2005, a special report was issued analyzing the first set of NAPs from the 10 acceding states. This recognized that most of these states had relatively small immigrant populations, but that issues of ethnic inequality arose in relation to national minorities. Roma were identified as a key target group, but also Russian-speaking minorities in the Baltic States.[59] Although subsequent reports have not assigned much attention to the latter, the Roma are specifically

[53] ibid 43. [54] ibid 53. [55] ibid 80.

[56] Council, 'Fight against poverty and social exclusion: common objectives for the second round of National Action Plans' Ref 14164/1/02 SOC 508, 25 November 2002.

[57] Commission (n 35 above) 34. [58] ibid 102. [59] Commission (n 9 above) 33.

mentioned in the seven 'key policy priorities' found within the 2005 and 2006 Joint Reports.[60]

By 2006, combating ethnic inequalities had consolidated within the Social Inclusion Process. Even if the various EU level reports reiterate concerns about shortcomings in the NAPs, this issue had an established profile as a fairly central endeavour of the process. This picture was disrupted by the changes to the Social Inclusion Process consequent upon its streamlining with the health and social protection OMCs. The Common Objectives were rewritten in 2006, distinguishing between several 'overarching objectives' and other objectives specific to each of the three strands (social inclusion, social protection, and health). During the Commission's consultation on streamlining the OMCs, Slovakia and Latvia contended that 'too much emphasis was given to social inclusion among immigrants', although Spain argued in the opposite direction.[61] Strikingly, the reference in the Common Objectives to 'immigrants' disappeared altogether, with a reversion to general expressions such as 'equal opportunities for all' and 'fighting all forms of discrimination'.[62] In contrast, 'equality between women and men' is included as an overarching objective.

Another by-product of the new process is a significant thinning of the annual Joint Report. Despite covering a broader range of topics, it has been transformed into a short, strategic document, albeit accompanied by other reports which analyze the national reports in more depth. This has led to criticisms that the overall priority attached to social inclusion policy has diminished.[63] The limited space now afforded to social inclusion has reduced the attention to detailed sub-issues. The 2007 and 2008 Joint Reports contain scattered references to immigrants/ethnic minorities, although there is only one mention of Roma.[64] The streamlined process has only been fully functional since mid-2006, so it is still rather early to draw firm conclusions on its impact. Nevertheless, there is a risk that it is diluting the focus on ethnic inequalities. Indeed, the European Anti-Poverty Network has criticized the lack of action on migrants and ethnic minorities according to its analysis of national reports.[65]

[60] Commission, 'Social inclusion in Europe 2006' (Luxembourg: OOPEC, 2006) 164.

[61] Commission, 'Evaluation of the open method of coordination for social protection and social inclusion' SEC (2006) 345, 12.

[62] Council, 'Working together, working better: a new framework for the open coordination of social protection and inclusion policies in the European Union—Joint Social Protection Committee/Economic Policy Committee Opinion' Ref 6801/06 SOC 96, ECOFIN 67, SAN 45, 27 February 2006. This document was approved by the subsequent Employment, Social Policy, Health and Consumer Affairs Council: Press Release, 6705/1/06 REV 1, 10 March 2006.

[63] Ales (n 47 above) 34; European Anti-Poverty Network (EAPN), 'Strengthening the social dimension of the Lisbon Strategy' (Brussels: EAPN, 2007) para 3.2.

[64] Council, 'Joint Report on Social Protection and Social Inclusion 2008' Ref 7274/08, 4 March 2008, 8. There was no mention of Roma in the 2007 report: Commission, 'Joint Report on Social Protection and Social Inclusion 2007' (Luxembourg: OOPEC, 2007).

[65] EAPN, 'Light year: hard work! Assessing the impact on poverty' (Brussels: EAPN, 2007) 9.

Mainstreaming ethnic equality into social inclusion policy

Having considered the evolution of the Social Inclusion Process and specific evidence of how it has addressed ethnic inequalities, this section reflects on what this reveals about the extent to which mainstreaming has already occurred. Several issues are addressed: target groups, data collection, the concept of racism, and mainstreaming via the OMC.

Target groups

Initially, the dominant frame within the Social Inclusion Process was 'immigrants'.[66] This reflected the typical construction of ethnic inequalities within the then 15 Member States. The groups affected were foreign nationals or those who had acquired citizenship (and their descendants).[67] Scant references can be found to Roma and Travellers, but this issue grew in visibility following the 2004 enlargement. More recent Commission reports have drawn attention to the vagueness found in NAPs around the relevant target groups:

> The language used to describe these groups can be unclear with Member States frequently referring to 'immigrants' to describe all ethnic minorities—from refugees, to Roma or other people with the nationality of the country. Little distinction has been made between groups and at the same time there is little or no acknowledgement of the diversity within these groups, or indeed the multiple disadvantage that these people might face (e.g. older migrants, Romani women etc).[68]

The Commission's Network of Independent Experts on Social Inclusion goes further in its criticism of national reports, concluding that 'there is relatively little effort to focus attention on target groups among immigrants and ethnic minorities'.[69] Moreover, despite the fact that gender mainstreaming has been pursued from the outset of the Social Inclusion Process, a gender perspective has not infused analysis of ethnic inequalities. A first step in this direction has been taken by the Expert Group on Gender, Social Inclusion and Employment (the Commission's specialist network to monitor gender mainstreaming in these fields). Its studies have included sections devoted to Roma women and migrant women.[70]

Data collection

The ambiguity surrounding who is affected by ethnic inequalities is both caused by and reflected in the lack of data. This recurring lament can be traced from the

[66] eg the 2002 Common Objectives. [67] Commission (n 42 above) 26.

[68] Commission (n 60 above) 135. Niessen and Huddleston identify 11 different ways in which states described immigrant target groups in the 2006 NAPs: J Niessen and T Huddleston, 'Setting up a system of benchmarking to measure the success of integration policies in Europe' (Brussels: European Parliament, 2007) 197.

[69] I Begg and E Marlier, '"Feeding in" and "feeding out", and integrating immigrants and ethnic minorities' (Brussels: Commission, 2007) 35.

[70] Fagan et al. (n 15 above).

first Joint Report onwards.[71] Shortcomings in the relevant statistical information are not purely found in relation to ethnic inequalities; this has been a wider problem for many aspects of the Social Inclusion Process, especially in relation to housing and health. It was only following the first round of NAPs that efforts were made to identify Common Indicators which could be used as European benchmarks for measuring social inclusion. This was accompanied by the creation of a new statistical dataset: the European Survey on Income and Living Conditions (EU-SILC). This survey will regularly gather information across all Member States on topics such as income, education, employment, housing, and health. Importantly, it includes the collection of data on respondents' country of birth and citizenship, although not ethnic origin.[72] The technical work of developing indicators has been the responsibility of the Indicators Sub-Group of the Social Protection Committee. Marlier et al. note that no consensus could be found on defining 'ethnic minority';[73] however, one sign of change was the inclusion of a 'commonly agreed national indicator' on immigrant employment in the 2006 version of the Common Indicators.[74] States report the employment rate for those born in the country, those born elsewhere in the EU, and those born outside the EU. The first results of this indicator have revealed the diversity of the situation in the Member States.[75] In six 'old' EU states, the employment rate of those born outside the EU is more than 15 percentage points lower than the rate of those born in the country.[76] In contrast, in 11 states, those born outside the EU have a higher employment rate than those born in the country. Seven of these eleven are states which joined the EU since 2004, revealing a considerable gap in the social context. Yet, the indicator chosen does not reveal the employment situation of Roma, many of whom will have been born within the country in which they reside. Similarly, it is unclear how Russian-speakers in the Baltic States are treated. In short, although the lack of data relating to ethnic inequalities has been consistently recognized as a problem within the process, actions to address this deficiency remain limited.[77]

[71] Commission (n 42 above) 80. See also Commission (n 35 above) 136; Commission (n 9 above) 80.

[72] Commission Regulation (EC) 1983/2003 implementing EP and Council Regulation 1177/2003 concerning Community statistics on income and living conditions (EU-SILC) as regards the list of target primary variables [2003] OJ L298/34, 64.

[73] E Marlier, A Atkinson, B Cantillon, and B Nolan, *The EU and Social Inclusion—Facing the Challenges* (Bristol: Policy Press, 2007) 66–7.

[74] Commission, 'Portfolio of overarching indicators and streamlined social inclusion, pensions and health portfolios' D(2006), 7 June 2006: <http://ec.europa.eu/employment_social/social_inclusion/docs/2006/indicators_en.pdf> accessed 18 June 2008.

[75] See Table 5.1 in Ch 5.

[76] Belgium, Denmark, Finland, Germany, the Netherlands, and Sweden.

[77] One sign of progress is the new data being yielded by the EU-SILC. A 2008 report from the Commission uses this to highlight the over-representation of children with migrant parents amongst those at risk of poverty: Commission, 'The social situation in the European Union 2007' (Luxembourg: OOPEC, 2008) 62–81.

Concept of racism

A preliminary observation is that the term racism is very rarely used in the documentation surrounding the Social Inclusion Process. A dichotomy can be identified between approaches based on 'integration' and those based on 'combating discrimination'. In the former, the causes of social exclusion are predominantly located within the affected persons, such as insufficient linguistic ability or a way of life divergent from that of the dominant population. In the latter, social exclusion is linked to prejudicial treatment of vulnerable groups, such as forced segregation in schooling or housing. For the most part, Member States have oriented towards integration measures, in other words, requiring change on the part of vulnerable groups to address their social exclusion. The 2004 Joint Report commented:

> In many cases the emphasis is on the need for immigrants to adapt, most notably through training and support measures. In Austria, Italy and Luxembourg, for example, a primary focus is on providing language courses.[78]

A corollary of this outlook is that few states initially made any link between the Social Inclusion Process and the implementation of the Racial Equality Directive.[79] In its 2006 analysis of the NAPs, the Commission noted more frequent citation of the Directive, but queried 'what, if any, practical impact it is having on the ground'.[80] The tendency to focus on integration rather than anti-discrimination was already observed in Chapter 5 in relation to the EES. By concentrating on adaptations by minorities, an analysis based on institutional racism is neglected.

Mainstreaming via the OMC

Placed alongside the EES, the Social Inclusion Process is arguably a more successful example of mainstreaming ethnic equality. Ethnic minorities were recognized as a key priority from early in the life of the process, even if not at its very outset. Despite flaws and shortcomings, the Joint Reports are woven with references to issues relating to ethnic inequality, in a manner which has not been replicated in the EES. Indeed, the 2006 Joint Report drew attention to the inconsistency between the priority devoted to immigrants in the Social Inclusion Process and its relative invisibility in the EES national reports.[81] At the same time, the strongest focus within the Social Inclusion Process has been on employment as a barrier to social inclusion. This is the field where most detail emerges in the Joint Reports and the sole indicator relating to ethnic inequalities

[78] Commission (n 35 above) 96. See also Commission (n 60 above) 137; Begg and Marlier (n 69 above) 20.

[79] Commission (n 9 above) 81.

[80] Commission (n 60 above) 137.

[81] Commission, 'Joint report on social protection and social inclusion 2006' (Luxembourg: OOPEC, 2006) 8.

concerns employment rates. This could be read as offering a synergy with the EES; both OMCs are pushing in the same direction. Yet, it suggests that the process has been less effective in promoting social inclusion in other fields. A detailed study in 2004 concluded that 'most of the NAPs/Inclusion have not generally presented coherent and integrated policies in relation to access to housing for migrants and ethnic minority groups'.[82] The streamlining of social inclusion into a broader OMC has arguably accentuated the emphasis on employment as the main 'lever for inclusion'.[83]

A broader question which troubles the Social Inclusion Process is its practical impact on shaping national policies. This preoccupation concerns all OMC processes,[84] but it is more acute in connection to a process which, at least initially, disclaimed normative policy evaluation. Concerns have been expressed that NAPs are not genuine strategies to tackle social exclusion, but simply a bundle of pre-existing measures which are pursued in accordance with domestic agendas.[85] Initial empirical research tends to reinforce the reasons to doubt the efficacy of the process. A 2007 study of the NAPs in the Czech Republic, France, and Portugal noted a substantial gap between what the NAP promised in relation to Roma and what was actually delivered.[86] There was often a low level of awareness of the NAP amongst the officials responsible for its implementation and adequate budgetary resources had not been allocated to match the undertakings. Moreover, there was limited evidence of Roma organizations participating in the design or implementation of the NAP. A vicious cycle emerges here: if the process is perceived to be ineffective, then NGOs may be reluctant to invest precious time and resources in trying to shape its contents. At EU level, the European Network Against Racism (ENAR) has started to work more extensively on the Social Inclusion Process, but mainly in the period since 2006.[87]

Taking an overview, the Social Inclusion Process does provide evidence of mainstreaming ethnic equality. Although this has not been based on an announced strategy (in contrast to gender mainstreaming), ethnic inequalities have in practice filtered onto the policy agenda. The open character of the OMC facilitates regular redefinition of its goals and instruments. This allowed

[82] B Edgar, 'Policy measures to ensure access to decent housing for migrants and ethnic minorities' (Dundee: Joint Centre for Scottish Housing Research, Universities of Dundee/St Andrews, 2004) 76.

[83] S Bernhard, 'The European paradigm of social exclusion' (2006) 2 JCER 41, 49.

[84] V Hatzopoulos, 'Why the open method of coordination is bad for you: a letter to the EU' (2007) 13 ELJ 309.

[85] Begg and Marlier (n 69 above) 44; EAPN (n 63 above) 11.

[86] ERRC and Númena Centro de Investigação em Ciências Sociais e Humanas, 'Social inclusion through social services: the case of Roma and Travellers. Assessing the impact of National Action Plans for Social Inclusion in the Czech Republic, France and Portugal' (Budapest: ERRC and Númena Centro de Investigação em Ciências Sociais e Humanas, 2007) 13.

[87] ENAR organized two public conferences on social inclusion during 2007 as well as setting up an ad hoc expert group on social and economic inclusion of disadvantaged ethnic and religious minorities: see further <http://www.enar-eu.org> accessed 10 April 2008.

'immigrants' to be added to the Common Objectives in 2002, despite having been omitted in 2000. It is testament to the fluidity of the OMC that this reference slipped away in 2006. This experience echoes that found in relation to the EES, as described in Chapter 5. Furthermore, just as with the EES, the major lack of data on ethnic inequalities has been a persistent obstacle to forging a more elaborate European policy. In the absence of data, the contours of inequality remain fuzzy and there is no external benchmark against which to measure the relative effectiveness of competing policy prescriptions.

D. EU Policies on Education and Health

This chapter has concentrated on measures taken under the auspices of the social inclusion OMC. This is not the only context in which the European Union engages with social policy. The EU also possesses well-established policies on education and public health which exist outside of the Social Inclusion Process and pre-date its creation. This section considers the extent to which evidence of mainstreaming may be found in the other activities of the Union in these two areas. Housing is not considered further because of the limited competence which the EU possesses in this field. Unlike education and health, there is no explicit EC Treaty foundation for a policy on housing. Whilst EU law and policy may have impacts on national housing policy,[88] the Union has not established dedicated housing programmes comparable to those discussed below on education and health. Therefore, the policy space for mainstreaming in housing policy (outside the Social Inclusion Process) is highly restricted.

Education

EU education law and policy can be traced back to the 1970s.[89] The initial impulse for intervention stemmed from issues relating to the education of migrant workers' children. Whilst this was an internal market-based rationale, it opened the door to address broader policy issues around how educational systems should respond to cultural diversity. Notably, the first piece of binding legislation adopted was a Directive on the education of the children of migrant workers.[90] This aimed to ensure free access to teaching of an official language of the host Member State, alongside encouraging teaching of the language and

[88] eg measures designed to restrict property ownership to permanent residents may contravene internal market free movement rights under the EC Treaty: Case C-302/97 *Konle v Austria* [1999] ECR I-3099.

[89] For a comprehensive overview, see G Gori, *Towards an EU Right to Education* (The Hague: Kluwer Law International, 2001).

[90] Council Directive (EC) 77/486 on the education of the children of migrant workers [1977] OJ L199/32.

culture of the child's country of origin. Due to legal competence concerns, it did not apply to children of third country nationals, although a Council Declaration stated the political will of Member States to apply the Directive's principles to non-EU children.[91] In practice, compliance with the Directive was poor,[92] but, in deference to political sensitivities, the Commission declined to issue any infringement proceedings.[93]

The Directive was a rare instance of 'hard law' during a period where the EC legal competence in relation to education was highly contested. Contemporary policy is based on the powers conferred in EC Treaty Articles 149 and 150. Whilst these permit the adoption of EC 'measures' on education and vocational training, this is heavily circumscribed by the proviso 'excluding any harmonization of the laws and regulations of Member States'.[94] Two main strands in education policy have emerged: programmes and the OMC.

Education programmes

From the mid-1980s onwards, various funding programmes have sought to promote European collaboration in relation to education, vocational training, and youth. Significantly, these programmes offer clear evidence of mainstreaming from the mid-1990s onwards. 'Socrates' was an umbrella programme which embraced programmes on themes such as higher education (Erasmus), schools (Comenius), and language-learning (Lingua). Frustrated with the limited impact of Directive 77/486, Cullen charts how the Parliament placed pressure on the Commission in the early 1990s to advance an 'intercultural' approach to education.[95] Specifically, the Parliament introduced amendments to the 1995 Socrates programme where promoting 'the intercultural dimension of education' was identified as a general objective of all Socrates actions.[96] In addition, one of the three objectives of Comenius was the 'education of the children of migrant workers, as well as the children of occupational travellers, travellers, and gypsies'.[97] In 2000, the Commission reported that around €5 million per year had been devoted to this objective under Comenius.[98]

Mainstreaming was taken further during the renewal of Socrates in 2000. In relation to Comenius, school partnerships were to include projects 'aimed at promoting intercultural awareness and in particular those designed to help

[91] Gori (n 89 above) 215.

[92] Commission, 'Report on the implementation in the Member States of Directive 77/486/EEC on the education of the children of migrant workers' COM (88) 787, 9.

[93] H Cullen, 'From migrants to citizens? European Community policy on intercultural education' (1996) 45 ICLQ 109, 124.

[94] EC Treaty, Arts 149(4) and 150(4).

[95] Cullen (n 93 above) 125.

[96] Art 3(b), EP and Council Decision (EC) 819/95 establishing the Community action programme 'Socrates' [1995] OJ L87/10.

[97] ibid Annex, ch II.

[98] Around 100 projects per year were funded. Commission, 'Report on the implementation of the action plan against racism—mainstreaming the fight against racism' (Brussels: Commission, 2000) 27.

combat racism and xenophobia'.[99] Staff training projects would include activities related to 'the integration and improved educational achievement of children of migrant workers, gypsies and travellers and occupational travellers'.[100]

In 2006, the existing education and vocational training projects were wrapped up under the new umbrella of 'Lifelong Learning'. Article 12 of the Decision establishing this seven-year programme evokes the mainstreaming ethos by referring to 'horizontal policies' that cut across all its activities. Three horizontal policies are identified, the first of which is 'promoting an awareness of the importance of cultural and linguistic diversity within Europe, as well as of the need to combat racism, prejudice and xenophobia'.[101] In the Commission's 2007 call for proposals under the Lifelong Learning programme, combating racism is one of six key priorities for funding networks under Comenius, whilst 'promoting interculturalism and supporting integration of migrants' is one of seven priorities for projects under 'Grundtvig', the adult education strand of the Lifelong Learning programme.[102]

Applying the OMC to education

One by-product of the Lisbon Strategy's focus on a knowledge-based economy was to spawn an OMC process dedicated to education and training. This shares many of the characteristics of the Social Inclusion Process, although it has unfolded at a slower pace. The education OMC is guided by its pursuit of three 'strategic objectives': improving quality, facilitating access for all, and opening up education and training systems to the wider world.[103] These have been subdivided into 13 'associated objectives' including 'supporting active citizenship, equal opportunities and social cohesion'.[104] A set of working groups was subsequently established in order to explore how to achieve each of the associated objectives, whilst work has been ongoing on defining benchmarks and indicators by which progress could be measured. Kate and Niessen note that although issues relating to immigrants are occasionally mentioned in the documentary trail surrounding this OMC, 'there is no overarching structure to incorporate the concerns of immigrants' and consequently measures are 'piecemeal'.[105]

[99] Annex, EP and Council Decision (EC) 253/2000 establishing the second phase of the Community action programme in the field of education 'Socrates' [2000] OJ L28/1.

[100] ibid.

[101] EP and Council Decision (EC) 1720/2006 establishing an action programme in the field of lifelong learning [2006] OJ L327/45.

[102] Commission, 'Lifelong Learning Programme: Part 1—priorities of the 2007 general call for proposals' EAC/61/2006, 20 December 2006.

[103] Council, 'Detailed work programme on the follow-up of the objectives of education and training systems in Europe' [2002] OJ C142/1.

[104] ibid.

[105] M Kate and J Niessen, 'Locating immigrant integration policy measures in the machinery of the European Commission' (Brussels: Migration Policy Group, 2007) 74. See also Niessen and Huddleston (n 68 above) 214–21.

Moreover, some national reports have omitted any reference to the specific situation of Roma in relation to education.[106] Interestingly, the Commission had originally proposed that one indicator for the equal opportunities objective could have been 'attitudes and opinions of young people to fighting racism'.[107] This was not, though, adopted and none of the indicators or benchmarks currently used expressly relates to racism or is disaggregated by ethnic origin.[108] More recently, there are some signs that ethnic equality issues are creeping up the agenda of the education OMC. In 2008, the Council recommended that improving the achievement levels of learners with a migrant background should be one of four key objectives for lifelong learning within the OMC.[109]

Mainstreaming ethnic equality and education policy

Taking an overview, it is possible to observe clear evidence of mainstreaming within EU funding programmes on education. In contrast, ethnic equality issues have remained a marginal concern for the education OMC. This recalls a pattern found in employment policy where more decisive evidence of mainstreaming was identified within the European Social Fund in comparison to the EES. Various explanations can be offered for why mainstreaming managed to advance within education programmes. First, it is notable that since the mid-1990s these programmes have been subject to the co-decision procedure where legislation is adopted jointly by the European Parliament and the Council (often following a process of inter-institutional bargaining).[110] The Parliament was one of the strongest advocates for extending EU anti-racism policy during the 1990s, including within education programmes. In contrast, the Parliament has a limited role in the OMC and here mainstreaming has not flourished. Second, Pollack and Hafner-Burton argue that *resonance* with wider objectives is a critical variable in determining the openness of a policy field to mainstreaming.[111] A basic premise of contemporary EU education policy is valuing interculturalism, such as student mobility or exchange of experience between diverse systems. Although this initially sprung from a focus on the children of EC migrant workers, moving to a broader notion of cultural diversity (and hence recognizing issues of racism) represented a logical evolution of existing policy objectives. Third, when pressure grew during the 1990s for a stronger response from the EU to racism, education was frequently identified as a key area. For instance, in

[106] Commission (n 7 above) 20.

[107] Commission, 'Draft detailed work programme for the follow-up of the report on the concrete objectives of education and training systems' COM (2001) 501, 12.

[108] Commission, 'Progress towards the common objectives in education and training—indicators and benchmarks' SEC (2004) 73.

[109] Council, 'Key messages to the Spring European Council in the field of education and training' Ref 5586/08 EDU 25 SOC 40, 25 January 2008, 4.

[110] EC Treaty, Art 251.

[111] M Pollack and E Hafner-Burton, 'Mainstreaming gender in the European Union' (2000) 7 JEPP 432, 435.

1994, the Council established a commission of national representatives to review the role of the EU in combating racism. Many of the recommendations which emerged flowed from its sub-committee on education and training.[112] This was followed by a Council Resolution inviting the Commission to 'exploit fully' EC education programmes in the 'struggle against racism and xenophobia'.[113] Similarly, when the Commission launched its 1998 'Action Plan Against Racism',[114] education was one of the main areas identified as amenable to mainstreaming. The greater susceptibility of the Member States to including anti-racism within education policy may, though, flow from the inherent limits on EU action in this field. The exclusion of any competence to adopt harmonizing legislation ensures that policy impact at the national level remains soft. As will be illustrated in Chapter 8, adopting binding legal instruments against racism has proven more divisive within the Council.

Notwithstanding the evidence of mainstreaming presented above, a number of shortcomings can be identified. On the one hand, it is noticeable that the term 'racism' is actually used within education programmes, whereas this word is often not expressly mentioned in other EU policies (such as the Social Inclusion Process or the EES). On the other hand, the underlying concept of racism reflects the cultural model:

> Intercultural initiatives and exchange in the EU context has [sic] so far focused on promoting understanding between national cultures and differences, and not on the issue of cultural and value conflicts or the power differentials between minority/majority cultures. This approach ignores the fact that intercultural contact in relation to ethnic minorities is often characterised by asymmetrical power relations and underpinned by ideologies of racism.[115]

Commenting on the experience of UK educational policies, Radcliffe highlights the risk that (ill-designed) intercultural projects can 'essentialize cultural difference and generate crude caricatures'.[116] A comparative study in 2004 for the Commission found great diversity in the way in which Member States conceived intercultural education, including variation in the extent to which anti-racism is a central part of this approach.[117] There is little evidence that the institutional racism perspective has penetrated EU educational policy. This is well illustrated in a 2008 Green Paper on education policy.[118] When considering the reasons for

[112] Consultative Commission on Racism and Xenophobia, 'Final Report' Ref 6906/1/95 Rev 1 Limite RAXEN 24 (Brussels: General Secretariat of the Council of the European Union, 1995).

[113] Council Resolution on the response of educational systems to the problems of racism and xenophobia [1995] OJ C312/1.

[114] COM (1998) 183.

[115] Bhandal and Hopkins (n 3 above) 34.

[116] Radcliffe (n 18 above) 77.

[117] Eurydice, 'Integrating immigrant children into schools in Europe' (Brussels: Eurydice, 2004) 57. See also, A Osler and H Starkey, 'Education for citizenship: mainstreaming the fight against racism?' (2002) 37 *European Journal of Education* 143, 156.

[118] Commission, 'Migration and mobility: challenges and opportunities for EU education systems' COM (2008) 423.

poorer educational outcomes amongst migrant children, no mention is made of discrimination within the education system.[119] Instead the reasons cited (loss of recognition of qualifications, language barriers, family expectations, lack of role models) tend to locate the causes for educational inequality in the migrants' own backgrounds.

Finally, on a practical level, it is very difficult to quantify the overall impact of the many different projects on anti-racism that the EU has funded. Although the significant financial support extended since the mid-1990s is one indicator of mainstreaming, further empirical research would be needed to evaluate the effectiveness of these projects. A recent study by Bhandal and Hopkins concluded that even though individual projects were meritorious, 'their impact remains limited, short term and not embedded in mainstream educational policy and practice'.[120] In addition, there are no data available on ethnic minority participation in EU education programmes.[121]

Health

In comparison to education, there is little evidence of mainstreaming ethnic equality in EU health law and policy. This field has steadily evolved, in particular since the 1993 amendment of the EC Treaty to insert a specific competence for public health (Article 152).[122] Like education, this Treaty base primarily authorizes the adoption of 'incentive measures' rather than harmonizing legislation. In this connection, a series of EC action programmes on public health has been adopted. Since 2004, there have been efforts to complement these programmes with a specific OMC on health.[123] This was slow to develop and, as described earlier, it has now been subsumed within the streamlined Social Protection and Social Inclusion Process.

Considering first the Action Programmes, these were initially targeted at specific health issues and diseases, such as cancer or AIDS.[124] In a shift in approach, the 2003–2008 Public Health Action Programme focused on broader goals of health promotion and action on 'health determinants', such as nutrition, tobacco, or alcohol.[125] A theme of growing importance within health policy has been tackling 'health inequalities' and this is one of the key objectives of the Action Programme.[126] Although the Decision establishing the programme refers only to taking into consideration gender and age,[127] several individual projects

[119] ibid 8. [120] Bhandal and Hopkins (n 3 above) 20. [121] ibid 18.

[122] For a comprehensive overview, see T Hervey and J McHale (eds), *Health Law and the European Union* (Cambridge: Cambridge University Press, 2004).

[123] T Hervey, 'The European Union and the governance of health care' in G de Búrca and J Scott (eds), *Law and New Governance in the EU and the US* (Oxford: Hart Publishing, 2006) 179, 192.

[124] Hervey and McHale (n 122 above) ch 9.

[125] Art 2(2)(c), EP and Council Decision (EC) 1786/2002 adopting a programme of Community action in the field of public health (2003–2008) [2002] OJ L271/1.

[126] Art 2(3)(b). [127] Recitals 12 and 18.

have touched directly on ethnic minority health. Under the 'health determinants' strand, a multinational project on reducing health inequalities in the Roma community was financed,[128] whilst a network of national organizations working on HIV/AIDS prevention and migrant communities has been funded under successive programmes for around 15 years.[129]

Given that minority health issues have filtered into individual projects under the 2003–2008 Action Programme, a logical next step for mainstreaming would be to ensure that this is expressly mentioned in the objectives of any successor programme. Nonetheless, when the Commission proposed a Health and Consumer Protection programme for 2007–2013, no reference to the health situation of ethnic minorities or migrants was included.[130] The Parliament amended the proposal during its first reading by adding the following overarching objective:

> tackling inequalities of all kinds in the field of health which exist both amongst and within Member States so that all EU citizens have access to healthcare of a comparable standard, irrespective of sex, age, ethnic origin, education or place of residence.[131]

An amendment to the data collection strand of the programme sought to include gathering health data according to ethnic background.[132] In responding to these amendments, the Commission noted that the anticipated budget for the programme had since been reduced to one-third of the originally expected allocation.[133] Accordingly, the programme would have to be more narrowly tailored. Amongst many adjustments to the original text, the Commission rejected (without detailed explanation) the Parliament's amendments which inserted reference to ethnic origin, whilst keeping references to gender and age.[134] The final text of the programme was adopted in October 2007 and no mention is made of groups such as Roma, immigrants, or ethnic minorities.[135] In a somewhat contradictory step, the Council subsequently requested the Commission to use this programme to support projects on the health of migrants, as well as more generally to give greater priority to this issue within health policy.[136]

128 See: <http://ec.europa.eu/health/ph_projects/2004/action3/action3_2004_01_en.htm> accessed 10 April 2008.

129 Funding for this project ceased at the end of 2006. See further: <http://www.aidsmobility.org> accessed 18 June 2008.

130 Commission, 'Healthier, safer and more confident citizens: a health and consumer protection strategy' COM (2005) 115.

131 Art 2(3), Position of the EP adopted at first reading on 16 March 2006 with a view to the adoption of Decision No.../2006/EC of the EP and of the Council establishing a *second* programme of Community action in the field of health (2007–2013) [2006] OJ C291E/372.

132 Annex, para 5.1.2.

133 Commission, 'Amended proposal for an EP and Council Decision establishing a second programme of Community action in the field of health and consumer protection (2007–2013)' COM (2006) 234, 2.

134 ibid 12.

135 EP and Council Decision (EC) 1350/2007 establishing a second programme of Community action in the field of health (2008–13) [2007] OJ L301/3.

136 Council, 'Health and Migration in the EU' Ref 15609/07, 29 November 2007, para 12.

In relation to the health strand of the Social Protection and Social Inclusion OMC, one of its three objectives is 'access for all to adequate health and long-term care', including the need to address 'inequities in access to care and in health outcomes'.[137] The 2007 Joint Report made no reference to ethnic minorities in this context, although the 2008 Joint Report acknowledges that there are 'striking differences in health outcomes' according to, inter alia, 'ethnic group, and gender'.[138] There is a degree of overlap here with the social inclusion strand of the OMC, which has also considered health status as a dimension of social exclusion. Occasional references have been made to the health situation of minorities, such as Roma,[139] but the level of analysis remains thin.

One general explanation for the limited evidence of anti-racism mainstreaming in this area is the slower development of health as an EU policy domain. When the Commission began to elaborate a wider range of anti-racism initiatives in the late 1990s, its education programmes were already well established. In contrast, health programmes commenced later and remain much smaller in financial terms.[140] Similarly, the health strand of the OMC developed very slowly and it has only taken on a more defined format following its streamlining with the social inclusion and social protection processes. There also seems to be a lower degree of resonance between health policy objectives and anti-racism. A key rationale for EU intervention in health policy was initially to tackle 'cross-border health threats' such as communicable diseases and pollution. The transition towards broader health policy goals, such as combating health inequalities, suggests that there may be more space for mainstreaming in the future. Finally, European-level information about ethnic inequalities in health remains sparse. When the EUMC commissioned a series of benchmark comparative studies on migrants and minorities, none of these addressed health.[141] Few projects under the Anti-Discrimination Action Programme have concerned health and this was not mentioned as an area for mainstreaming in the Commission's 1998 Action Plan against Racism.[142]

E. Conclusions

Ethnic equality mainstreaming has penetrated EU law and policy relating to social inclusion, both in its OMC form and within the dedicated policy on

[137] Council (n 62 above) 9. [138] Council (n 64 above) 11.

[139] Commission (n 9 above) 83.

[140] The total budget for the 2003–2008 public health programme was €312 million, whereas the budget for the 2007–2013 Lifelong Learning programme is €6,970 million.

[141] The topics covered were legislation, policing racist crime and violence, employment, education and housing. In 2003, the EUMC did publish the report 'Breaking the Barriers—Romani Women and Access to Public Health Care'. See further: <http://fra.europa.eu> accessed 18 June 2008.

[142] COM (1998) 183.

education. In relation to the OMC, there is less evidence that a *deliberate* strategy of mainstreaming has been pursued; even so, issues relating to ethnic inequalities have found their way onto the policy agenda. In neither instance is there a clear *process* through which mainstreaming takes place. The OMC has a specialist group devoted to gender mainstreaming, whilst DG Education and Culture has an in-house 'equal opportunities network'. It was reported in 2007 that this network was beginning to consider ethnicity issues.[143] The lack of any overarching structure for mainstreaming may help explain why some issues get neglected, such as health policy. Within the streamlined OMC, there is little evidence that the work on ethnic inequalities in the social inclusion strand has yet provoked any mainstreaming within the social protection or health strands.

It is difficult to identify any shared conceptual understanding of racism or the key groups vulnerable to discrimination. Education policy is distinct because it explicitly uses terms such as racism and xenophobia in its programme objectives. In practice, this mainly manifests itself in intercultural education projects. The Social Inclusion Process rarely mentions racism, but its documentary trail includes fairly regular recognition of inequalities linked to ethnicity or nationality. The policy response to such inequalities is variable. The dichotomy in national plans between those based on integration measures and those which acknowledge the role played by discrimination confirms that institutional racism is a concept not yet embraced in many Member States. Disparities also emerge regarding the target groups. Unsurprisingly, immigrants were highlighted as a key group within the Social Inclusion Process. Post-enlargement, this has been accompanied by attention to the situation of Roma. EU education policy was concerned with migrants and their descendants from the outset, but it is notable that the education of Roma children was also recognized at an early stage. In 1989, the Council adopted a resolution[144] on this issue and actions to improve the education of Gypsy children have been explicitly included in the programme objectives of Comenius since 1995. This is a rare example of Roma disadvantage being acknowledged in EU policy prior to the 2004 enlargement. If contemporary social inclusion policy focuses on immigrants/ethnic minorities and Roma, an intersectionality perspective has yet to make much headway. The new common indicator on immigrant employment rates is intended to be disaggregated by gender which constitutes a small step in this direction.[145]

Finally, a comment can be made in relation to regulatory style and mainstreaming. The policy areas considered in this chapter are mainly built upon the application of new governance techniques; however, it is difficult to detect any common pattern. In relation to the OMC, the Social Inclusion Process has been a moderately fruitful site for mainstreaming, whereas this is less true with regard

143 Bhandal and Hopkins (n 3 above) 22.
144 Council Resolution on school provision for gypsy and traveller children [1989] OJ C153/3.
145 Commission (n 74 above) 21.

to either the education or the health processes. As regards funding programmes, education offers an example where mainstreaming has had some success, yet this is contradicted by the experience with health programmes. This suggests that while regulatory style may be one variable in shaping the opportunity for mainstreaming, the individual policy context is more influential.

7

Immigration and Integration

Law and policy concerning immigration are inherently sensitive from the perspective of combating racism. Migrants are one of the principal groups vulnerable to discrimination on grounds of ethnic origin. The information presented at the beginning of Chapters 5 and 6 has already demonstrated widespread evidence of unequal outcomes for migrants (compared to nationals or EU citizens) in fields such as employment or education. Immigration law and policy can play a crucial role in promoting ethnic equality by addressing how migrants are treated by the state, as well as by society at large.

The European Union has always been an organization involved in regulating migration, initially that of EU citizens. This chapter focuses, however, on law and policy relating to third country nationals. Here, the Union's role has evolved gradually, albeit following a 'tortuous path'.[1] Following years dominated by intergovernmental cooperation outside the ambit of the EC Treaty, in 1999 the Treaty of Amsterdam inserted new legal competences covering most dimensions of immigration law, ranging from external border controls and visas, to asylum and resident third country nationals.[2] Since then, there has been a very active legislative programme which has established rules governing different strands of migration, such as asylum, family reunion, and irregular migration.[3] In contrast to the previous chapter, this is a field where the traditional regulatory tool of binding legislation has been deployed. Nevertheless, new governance techniques are also in evidence. Although a full-bodied open method of coordination on immigration has yet to emerge,[4] a nascent policy coordination process can be witnessed in relation to the integration of migrants.

Given the elaborate legislative architecture which has been built on immigration, it is not possible, in the space of a single chapter, to consider the extent

[1] S Giubboni, 'Immigrazione e politiche dell'Unione Europea: dal Trattato di Roma alla Costituzione per l'Europa' (2005) no. 106 / anno XXVII *Giornale di diritto del lavoro e di relazioni industriali* 205, 206.

[2] EC Treaty, Arts 62 and 63.

[3] For a detailed overview, see S Peers, *EU Justice and Home Affairs Law* (2nd edn, Oxford: OUP, 2006).

[4] A more elaborate policy coordination mechanism has been proposed: Commission, 'A common immigration policy for Europe: principles, actions and tools' COM (2008) 359.

to which ethnic equality objectives have been mainstreamed into all aspects of this field. In selecting which elements to scrutinize in more depth, guidance was taken from the material scope of the Racial Equality Directive. This prohibits discrimination on grounds of racial or ethnic origin in key social goods, such as employment, education, health, and housing.[5] Immigration law is directly relevant here because it regulates the access of migrants to these social goods. Moreover, it assumes a special importance as a result of Article 3(2) of the Racial Equality Directive:

> This Directive does not cover difference of treatment based on nationality and is without prejudice to provisions and conditions relating to the entry into and residence of third-country nationals and stateless persons on the territory of Member States, and to any treatment which arises from the legal status of the third-country nationals and stateless persons concerned.

Given this restriction, immigration law is potentially an alternative venue where equality for third country nationals in access to social goods can be advanced. This chapter divides this topic into three parts. First, it considers irregular migrants.[6] The precariousness of their residence status renders it complicated to consider equality claims. Yet, for the same reason, such persons are highly vulnerable to discrimination; an employer knows that an irregular migrant risks removal if she publicly complains about her working conditions. Second, the situation of legal migrants is examined. Quite a substantial body of EC legislation has been introduced which regulates the access to social goods by different categories of lawful resident, such as family members or refugees. Consequently, it will be relevant to consider if these laws contribute to promoting ethnic equality. Finally, the embryonic integration policy is considered. This also concerns access to social goods by third country nationals, but it is largely based on non-legislative instruments. Before examining these three examples, it is appropriate to reflect further on what mainstreaming ethnic equality means in the context of immigration law and policy. Unlike employment or social inclusion policies, this is a field which is, to a large extent, premised on the *different* treatment of third country nationals. A state's citizens are not normally subject to immigration control, aside from establishing their nationality. Moreover, the extensive free movement rights enjoyed by EU citizens mean that only in very limited circumstances can states restrict their movement within the Union or deny them equal treatment in access to social goods.[7]

[5] Art 3; Council Directive (EC) 2000/43 implementing the principle of equal treatment between persons irrespective of racial or ethnic origin [2000] OJ L180/22.

[6] This encompasses various situations, ranging from unauthorized entry into the EU, to those who originally enjoyed permission to be present but have since forfeited this, for example, because they have overstayed a time-limited visa.

[7] For an overview of the case-law on EU citizenship rights, see R White, 'Free movement, equal treatment and citizenship of the Union' (2005) 54 ICLQ 885.

A. Can Ethnic Equality Objectives be Mainstreamed into Immigration Law?

There is nothing inherently fixed about the existence of borders and their accompanying restrictions on the international movement of people.[8] It can be argued that any form of immigration control tends towards racial discrimination as it seeks to exclude outsiders who are typically of different ethnic origins to the existing residents. Similarly, any form of citizenship inevitably creates a boundary between those who are citizens and those who are not. Again, non-citizens are likely to be disproportionately from a different ethnic background to that of the current citizens. Therefore, a debate could be opened as to whether the very concept of borders and bounded citizenship categories are incompatible with promoting ethnic equality. Nevertheless, it is not unusual for commentators to proceed from the assumption that these are fixed elements of immigration law for the foreseeable future.[9] As Kymlicka remarks, some degree of limitation of rights and benefits according to citizenship is inevitable, 'unless one is willing to accept either a single world-government or completely open borders between states—and very few liberal theorists have endorsed either of these'.[10]

A further factor to consider is that immigration law tends to distinguish not just between nationals and non-nationals, but also between different categories of non-nationals. Within the EU, nationals of other Member States obviously receive preferential treatment in the field of immigration compared to non-EU nationals. Additionally, nationals of some countries enjoy visa-free access to the Union, whilst stricter immigration controls apply to others. Some groups of nationals enjoy more favourable treatment based on international agreements; nationals of the European Economic Area (EEA)[11] receive treatment in immigration law very similar to that of EU nationals.

Given that immigration law is premised on an insider/outsider construction and seemingly riddled with differences in treatment linked to nationality, it is tempting to conclude that mainstreaming ethnic equality is structurally impossible or amounts to little more than recommending a more open approach to migration. Indeed, immigration law and policy were given very little attention in the Commission's 1998 Action Plan Against Racism.[12] In contrast, this chapter argues that mainstreaming can be productively applied. A point of departure

[8] Juss observes that 'prior to the 19th century, closed cities and closed territories had been rare': S Juss, 'Free movement and the world order' (2004) 16 *International Journal of Refugee Law* 289, 299.

[9] eg S Spencer, 'The impact of immigration policy on race relations' in T Blackstone, B Parekh, and P Sanders (eds), *Race Relations in Britain—A Developing Agenda* (London: Routledge, 1998) 74, 90.

[10] W Kymlicka, *Multicultural Citizenship* (Oxford: OUP, 1995) 124–5.

[11] Norway, Iceland, and Liechtenstein.

[12] COM (1998) 183.

is recognizing that fundamental human rights, including the right to non-discrimination, apply to all persons, regardless of citizenship or immigration status. This is affirmed in the preamble of the Racial Equality Directive which states that 'the right to equality before the law and protection against discrimination for all persons constitutes a universal right'.[13] The difficulty lies in reconciling the global nature of this right with the widely accepted possibility for states to treat non-citizens less favourably. Article 1(2) of the International Convention on the Elimination of All Forms of Racial Discrimination states: 'this Convention shall not apply to distinctions, exclusions, restrictions or preferences made by a State Party to this Convention between citizens and non-citizens.' At first glance, this seems to excuse immigration law from the risk of contravening laws against racial discrimination. The UN Committee on the Elimination of Racial Discrimination (CERD) has, though, argued for a narrow interpretation of this exception. The Committee observes that 'xenophobia against non-nationals, particularly migrants, refugees and asylum-seekers, constitutes one of the main sources of contemporary racism', as well as the treatment of undocumented and stateless persons.[14] Given this reality, the Committee holds that:

> differential treatment based on citizenship or immigration status will constitute discrimination if the criteria for such differentiation, judged in the light of the objectives and purposes of the Convention, are not applied pursuant to a legitimate aim, and are not proportional to the achievement of this aim.[15]

Similarly, the European Court of Human Rights has held that there must be 'very weighty reasons' to justify differences of treatment exclusively based on nationality.[16] Therefore, immigration law needs to be carefully scrutinized to ensure that it avoids discrimination and, as far as possible, is mobilized to favour equality. To this end, it is necessary to consider both *policy objectives* and *policy implementation*.

Without reopening the debate on whether restricting immigration is per se discriminatory, situations can arise where policy objectives constitute discrimination on grounds of racial or ethnic origin. A historical example can be found in 1968, when the UK government changed immigration law in order to restrict the possibility of British citizens of Asian ethnic origin using their citizenship in order to migrate to the UK. The European Commission of Human Rights held that the legislation contravened Article 3 ECHR on the right to be free from degrading treatment because 'the 1968 Act had racial motives . . . it was directed

[13] Recital 4.
[14] General recommendation no 30: discrimination against non-citizens, 1 October 2004.
[15] ibid para I(4).
[16] eg para 42, *Gaygusuz v Austria* (1997) 23 EHRR 364. The Court has not been entirely consistent in its application of this standard: see J Gerards, 'Discrimination grounds' in D Schiek, L Waddington, and M Bell (eds), *Cases, Materials and Text on National, Supranational and International Non-discrimination Law* (Oxford: Hart Publishing, 2007) 33, 66–7.

against the Asian citizens of the United Kingdom'.[17] Even if immigration policy objectives are ostensibly neutral, ethnic equality considerations also need to be mainstreamed into *policy implementation*. An obvious example here is the way in which people are selected for immigration checks. In *R (European Roma Rights Centre) v Immigration Officer at Prague Airport and another*,[18] the UK introduced a scheme where passengers seeking to travel to the UK would be first examined by UK immigration officials in Prague Airport. Statistics showed that only 0.2% of non-Roma Czech passengers were refused leave to enter the UK, compared with a refusal rate of 87% for Roma passengers. The House of Lords held that this application of immigration controls constituted direct discrimination contrary to the Race Relations Act 1976. A different example concerns visa requirements. The EU has chosen to require some non-EU nationals to apply for a visa in order to get permission to enter the Union. Concerns arise around the implementation of this scheme by the Union. Peers argues that:

> The visa list arguably breaches the principle of non-discrimination, particularly given the application of the visa requirement to all countries with a majority black population and nearly every country with a Muslim majority.[19]

In summary, mainstreaming calls for close scrutiny of immigration policy objectives and their implementation. This is both with a view to eliminating discrimination within immigration law and policy, but also in order to identify how this field can contribute to promoting ethnic equality. Specifically, immigration law can be used constructively to provide rights for equal treatment irrespective of citizenship or immigration status. The remainder of this chapter examines three elements of EU immigration law and policy in order to consider the extent to which mainstreaming can be identified.

B. Irregular Migrants

The first aspect to be examined is irregular migration. By virtue of its nature, accurate statistics are impossible to ascertain.[20] In 2007, the Commission estimated that there were 2–8 million irregular migrants in the Union.[21] Cholewinski argues that 'the EU's primary concern with irregular migration focuses on preventing the phenomenon, detecting and punishing those who

[17] Cited in A Lester, 'Thirty years on: the East African Asians case revisited' [2002] PL 52, 60.

[18] [2005] 2 AC 1, HL.

[19] Peers (n 3 above) 167.

[20] V Mitsilegas, 'Measuring irregular migration: implications for law, policy and human rights' in B Bogusz, R Cholewinski, A Cygan, and E Szyszczak (eds), *Irregular Migrants: Theoretical, European and International Perspectives* (Leiden: Martinus Nijhoff Publishers, 2004) 29.

[21] Commission, 'Proposal for a EP and Council Directive providing for sanctions against employers of illegally staying third-country nationals – impact assessment' SEC (2007) 603, 6.

facilitate it, and returning irregular migrants to their countries of origin'.[22] This rests on a long-standing policy mix which seeks to balance 'fair treatment' of legally resident third country nationals with firm measures to combat 'illegal immigration'.[23] A variety of instruments has been deployed in relation to irregular migration. On the preventative side, sanctions have been targeted at those who assist in illegal entry into the EU. Member States are required to impose criminal penalties on those who facilitate unlawful entry,[24] with more severe sanctions where this takes the form of human trafficking.[25] Preventative measures are combined with a policy of returning irregular migrants to their countries of origin. This is clearly reflected in the proposed 'Returns Directive', which establishes a presumption that irregular migrants should be returned to their country of origin, subject to certain exceptions.[26]

Taking an overview of EU policy on irregular migrants, tensions with ethnic equality objectives emerge. The Commission bases its return policy on the mantra that the public will accept legally resident third country nationals only if they are convinced that a robust approach has been adopted in respect of irregular migrants.[27] Yet, it is hard to verify whether the basic premise is correct. Repressive measures against irregular migrants could also be interpreted by the public as an indication that these people are dangerous and harmful to society and that security can be maintained only by their removal. It is at least doubtful whether this will inspire the public to value legal migrants, particularly given that a significant number of lawful migrants were previously in an irregular situation.[28] Kymlicka argues that policies based purely on return are fundamentally unrealistic and 'the likely result of such a policy is to create a permanently disenfranchised, alienated, and racially-defined underclass'.[29] Given the estimated scale of the irregular migrant population, it seems highly improbable that

[22] R Cholewinski, *Irregular Migrants: Access to Minimum Social Rights* (Strasbourg: Council of Europe Publishing, 2005) 20.

[23] eg Presidency Conclusions – Tampere European Council, 15–16 October 1999.

[24] Council Framework Decision (EU) 2002/946 on the strengthening of the penal framework to prevent the facilitation of unauthorised entry, transit or residence [2002] OJ L328/1.

[25] Council Framework Decision (EU) 2002/629 on combating trafficking in human beings [2002] OJ L203/1. Trafficking (as opposed to mere facilitation) is linked to the additional element of assisting unlawful entry with a view to exploitation either for labour or sexual purposes (Art 1(1)).

[26] Art 6, Position of the EP adopted at first reading on 18 June 2008 with a view to the adoption of Directive 2008/ . . . /EC of the EP and of the Council on common standards and procedures in Member States for returning illegally staying third country nationals, P6_TC1-COD(2005)0167.

[27] eg in the following Commission documents: 'Communication on a common policy on illegal immigration' COM (2001) 672, 8; 'Green paper on a Community return policy on illegal residents' COM (2002) 175, 8; 'Communication on a Community return policy on illegal residents' COM (2002) 564, 8; 'Communication on policy priorities in the fight against illegal immigration of third-country nationals' COM (2006) 402, 10.

[28] This is evident from the substantial regularization programmes which have taken place in various European countries: Commission, 'Policy plan on legal migration' COM (2005) 669, 28.

[29] W Kymlicka, 'Western political theory and ethnic relations in Eastern Europe' in W Kymlicka and M Opalski (eds), *Can Liberal Pluralism be Exported? Western Political Theory and Ethnic Relations in Eastern Europe* (Oxford: OUP, 2001) 13, 41.

return policies will, by themselves, be a sufficient response. This was tentatively recognized in the Commission's first major policy document on migrant integration. It admitted that many irregular migrants could not be returned for 'legal, humanitarian or practical reasons'.[30] Nevertheless, the Commission has since voiced its hostility to 'wide-scale regularisation measures'.[31] To date, EU policy has paid little attention to the social situation of irregular migrants. From the perspective of promoting equality, this is problematic. It implies that a significant group of people, often characterized by ethnic difference from the majority population, will be consigned to a highly marginalized status. Although their residence is an ongoing social reality, they are cut off from legal protection and rendered vulnerable to discrimination.

In the light of the above, it is difficult to find evidence that ethnic equality objectives have been taken into account in this area of immigration policy. This is well illustrated by the Commission's 2007 proposal for a Directive 'providing sanctions against employers of illegally staying third-country nationals'.[32] The Directive aims to reduce the employment of irregular migrants and thereby discourage irregular migration. To this end, Member States are required to prohibit the employment of irregular migrants and to impose financial penalties on any employer in breach of this provision. Furthermore, this must be punishable as a criminal offence in any of the following circumstances: where the offence is repeated; where it involves more than four employees; where it is accompanied by 'particularly exploitative working conditions'; or where the employer knows that the employee is a victim of trafficking.[33]

Considering first the policy objectives of the proposed Directive, they are, in part, consistent with combating inequality. The vulnerability of irregular migrants in the informal economy places them at risk of abusive working conditions. Consequently, attempts to repress informal employment can be viewed as desirable. The Directive also takes initial steps towards recognizing minimum social rights of irregular migrants. Article 7 would require the employer to pay any outstanding remuneration to the irregular migrant and, where working conditions have been exploitative, the migrant is entitled to remain in the Member State until any unpaid remuneration has been received.

Despite the above, the objectives of the proposal are unlikely to improve the social situation of irregular migrants. The Directive's legal base[34] implies that its principal orientation is repression of irregular migration rather than attempting to redress the workplace discrimination faced by irregular migrants. Whilst it does protect unpaid remuneration, there is no mention of enforcing other labour law

[30] Commission, 'Communication on immigration, integration and employment' COM (2003) 336, 26.

[31] Commission, 'Study on the links between legal and illegal migration' COM (2004) 412, 17.

[32] COM (2007) 249.

[33] Art 10.

[34] EC Treaty, Art 63(3)(b).

entitlements, such as compensation for unequal pay or violations of working time rules. A coalition of trade unions and European NGOs, including the European Network Against Racism, has argued that enforcing labour law should be disentangled from immigration law.[35] The Directive tends to conflate the two issues and places clear priority on immigration control. Moreover, the Directive does not derogate from the underlying policy that, upon discovery, any irregular migrants must be returned.[36]

Turning to consider *policy implementation*, applying sanctions to employers has often provoked concern that this will have spillover effects on both legally resident migrants and ethnic minority citizens.[37] This is based on the reasoning that: (a) it can be difficult for employers to know exactly who is or is not entitled to work, so concerned employers might be deterred from recruiting legally resident migrants or citizens of migrant origin; (b) employers might disproportionately apply documentation checks to ethnic minority employees assuming that these individuals are more at risk of being irregular migrants. The Commission conducted an extended impact assessment prior to issuing the proposed Directive, but surprisingly this did not even recognize the potential for increased ethnic discrimination. It suggested that less irregular migration could reduce xenophobia amongst EU nationals,[38] but that mostly there would be an unchanged situation for non-discrimination.[39] The Commission's conclusions can be contrasted with a similar impact assessment process in the UK. There, the government wanted to introduce new civil penalties on employers of irregular migrants with a view to complementing the existing criminal law offence.[40] An equality impact assessment of the proposal was conducted which recognized the potential for various negative effects:

- stigma for those required to demonstrate their immigration status;
- caution amongst employers about employing a person who 'is or might appear to be a foreign national';
- as illegal working is concentrated in certain sectors, ethnic minority *employers* might be more likely to be subject to investigation.[41]

[35] para 5, ETUC, PICUM, and Solidar, 'Joint comments of ETUC, PICUM and Solidar on expected Commission proposals to fight "illegal" employment and exploitative working conditions', 26 April 2007.

[36] In cases of exploitative working conditions, time-limited residence permits could be issued to irregular migrants who cooperate in proceedings against the employer: Art 14.

[37] This is a long-running debate in the USA: eg P Martin and M Miller, 'Employer sanctions: French, German and US experiences' International Migration Papers No 36 (Geneva: International Labour Office, 2000) 36.

[38] Commission (n 21 above) 9.

[39] ibid 33.

[40] para 4.2, Home Office, 'Consultation on the implementation of new powers to prevent illegal migrant working in the UK' (London: Home Office, 2007).

[41] Home Office, 'Prevention of illegal working—Immigration, Asylum and Nationality Act 2006. Equality impact assessment' (London: Home Office, 2007) 7.

Recognizing these potential impacts did not cause the UK government to abandon the policy, but it did adopt complementary measures in mitigation. Namely, a Code of Practice has been prepared to guide employers on how to comply with the law without engaging in racial discrimination.[42] The failure of the Commission's impact assessment procedure to identify these issues illustrates its shortcomings as a vehicle for mainstreaming. In addition, the specific impact assessment on this proposed Directive was selected for review by the Commission's Impact Assessment Board.[43] Although this made several criticisms of the impact assessment, it made no comment on the omission of any analysis of the potential for the proposal to give rise to racial discrimination.[44]

Mainstreaming ethnic equality into policy on irregular migration neither implies that all persons should be regularized, nor that return policies can never be used. It does, though, call attention to the impact of a situation where a large group of persons, usually from ethnic minority communities, is stigmatized in the public mind and deprived of legal protection. These ingredients seem a recipe for aggravating ethnic inequality and perpetuating, in Kymlicka's words, 'a racially-defined underclass'.[45] EU policy has done little to improve the living and working conditions of irregular migrants or to reduce their vulnerability to discrimination.

C. Legal Migrants

EC Treaty, Article 63(3)(a) confers a legal competence in relation to the 'conditions of entry and residence' of third country nationals. In relation to *entry*, EU policy has not flourished and decisions on the volume of legal migration remain a matter of national discretion, at least as regards economic migration.[46] Therefore, this section focuses on various instruments which regulate the *conditions* of residence for legal migrants.

[42] Home Office, 'Guidance for employers on the avoidance of unlawful discrimination in employment practice whilst seeking to prevent illegal working—Code of Practice' (London: Home Office, 2008).

[43] On the role of the Impact Assessment Board, see Ch 3.

[44] Impact Assessment Board, Document SG C-2 D(2007) 3497, 18 April 2007.

[45] Kymlicka (n 29 above).

[46] See further B Ryan, 'The European Union and labour migration: regulating admission or treatment?' in A Baldaccini, E Guild, and H Toner (eds), *Whose Freedom, Security and Justice? EU Immigration and Asylum Law and Policy* (Oxford: Hart Publishing, 2007) 489.

Overview of the current legal framework

Since immigration law was inserted into the EC Treaty in 1999, multiple Directives have been adopted which contain provisions on the treatment of legally resident third country nationals:

- free movement of EU citizens (and their family members);[47]
- long-term residents (LTR);[48]
- family reunion of third country nationals;[49]
- scientific researchers;[50]
- students (in higher education);[51]
- refugees and beneficiaries of subsidiary protection;[52]
- temporary protection;[53]
- asylum applicants.[54]

One feature which immediately emerges is the way in which the legislation stratifies migrants according to their immigration status. This is significant because equal treatment rights vary depending on which status is enjoyed. Table 7.1 summarizes these provisions in relation to the labour market. A similar diversity in the legal situation exists regarding other social rights, such as education, housing, and healthcare, which have not been listed here for reasons of space.[55] In addition, equal treatment rights can be derived from agreements between the EU and third countries. Such agreements extend to some European states which are not currently in the EU (eg Turkey, Croatia, Macedonia); several north African states (Algeria, Morocco, Tunisia); the Russian Federation and some former Soviet states; as well as more than 70 African, Caribbean, and

[47] Art 24(1), EP and Council Directive (EC) 2004/38 on the right of citizens of the Union and their family members to move and reside freely within the territory of the Member States . . . [2004] OJ L229/35.

[48] Arts 11 and 21, Council Directive (EC) 2003/109 concerning the status of third country nationals who are long-term residents [2004] OJ L16/44.

[49] Art 14, Council Directive (EC) 2003/86 on the right to family reunification [2003] OJ L251/12.

[50] Arts 11–12, Council Directive (EC) 2005/71 on a specific procedure for admitting third-country nationals for the purposes of scientific research [2005] OJ L289/15.

[51] Art 17, Council Directive (EC) 2004/114 on the conditions of admission of third-country nationals for the purposes of studies, pupil exchange, unremunerated training or voluntary service [2004] OJ L375/12. The limited right to work is expressly for 'students', but Member States may decide to apply the Directive to secondary school exchange pupils, or those engaging in unremunerated training or voluntary service (Art 3).

[52] Arts 26–27, Council Directive (EC) 2004/83 on minimum standards for the qualification and status of third-country nationals or stateless persons as refugees or as persons who otherwise need international protection and the content of the protection granted [2004] OJ L304/12.

[53] Arts 12–14, Council Directive (EC) 2001/55 on minimum efforts for giving temporary protection in the event of a mass influx of displaced persons and on measures promoting a balance of efforts between Member States in receiving such persons and bearing the consequences thereof [2001] OJ L212/12.

[54] Arts 10–11, Council Directive (EC) 2003/9 laying down minimum standards for the reception of asylum seekers [2003] OJ L31/18.

[55] See further M Bell, 'Civic citizenship and migrant integration' (2007) 13 EPL 311, 325–6.

Table 7.1: EC legislation on third country nationals' (TCN) rights as regards employment

Type of migrant	Rights relating to employment
Member of EU citizen's family	Equal treatment with nationals. Limited exception for certain positions in the public service under EC Treaty, Art 39(4).
LTR	Equal treatment with nationals, but any measures restricting access to employment to national/EU/EEA citizens can be retained and jobs involving any exercise of public authority can be excluded.
LTR in another Member State	Equal treatment with nationals, but the receiving Member State may limit the range of permitted employment activities for 12 months.
Member of TCN family	Entitled to the same standard of treatment as the sponsoring migrant, but access to employment may be limited for up to 12 months; access to employment may be limited to first-degree relatives in ascending line and adult unmarried children permitted entry for health reasons.
Researcher	Access to teaching subject to maximum days/hours set by national law. Equal treatment in working conditions, including pay and dismissal.
Student	No rights regarding treatment at work specified. Permitted to work at least 10 hours per week, but this may be restricted during first 12 months.
Refugee	Access to employment subject to the rules generally applicable to the profession and the public service. General provisions of employment law shall apply.
Subsidiary protection	Access to employment subject to the rules generally applicable to the profession and the public service. May be subject to prioritization for other nationals for a limited period. General provisions of employment law shall apply.
Temporary protection	Access to employment may be subject to priority for EU/EEA nationals and legally resident TCNs receiving unemployment benefit. General provisions of employment law shall apply.
Asylum applicant	Access to employment must be granted if no first instance decision within 1 year (and this is not due to the applicant's actions). May be subject to priority for EU/EEA and legally resident TCNs.

Note: With the exception of Directive 2004/38, none of this legislation applies to Denmark. Ireland has accepted the Directives applying to scientific researchers, refugees, and beneficiaries of subsidiary protection. The UK has accepted the Directives applying to refugees, beneficiaries of subsidiary protection, temporary protection, and asylum applicants.

Pacific states which are party to the Cotonou Agreement.[56] The right to equal treatment conferred by each of these agreements varies and not all have yet been tested through litigation. Moreover, Ryan notes that it is doubtful whether such rights can be invoked against a private employer.[57]

[56] For more detail, see Ryan (n 46 above) 511–13; Peers (n 3 above) 202–10.
[57] ibid 513.

A framework for equality?

From the perspective of mainstreaming, the question to be considered is whether this framework is suitable for promoting ethnic equality. Considering the policy objectives, the existing legislation is consistent with mainstreaming insofar as it helps to provide a complementary layer of protection from nationality discrimination and thereby addresses some of the shortcomings in the Racial Equality Directive. Nevertheless, the legal framework has two major deficiencies. First, the protection against nationality discrimination is riddled with *gaps*. Not all legally resident third country nationals will be covered by any of these Directives. Notably, migrant workers who have not yet acquired enough length of residence to be treated as LTRs,[58] and who are neither researchers nor EU citizen family members, do not currently enjoy protection from nationality discrimination (unless this can be derived via an international agreement). As well as gaps in the personal scope of protection, the actual rights conferred vary greatly and 'equal treatment' is not always guaranteed. For example, students and asylum applicants are entitled to (limited) *access* to employment, but no guarantees are provided regarding their treatment once in employment. Some of these inconsistencies might be ironed out in the future. The Commission has proposed a Directive establishing a 'common set of rights' for all those who have been legally admitted to EU territory and are permitted to work.[59] This would include a right to 'equal treatment with nationals' in fields such as working conditions (including pay, dismissal, and health and safety); freedom of association; education; social security; and access to goods and services.[60]

Second, a *hierarchy* of equal treatment rights emerges which stratifies third country nationals into various 'status categories'.[61] Those with the most precarious residence rights are also those with the least protection against nationality discrimination. For example, asylum applicants can be excluded from any access to employment for one year and even then they are subject to priority for EU/EEA citizens or legally resident third country nationals. Elsewhere rights are evidently tied to economic status. This is most transparent in the Commission's recent proposal for a Directive on highly qualified employment.[62] This status is reserved to those third country workers performing jobs which normally require a higher education qualification and where the salary received is 'at least three

[58] In general, five years of legal and continuous residence are required: Art 4(1), Dir 2003/109.

[59] Commission, 'Proposal for a Council Directive on a single application procedure for a single permit for third-country nationals to reside and work in the territory of a Member State and on a common set of rights for third-country workers legally residing in a Member State' COM (2007) 638.

[60] ibid Art 12.

[61] Y Soysal, *Limits of Citizenship—Migrants and Postnational Membership in Europe* (Chicago: University of Chicago Press, 1994) 126.

[62] Commission, 'Proposal for a Council Directive on the conditions of entry and residence of third-country nationals for the purposes of highly qualified employment' COM (2007) 637.

times the minimum gross monthly wage as set by national law'.[63] These privileged workers would receive an 'EU Blue Card' enabling them to exercise free movement rights after two years, albeit only for highly qualified employment elsewhere in the Union. Unlike other third country nationals, family reunion rights would not be subject to any minimum period of residence within the EU. The linking of rights to residence status or, in essence, the migrant's economic attractiveness to the EU is difficult to reconcile with international human rights standards. As mentioned earlier, CERD takes the view that any different treatment based 'on citizenship or immigration status' must be thoroughly justified.[64] On one side, EC law (via international agreements) establishes a hierarchy of protection based on nationality. On the other, equal treatment rights in EC legislation are contingent upon the individual's immigration status.

Finally, the legal framework is further diminished by optional exceptions. This is particularly striking in relation to LTRs where the Directive permits Member States to maintain restrictions on access to any form of employment, public or private, where this is already reserved in legislation to nationals or EU/EEA citizens.[65] This preserves practices which institutionalize disadvantage for third country nationals in the labour market.

Overall, the various bits and pieces of immigration law provide some degree of protection against nationality discrimination and contribute to plugging the gaps in the Racial Equality Directive. Nevertheless, the jumbled nature of the rights on offer renders the law relatively inaccessible for individual victims of discrimination. The provisions are mainly confined to a bald statement of equal treatment; there is no detail on the concept of discrimination or procedures for enforcement as found within EC anti-discrimination legislation. Immigration law imperatives seem to trump equality concerns, as seen in the ongoing possibility to ring-fence certain occupations for EU citizens.

D. Integration Policy

As the Treaties currently stand, the EU has no express competence for migrant integration policy.[66] Policy coordination has gradually developed in this area,

[63] ibid Art 5(2). [64] CERD (n 14 above).

[65] Art 11(3)(a), Dir 2003/109. On the equality provisions of the LTR Directive, see further: S Peers, 'Implementing equality? The Directive on long-term resident third-country nationals' (2004) 29 ELR 437; L Halleskov, 'The Long-Term Residents Directive: a fulfillment of the Tampere objective of near-equality?' (2005) 7 EJML 181; S Boelaert-Suominen, 'Non-EU nationals and Council Directive 2003/109/EC on the status of third country nationals who are long-term residents: five paces forward and possibly three paces back' (2005) 42 CML Rev 1011; A Skordas, 'Immigration and the market: the Long-Term Residents Directive' (2006) 13 CJEL 201.

[66] The Treaty of Lisbon would create a competence for 'promoting the integration of third-country nationals residing legally': Art 79(4), Consolidated version of the TFEU [2008] OJ C115/78. This is limited to incentive and supporting measures and excludes any harmonization of legislation.

primarily through recourse to new governance instruments, such as exchange of experience and the pursuit of (non-binding) common policy objectives. This section begins with a summary of the main features of integration policy and then turns to consider the extent to which ethnic equality objectives have been mainstreamed therein.

The principal elements of EU integration policy

Integration policy could not be described as a fully fledged open method of coordination process, yet some of the techniques familiar to the OMC have been imported into this field.[67] A loose set of common policy objectives has been established via the 'Common Basic Principles for Immigrant Integration Policy in the European Union', which were adopted by the Council in 2004.[68] The 11 principles are fairly general in nature, but identify some shared orientations for integration policy. Integration is defined as 'a dynamic, two-way process of mutual accommodation by all immigrants and residents of Member States'.[69] On the one hand, immigrants should acquire 'the language and culture of the host society'; on the other, 'access for immigrants to institutions, as well as to public and private goods and services, on a basis equal to national citizens and in a non-discriminatory way is a critical foundation for better integration'.[70] A network of 'National Contact Points' was established, which reports to the Commission on developments in domestic law and policy relating to integration.[71] This information feeds into the Commission's annual report on 'migration and integration'.[72] The second annual report assumed a format more akin to an OMC process, taking each of the Common Basic Principles and considering how they are reflected in national law and policy.[73] In cooperation with the National Contact Points, an official 'Handbook on Integration' has been published.[74] This has a normative dimension, making explicit policy recommendations. It grounds these in numerous examples of 'good practices' found within the Member States which could be emulated elsewhere.

Policy analysis and transnational exchange of experience were promoted through a pilot project called INTI, which ran between 2003 and 2006 and

[67] S Velluti, 'What European Union strategy for integrating migrants? The role of OMC soft mechanisms in the development of an EU immigration policy' (2007) 9 EJML 53, 75.

[68] Council, 'Press Release: 2618th Council Meeting Justice and Home Affairs' 14615/04 (Presse 321), 19 November 2004, 15. See further, V Mitsilegas, 'Immigration, diversity and integration: the limits of EU law' in P Shah (ed), *Law and Ethnic Plurality: Socio-legal Perspectives* (Leiden: Koninklijke Brill NV, 2007) 31, 34.

[69] ibid 17. [70] ibid 20–1.

[71] H Urth, 'Building momentum for the integration of third country nationals in the European Union' (2005) 7 EJML 163, 172.

[72] The first 'annual' report was in 2004 (COM (2004) 508); however, no report appeared in 2006.

[73] COM (2005) 389.

[74] J Niessen and Y Schibel, *Handbook on Integration for Policy-makers and Practitioners* (Luxembourg: OOPEC, 2004). The second edition was published by the same authors in 2007.

received an annual budget of €4–6 million. This has now been greatly expanded. The 'European Fund for the integration of third country nationals' has a budget of €825 million, 2007–2013.[75] It is notable that this is substantially larger than the forecast budget of around €150 million for anti-discrimination projects during the same period.[76] Although the fund is based on a decentralized implementation structure, national programmes should be based on 'strategic guidelines' set by the Commission. Notably, these guidelines 'shall in particular give effect to the priorities of the Community with a view to promoting the Common Basic Principles'.[77]

Finally, integration policy has explicitly borrowed from the equality toolbox and there is an active commitment to 'mainstreaming integration'. Many of the sites identified for mainstreaming integration are similar to those considered elsewhere in this book: the European Employment Strategy, the Strategy for Social Protection and Inclusion, education and youth policies. Indeed, in an instance of what might be termed reflexive mainstreaming, anti-racism policy is noted as an area where integration policy objectives should be mainstreamed.[78]

Integration policy and mainstreaming ethnic equality

As elsewhere in this chapter, this section considers mainstreaming first from the perspective of policy objectives and then in relation to policy implementation. Considering policy objectives, it is possible to identify several points of convergence between integration policy and the pursuit of ethnic equality. Combating inequality in relation to immigrants is a thread running throughout the Common Basic Principles.[79] The Handbook on Integration expressly mentions institutional racism on the part of employers as one reason for immigrant disadvantage in the labour market.[80] It is also noticeable that integration policy recognizes the intertwining influences of ethnicity, nationality, and religion,[81] rather than the boundaries between these categories erected in EC anti-discrimination law. Nevertheless, the Common Basic Principles are restricted in application to legally resident third country nationals. The exclusion of EU

[75] Council Decision (EC) 2007/435 establishing the European fund for the integration of third country nationals for the period 2007 to 2013 as part of the general programme 'solidarity and management of migration flows' [2007] OJ L168/18.

[76] Art 17, EP and Council Decision (EC) 1672/2006 establishing a Community programme for employment and social solidarity – Progress [2006] OJ L315/1.

[77] Dec 2007/435, Art 16(2).

[78] Commission, 'Third annual report on migration and integration' COM (2007) 512, 6–7.

[79] eg Principle 3 states the need to combat ethnic discrimination in the labour market, whilst Principle 7 concerns the improvement of housing, healthcare, and education for immigrants: Council (n 68 above).

[80] J Niessen and Y Schibel, *Handbook on Integration for Policy-makers and Practitioners* (2nd edn, Luxembourg: OOPEC, 2007) 60.

[81] eg Art 2(1), Dec 2007/435.

citizens from the scope of integration policy is surprising; much of the debate surrounding integration in the Member States concerns not just those who are third country nationals, but also ethnic minority EU citizens.[82] It is also notable that there is little evidence of integration policy engaging with intersectionality issues. Although some projects funded under INTI occasionally touched on gender or age issues,[83] such themes are not pursued in any depth in the annual reports. Indeed, the first annual report concluded that 'a systematic mainstreaming of gender considerations seems to be lacking in most Member States'.[84]

The underlying importance of integration policy is the way in which it shapes an understanding of what constitutes equality. As discussed in Chapter 2, equality can be regarded as simply providing identical treatment (formal equality) or recognizing the need to accommodate diversity (substantive equality). The balance between formal and substantive equality in relation to ethnicity is often closely linked to the objectives of integration policy. Conventionally, national policies on integration have been described as falling between two points on an axis, ranging from assimilation to multiculturalism.[85] Alternatively, a typology exists between those which focus on the incorporation of immigrants as individuals or as groups.[86] Where policy tends towards assimilation or the incorporation of individuals, then this is likely to lead to an emphasis on formal equality. For example, individuals will be expected to accept pre-existing workplace dress codes and adapt accordingly. Alternatively, multicultural policies or approaches based on incorporating groups are often associated with revising pre-existing norms in order to accommodate cultural diversity.[87] EU integration policy has a potentially crucial role to play, therefore, in conveying a signal on how equality should be interpreted in relation to requests for cultural accommodation.

Unsurprisingly, EU integration policy does not expressly endorse any particular model. This can be explained by several factors. First, it must reach across

[82] P Watt, 'An intercultural approach to "integration"' (2006) 1 *Translocations—The Irish Migration, Race and Social Transformation Review* 154, 161.

[83] See further: <http://ec.europa.eu/justice_home/funding/2004_2007/inti/funding_inti_en.htm> accessed 13 May 2008. The integration fund includes an objective of adapting migrant integration courses to 'children, women, elderly, illiterate or persons with disabilities' (Art 4(2)(c), Dec 2007/435).

[84] COM (2004) 508, 6.

[85] J Monod, 'Quelle(s) politique(s) d'intégration au sein de l'Union européenne?' (2007) Fondation Robert Schuman Policy Papers, No 53.

[86] H Entzinger, 'The dynamics of integration policies: a multidimensional model' in R Koopmans and P Statham (eds), *Challenging Immigration and Ethnic Relations Politics* (Oxford: OUP, 2000) 97, 107.

[87] B Parekh, 'Integrating minorities' in T Blackstone, B Parekh, and P Saunders (eds), *Race Relations in Britain—A Developing Agenda* (London: Routledge, 1998) 1, 3.

states with rather different national traditions, such as France and the UK. Second, in recent years, those states with established approaches have often interrogated their effectiveness, leading to moderate or radical shifts in policy.[88] Finally, many Member States are historically recent countries of immigration, where it is often difficult to identify any settled model of integration.[89] As a consequence, EU integration policy is vulnerable to the criticism that it tries to be 'all things to all people' and lacks clarity on core concepts.[90] Its basic premise seems to be the 'two-way street' philosophy; in other words, adaptation is required from both sides of the integration equation. Although rather abstract, this indicates a rejection of an approach based purely on formal equality. The Handbook on Integration, for example, recommends diversity management strategies in the workplace, including recourse to positive action.[91] Yet, this message is not always consistently reflected throughout the policy. The integration fund is to be 'primarily' focused on 'newly arrived third-country nationals'.[92] Many of its objectives are oriented towards action by the individual migrant, especially training courses on social and cultural adaptation. Whilst some imply an element of change from the host society,[93] combating discrimination or promoting equality are not explicitly mentioned in any of the objectives of the fund. This is a missed opportunity from the perspective of mainstreaming. Although the EU has separate anti-discrimination programmes, their remit does not focus on equality in relation to nationality or immigration status.

Turning next to consider the implementation of integration policy, an initial observation is the difficulty of speaking of 'implementation' in an area where policy cooperation remains very loose. Notwithstanding this proviso, a few observations can be made. First, some of the objectives of integration policy that resonate well with ethnic equality show little sign of implementation in practice. A good illustration is the third Common Basic Principle, which includes promoting the recognition of qualifications obtained in another country. Opportunities to advance this objective elsewhere in EC law have been lost. In 2005, a wide-ranging Directive on the mutual recognition of qualifications was adopted.[94] This expressly provides that Member States must take into account qualifications acquired in third countries where one Member State has already provided recognition of this qualification and the EU citizen has subsequently

[88] eg the UK and the Netherlands: Monod (n 85 above).
[89] eg Italy: R Guolo, *Xenofobi e xenofili – gli italiani e l'islam* (Rome: Editori Laterza, 2003) 151.
[90] Watt (n 82 above) 160.
[91] Niessen and Schibel (n 80 above) 67.
[92] Art 2(1), Dec 2007/435.
[93] eg promoting 'diversity management' and 'intercultural training', Art 4(3).
[94] EP and Council Directive (EC) 2005/36 on the recognition of professional qualifications [2005] OJ L255/22.

accumulated three years of professional experience in that state.[95] This provision does not, though, extend to third country nationals.[96]

Second, the balanced, 'two-way process' formula found within integration policy risks being undermined by certain provisions of EC immigration legislation, where integration is posited as a *precondition* for the enjoyment of rights. Specifically, the Family Reunion Directive permits Member States to make the admission of children over the age of 12 conditional on meeting 'a condition for integration'.[97] There is also an option of requiring third country nationals applying for family reunion to 'comply with integration measures'.[98] In a similar vein, the LTR Directive permits Member States to 'require third country nationals to comply with integration conditions' as a criterion for access to LTR status.[99] These clauses reflect a trend in certain Member States to introduce mandatory courses relating to language and civic orientation.[100] In some instances, successful completion of these courses is a prerequisite to accessing a specific immigration law status, including citizenship and LTR status.[101] Indeed, some states are even moving in the direction of imposing integration requirements as a condition for initial permission to enter.[102] The mere fact that EC legislation permits the imposition of such requirements may not, by itself, give rise to ethnic discrimination. Whilst the Court of Justice upheld the legality of these clauses in the Family Reunion Directive, it affirmed that:

> the fact that the concept of integration is not defined cannot be interpreted as authorising the Member States to employ that concept in a manner contrary to general principles of Community law, in particular to fundamental rights.[103]

There are, though, reasons to question whether this trajectory is conducive to promoting ethnic equality. On the one hand, it accentuates the already wide gap between the legal status of EU citizens and non-EU citizens. Integration requirements cannot be imposed on the former because of their EC Treaty free movement rights. Consequently, this trend appears to move away from the original objective in the Tampere European Council conclusions of granting

[95] Art 3(3). See further, P Craig and G de Búrca, *EU Law—Text, Cases and Materials* (4th edn, Oxford: OUP, 2008) 841.

[96] Art 2(1) and Recital 10. The proposed Directive on a common set of rights for third country workers would extend the principles in Dir 2005/36 to third country nationals: Commission (n 59 above) 10.

[97] Art 4(1), Dir 2003/86.

[98] ibid Art 7(2).

[99] Art 5, Dir 2003/109.

[100] S Carrera, 'A comparison of integration programmes in the EU—trends and weaknesses' CHALLENGE Papers No 1/March 2006 (Brussels: Centre for European Policy Studies, 2006).

[101] J Niessen, M J Peiro, and Y Schibel, *Civic Citizenship and Immigrant Inclusion—A Guide for the Implementation of Civic Citizenship Policies* (Brussels: Migration Policy Group, 2005) 23.

[102] eg the Netherlands: L Besselink, 'Unequal citizenship: integration measures and equality' in S Carrera (ed), *The Nexus Between Immigration, Integration and Citizenship in the EU* (Brussels: Centre for European Policy Studies, 2006) 14, 15.

[103] para 70, Case C-540/03 *Parliament v Council* [2006] ECR I-5769.

third country nationals 'rights and obligations comparable to those of EU citizens'.[104] On the other hand, there is the latent risk that 'integration' is being used as a covert label for exclusion.[105] Integration requirements once again emphasize action by the individual migrant without necessarily being balanced by corresponding adjustments in the host society.

E. Conclusions

Promoting ethnic equality within immigration law and policy is inherently difficult, yet essential given that immigrants are one of the principal groups subject to discrimination on grounds of ethnic origin. A radical critique would argue that many of the basic premises of EU immigration law and policy give rise to ethnic discrimination. It is hard to deny that the overall effect of EU law has been to *increase* the gap between the rights of EU nationals and those of third country nationals by introducing a special set of immigration rights (free movement) which primarily remains the prerogative of EU citizens. This chapter has not sought to challenge such fundamental principles of the legal order; rather it has sought to illustrate the capacity for mainstreaming ethnic equality objectives even within the conventional parameters of immigration law and policy.

Some steps which favour ethnic equality can be identified, such as the scattered equality rights found in EC legislation on legal migrants or the promotion of good practice via the Handbook on Integration. Overall, these provide very little indication of how the key concepts of 'equality' or 'racism' are understood. It is readily apparent that mainstreaming ethnic equality has yet to be fully embedded in this field. The main procedural vehicle for mainstreaming seems to be the impact assessment process. Following the classification established in Chapter 3, this seems closer to the integrationist model of mainstreaming. In particular, doubts have been expressed about the general quality of impact assessments within immigration policy.[106] Certainly, the example of the proposed employer sanctions Directive reveals how potential discrimination issues can be overlooked even where a detailed impact assessment has been conducted. The limited nature of mainstreaming means that there is scant evidence of engagement with more detailed issues, such as intersectionality. In contrast to employment or social inclusion policies, it is notable that Roma are relatively invisible in immigration

[104] Presidency Conclusions—Tampere European Council, 15–16 October 1999.

[105] K Groenendijk, 'The Long-Term Residents Directive, denizenship and integration' in A Baldaccini, E Guild, and H Toner (eds), *Whose Freedom, Security and Justice? EU Immigration and Asylum Law and Policy* (Oxford: Hart Publishing, 2007) 429, 450.

[106] H Toner, 'Impact assessments: a useful tool for "better lawmaking" in EU migration policy?' in A Baldaccini, E Guild, and H Toner (eds), *Whose Freedom, Security and Justice? EU Immigration and Asylum Law and Policy* (Oxford: Hart Publishing, 2007) 109.

policy. This contrasts with the social reality that significant numbers of Roma have migrated within Europe since the 1990s.[107]

If a transformative model of mainstreaming was adopted, immigration law and policy could be mobilized to provide a firm legal foundation for equality irrespective of citizenship or immigration status. At various junctures, rhetorical commitments to promoting equality have been made, such as the Tampere European Council conclusions or the Common Basic Principles on Immigrant Integration. The underlying political dynamics around immigration control often seem to override such statements of intent when the Member States reach the point of adopting enforceable legislation in the Council of Ministers. A comprehensive right to equal treatment for third country nationals has not been instituted. Instead, a haphazard and inconsistent framework has been built which conditions equality rights on immigration status. Far from promoting equality, this seems likely to accentuate inequality, with those in the most precarious residence situation receiving the least legal protection.

[107] eg from the former Yugoslavia: N Sigona, 'Locating "the Gypsy problem". The Roma in Italy: stereotyping, labeling and "nomad camps"' (2005) 31 *Journal of Ethnic and Migration Studies* 741, 745.

8

Criminal Law

The last substantive chapter considers the extent to which the objectives of combating racism and promoting equality have been mainstreamed into EU criminal law. There are a number of reasons explaining the choice of this case study. Aside from the Racial Equality Directive, criminal law is the only area of EU law where legal instruments exclusively concerned with racism have been adopted. This reflects the objective set by the EU Treaty, Article 29:

> Without prejudice to the powers of the European Community, the Union's objective shall be to provide citizens with a high level of safety within an area of freedom, security and justice, by developing common action among the Member States in the fields of police and judicial cooperation in criminal matters and by preventing and combating racism and xenophobia.

Given this explicit Treaty mandate for action,[1] it would be strange not to consider mainstreaming in relation to criminal law. Indeed, the Commission identified 'justice and home affairs' as a key area for mainstreaming in its 1998 Action Plan Against Racism.[2] The role of the EU in criminal law also offers a useful contrast to the areas hitherto considered. Whilst employment, social inclusion, and immigration all fall within the scope of the EC Treaty, criminal law is currently governed by the rather different institutional arrangements applying under the EU Treaty. Therefore, it will be relevant to consider whether the different governance regime impacts upon the capacity for mainstreaming.

It is also evident that criminal law and the criminal justice system are key interfaces for promoting ethnic equality. There are two principal dimensions to be considered. First, criminal law can be used to combat racism, both through the designation of specific crimes (such as incitement to hatred) and through taking into account a racist motive in the investigation and penalization of any type of crime. The European Court of Human Rights has placed a positive duty on national authorities to pursue any evidence of racist motivation in the commission of crime.[3] Comprehensive data on the prevalence of racist crime in

[1] The Treaty of Lisbon would retain this objective, albeit reformulated within the Treaty on the Functioning of the European Union (TFEU). Article 67(3) states 'The Union shall endeavour to ensure a high level of security through measures to prevent and combat crime, racism and xenophobia . . . '; Consolidated version of the TFEU [2008] OJ C115/73.

[2] COM (1998) 183, 14.

[3] para 66, *Šečić v Croatia*, Application 40116/02, 31 May 2007.

the EU are currently lacking. The EU Fundamental Rights Agency (FRA) has concluded that only 11 Member States have data collection systems in this area which could be described as 'good'.[4] Amongst those states where data collection systems exist, specific numbers vary greatly; in 2005, the highest figure for racist incidents was 57,902 and the lowest was 85.[5] Given the variation in data collection systems, it is impossible to discern whether a higher level of recorded incidents truly reflects an elevated rate of racist crime or simply more efficient data collection.[6] The FRA identifies the following groups as the principal targets of racist crime in the EU: immigrants and 'visible' minorities, Jewish persons, Roma, Muslims, asylum-seekers, and refugees.[7] This list underlines that factors of ethnicity, religion, nationality, and immigration status are interconnected and hard to disentangle. Some forms of racist crime are more distinct.[8] For example, Holocaust denial is often a specific method of denigrating Jewish communities and the EU Monitoring Centre on Racism and Xenophobia observed how anti-Semitism often takes place against the backdrop of international political events in the Middle East.[9] Little information was found on how intersectionality with other grounds, such as disability or sexual orientation, affects the nature of racist crime. One instance which illustrates an intersection of gender, religion, and ethnic origin is attacks on women wearing a headscarf.[10]

The second role that law and policy can play is ensuring that the equal treatment of ethnic minorities is promoted throughout the criminal justice system. This ranges from those who are victims of crime to those who are subject to investigation, prosecution, and conviction. The UK gathers the most extensive data in the EU and its figures reveal significant ethnic disparities. Data for 2005–2006 showed that black people were 'seven times more likely than their white counterparts to be stopped and searched, three and a half times more likely to be arrested, and six times more likely to be in prison'.[11] Determining the reasons for such inequalities, and the extent to which they reflect racial discrimination, is complex. The UK data also reveal that not all ethnic groups experience similar levels of disadvantage; persons of Chinese ethnic origin are *less*

[4] FRA, 'Trends and developments 1997–2005—combating ethnic and racial discrimination and promoting equality in the European Union' (Hungary: Printer Elanders Hungary, 2007) 37.

[5] ibid 39; England/Wales and Denmark respectively.

[6] J Goodey, 'Racist violence in Europe: challenges for official data collection' (2007) 30 *Ethnic and Racial Studies* 570, 579.

[7] FRA (n 4 above) 41–2.

[8] On Islamophobia, see N Chakraborti, 'Policing Muslim communities' in M Rowe (ed), *Policing Beyond MacPherson—Issues in Policing, Race and Society* (Cullompton: Willan Publishing, 2007) 107, 112.

[9] EUMC, 'Antisemitism: summary overview of the situation in the European Union 2001–2005' (Vienna: EUMC, 2006) 5.

[10] No statistical evidence on this phenomenon was located, but such incidents have been reported in the UK media: eg 'Man admits he "pulled off" hijab' *BBC News* (30 August 2007) <http://news.bbc.co.uk/1/hi/wales/6970761.stm> accessed 19 May 2008.

[11] Ministry of Justice, 'Statistics on race and the criminal justice system—2006' (London: Ministry of Justice, 2007) ix.

likely to be in prison than white persons.[12] The data from other countries are less detailed, but there is little doubt that ethnic minorities are not always treated equally by law enforcement agencies. Recent empirical research found that Roma persons were more likely to be subject to a pedestrian police stop in Hungary and Bulgaria, whilst the same was true of immigrants in Spain.[13] Evidence that ethnic minorities are systematically subject to less favourable treatment by the police has been viewed as a classic illustration of the concept of institutional racism, discussed in Chapter 1. It can be very hard to isolate (and prove) racist behaviour by individual officers, yet disproportionate rates of stop and search show how organizational practices generate unequal outcomes for ethnic minority groups. The European Commission against Racism and Intolerance (ECRI) has warned that the situation is actually deteriorating: 'cases of racism and racial discrimination in policing, including racial profiling, have intensified and taken on a new dimension, particularly as a result of the fight against terrorist crime.'[14] Moreover, a string of cases at the European Court of Human Rights has uncovered evidence of racist treatment of Roma by police and judicial authorities in EU Member States.[15]

In the light of the above, mainstreaming ethnic equality objectives into criminal law implies (1) taking specific measures against racist crime and (2) ensuring equality for ethnic minorities throughout the criminal justice system. This chapter considers first those measures specifically designed to combat racist crime, principally the Framework Decision on racism and xenophobia. Following this discussion, the chapter turns to consider ways in which the European Union has promoted equal treatment of ethnic minorities in the criminal justice system. Given that the EU Treaty legal framework is distinct from that examined elsewhere in this book, this chapter begins with a brief introduction to the role of the Union in criminal law.

A. Criminal Law and the EU Treaty

Although EC Treaty provisions can be relevant to criminal law, the Court of Justice has observed that 'as a general rule, neither criminal law nor the rules of

[12] ibid xii.

[13] Open Society Institute Justice Initiative, '"I can stop and search whoever I want"—police stops of ethnic minorities in Bulgaria, Hungary, and Spain' (New York: Open Society Institute, 2007). See also, M Duvall, 'Evidence of ethnic profiling in selected European countries' in Open Society Institute Justice Initiative (eds), *Ethnic Profiling by Police in Europe* (New York: Open Society Institute, 2005) 14.

[14] para 24, ECRI, General policy recommendation no 11 on combating racism and racial discrimination in policing, CRI (2007) 39, 29 June 2007.

[15] *Nachova and others v Bulgaria* [GC] (2006) 42 EHRR 43; *Moldovan and others v Romania* (2007) 44 EHRR 16; *Bekos and Koutropoulous v Greece* (2006) 43 EHRR 2; *Cobzaru v Romania*, Application 48254/99, 26 July 2007; *Petropoulou-Tsakiris v Greece*, Application 44803/04, 6 December 2007; *Stoica v Romania*, Application 42722/02, 4 March 2008.

criminal procedure fall within the Community's competence'.[16] Instead, Title VI of the EU Treaty provides the legal framework for 'police and judicial cooperation in criminal matters'. As this heading suggests, the main emphasis is on the *coordination* of police and judicial activities, notably where there is a significant cross-border dimension, such as the transfer of suspects or tackling international forms of organized crime. Although this process of coordination generally preserves a wide discretion for Member States over the domestic organization of the criminal justice system, the EU Treaty does include a legal competence for the 'approximation, where necessary, of rules on criminal matters in the Member States'.[17] Based on this power, a body of EU criminal legislation has accumulated covering a diverse range of topics, from money laundering to terrorism.[18] Compared to the EC Treaty, there are significant differences in the nature of this legislation. These include the legislative process,[19] as well as the actual legal instruments. In the context of this chapter, the most important instrument to note is the 'Framework Decision'. This is akin to an EC Directive, although EU Treaty, Article 34(2)(b) expressly states that Framework Decisions 'shall not entail direct effect'. This implies that an individual cannot directly enforce rights found within a Framework Decision in proceedings before national courts. Notwithstanding this injunction, the Court of Justice has held that an individual may invoke a Framework Decision in order to ensure that national courts fulfil their duty to interpret national law 'as far as possible in the light of the wording and purpose of the Framework Decision in order to attain the result which it pursues'.[20] This equates to the EC law doctrine of 'indirect effect'.[21]

Even if there may be some situations when individuals can rely upon Framework Decisions, this possibility must be read alongside the purely optional jurisdiction of the Court of Justice in this Title of the EU Treaty. Peers reports that only 14 Member States have accepted its jurisdiction.[22] Furthermore, there is no power for the Commission to bring infringement proceedings against a Member State for non-compliance with a Framework Decision. The cumulative impact of these departures from the normal practices of the EC Treaty is to render legislation adopted under the EU Treaty much less amenable to enforcement. The Treaty of Lisbon, if ratified, would have a dramatic effect on these complex arrangements. In effect, it would apply most of the current

[16] para 47, Case C-176/03 *Commission v Council* [2005] ECR I-7879. On the extent of EC competence in criminal law, see S Peers, *EU Justice and Home Affairs Law* (2nd edn, Oxford: OUP, 2006) 392 and Case C-440/05 *Commission v Council* [2007] OJ C315/9.

[17] EU Treaty, Art 29. See also Art 31(1)(e).

[18] For an overview, see Peers (n 16 above) 402–3.

[19] The Commission shares the right of initiative with the Member States (EU Treaty, Art 34(2)).

[20] para 43, Case C-105/03 *Criminal proceedings against Pupino* [2005] ECR I-5283.

[21] See further, V Mitsilegas, 'Constitutional principles of the European Community and European criminal law' (2006) 8 *European Journal of Law Reform* 301, 311.

[22] Peers (n 16 above) 41. States may further restrict the possibility for making preliminary references to those courts 'against whose decisions there is no judicial remedy in national law' (Art 35(3)(a)).

practices of the EC Treaty to police and judicial cooperation, albeit within the framework of the new Treaty on the Functioning of the European Union (TFEU).[23] The Court's jurisdiction would become mandatory, the Commission could bring infringement proceedings, and the standard legal instruments, such as Directives, would be used. This is subject to the caveat that Denmark, Ireland, and the UK have negotiated opt-outs, so future legislation in this field might not apply to some or all of these states.[24] As discussed further in the next section, political agreement was reached in 2007 on a Framework Decision on racism and xenophobia. If the Treaty of Lisbon is ratified, Framework Decisions will no longer exist; provision is made, though, to ensure that any such instruments already adopted will continue to be legally binding until such time as they are replaced.[25]

B. Using Criminal Law to Combat Racism

As discussed in Chapter 3, mainstreaming is one element of a twin-track strategy which combines specialized measures to promote equality on the one hand, and the mobilization of all areas of law and policy via mainstreaming on the other. Anti-discrimination law and policy are typically seen as the venue for the Union's specialized measures, whilst mainstreaming is relevant elsewhere. EU criminal law challenges these boundaries as it is a hybrid case. Specialized measures devoted to combating racist crime have been adopted, yet mainstreaming is also relevant in order to integrate ethnic equality objectives across the full range of measures in this field. This section focuses on the specialized measures against racist crime, which have occasionally been cited by the Commission as an instance of mainstreaming.[26]

The 1996 Joint Action on racism and xenophobia

During the 1990s, a debate emerged around how best to tackle cross-border forms of racist crime. In part, this was sparked by some high-profile incidents, such as the Verbeke case, where a Belgian national sent leaflets denying the

23 For a detailed analysis, see S Peers, 'EU Reform Treaty: Analysis 1: Version 3: JHA provisions' <http://www.statewatch.org/news/2007/oct/eu-refrom-treaty-jha-anal-1-ver-3.pdf> accessed 19 May 2008.

24 The exact arrangements applying to each of these three states are slightly different. A crude summary would be that Denmark has opted out from any participation in this field of EU law, whereas Ireland and the UK retain the possibility to opt in, on a case-by-case basis, to such legislation. See further: S Peers, 'British and Irish opt-outs from EU Justice and Home Affairs law' <http://www.statewatch.org/news/2007/oct/eu-reform-treaty-uk-ireland-opt-outs.pdf> accessed 19 May 2008.

25 Art 9, Protocol 36 on Transitional Provisions [2008] OJ C115/322.

26 Commission 'Report on the implementation of the action plan against racism—mainstreaming the fight against racism' (Brussels: Commission, 2000) 9.

Holocaust from Belgium to Jewish persons in the Netherlands.[27] At the time, this activity was not unlawful in Belgium, but, after lengthy proceedings, the Dutch Supreme Court held that this was a criminal act in the Netherlands.[28] The capacity for individuals and groups to exploit differences in national legislation was heightened by the emergence of the Internet in this period,[29] yet also intertwined with the Union's internal market project which emphasized an absence of restrictions on the movement of persons or products. Attempts to restrict access to Internet content hosted in another Member State had been contested by Internet service providers as potentially in breach of the free movement of services.[30]

An early sign that the Member States were recognizing the need for collaboration in this field was the 1995 Europol Convention. Europol aims to assist national authorities in tackling international organized crime in various ways, such as facilitating the exchange of information or collating intelligence.[31] Although its mandate was initially restricted to specific crimes, an annex to the Convention listed further 'serious forms of international crime' in respect of which it could eventually assume powers. Notably this list included 'racism and xenophobia'. In 2001, its mandate was duly extended to cover all the crimes listed in the annex.[32] Nevertheless, a search of Europol's annual reports and its website uncovered no information relating to specific actions on racist crime.[33]

More substantively, in 1996, the Council adopted a 'Joint Action' on combating racism and xenophobia.[34] Joint Actions were one of the original legal instruments available under the EU Treaty during the period 1993–1999. The subsequent reforms of the Treaty of Amsterdam removed this instrument, in effect replacing it with the 'Framework Decision' (discussed earlier). Whilst most Member States agreed that Joint Actions were legally binding commitments,[35] the absence of any jurisdiction for the Court of Justice over Joint Actions meant that the main lever for compliance was political will. The rationale for the Joint Action was defined as the following: 'to prevent the perpetrators of such offences from exploiting the fact that racist and xenophobic activities are classified

[27] P Rodrigues, 'Cross-border discrimination: private international law, the denial of the Holocaust and the internet' in T Loenen and P Rodrigues (eds), *Non-discrimination Law: Comparative Perspectives* (Kluwer, The Hague, 1999) 397.

[28] ibid 404.

[29] See further, M Fernández Esteban, 'The internet: a new horizon for hatred?' in S Fredman (ed), *Discrimination and Human Rights—The Case of Racism* (Oxford: OUP, 2001) 77.

[30] Commission, 'Illegal and harmful content on the internet' COM (96) 487, 15.

[31] Convention on the establishment of a European Police Office (Europol Convention) [1995] OJ C316/2.

[32] Council Decision (EU) extending Europol's mandate to deal with the serious forms of international crime listed in the Annex to the Europol Convention [2001] OJ C362/1.

[33] Conducted 19 May 2008.

[34] Joint Action (EU) 96/443 concerning action to combat racism and xenophobia [1996] OJ L185/5.

[35] Peers (n 16 above) 17.

differently in different states'.[36] To that end, it offered two choices: states can either choose to adjust their criminal law to ensure that it prohibits all of the offences listed in the Joint Action *or* states can derogate from the principle of 'double criminality' in relation to these offences. The latter is a central concept to international cooperation in the field of criminal law. Double criminality implies that where a state requests assistance from other national authorities, then the state receiving the request should act only if the offence concerned is also a crime in its jurisdiction. For example, if the Austrian authorities request the Irish authorities to seize documents which they believe may contain evidence of a racist offence, then the principle of double criminality implies that the latter should comply with the Austrian request only if the activity under investigation would also constitute an offence in Irish law. By requesting states either to harmonize national criminal law or to waive double criminality, the Joint Action sought to ensure that cross-border judicial cooperation would not be obstructed even where the substantive national criminal law was divergent. Concretely, Title I.A of the Joint Action identified five criminal acts relating to racism and xenophobia:

(a) public incitement to discrimination, violence or racial hatred in respect of a group of persons or a member of such a group defined by reference to colour, race, religion or national or ethnic origin;
(b) public condoning, for a racist or xenophobic purpose, of crimes against humanity and human rights violations;
(c) public denial of the crimes defined in Article 6 of the Charter of the International Military Tribunal appended to the London Agreement of 8 April 1945 insofar as it includes behaviour which is contemptuous of, or degrading to, a group of persons defined by reference to colour, race, religion or national or ethnic origin;
(d) public dissemination or distribution of tracts, pictures or other material containing expressions of racism and xenophobia;
(e) participation in the activities of groups, organizations or associations, which involve discrimination, violence, or racial, ethnic or religious hatred.

To a large extent, this list of offences is inspired by the International Convention on the Elimination of All Forms of Racial Discrimination (ICERD). Paragraphs (a), (d), and (e) resemble Article 4 ICERD.[37] Paragraphs (b) and (c) go further and reflect the fact that Holocaust denial was a classic example of a situation where divergence in Member States' laws could be exploited by perpetrators. Even though the Joint Action did not require harmonization of national law regarding these offences, several states entered declarations regarding how they

[36] Preamble.

[37] See further, T McGonagle, 'The international and European legal standards for combating racist expression' in ECRI (eds), *Combating Racism While Respecting Freedom of Expression* (Strasbourg: Council of Europe, 2007) 77.

would apply its provisions. The UK and Denmark both indicated that they would apply a higher threshold, such as imposing the additional requirement that any such behaviour was threatening and insulting.[38]

There is very little evidence on how the Joint Action has been applied in practice. The Council reviewed its application in 1998 and noted that just two states (Austria and Luxembourg) had felt it necessary to introduce legal reforms in response to the Joint Action, whilst others were contemplating amendments of national law.[39]

The Framework Decision on racism and xenophobia

The reforms to the EU Treaty by the Treaty of Amsterdam inserted a specific reference to the objective of combating racism and xenophobia into Article 29 and simultaneously created a legal competence for the approximation of criminal law.[40] Exercising these powers, in 2001 the Commission proposed a 'Framework Decision on combating racism and xenophobia'.[41] Unlike the Joint Action, this measure went beyond merely promoting judicial cooperation and required a minimum level of convergence in the substantive content of national criminal law. This marks a transition away from a classic EU integration rationale based around the coordination of divergent legal systems and a step towards strengthening the law on racist crime as an autonomous EU objective. To this end, the Commission's proposal went further than the Joint Action, such as regulating the penalties for racist crimes and the rules on the liability of natural and legal persons.

In contrast to the rapid adoption of the Racial Equality Directive, the Framework Decision has endured a turbulent legislative history. From the outset, certain states expressed serious reservations, principally the UK and Denmark.[42] Agreement was almost reached in spring 2003, but the Italian Presidency then proposed an alternative text which received no support.[43] Notably, the Casa delle Libertà coalition which governed Italy during this period included the Lega Nord party which is well known for anti-immigrant and anti-Muslim rhetoric.[44] In 2005, the Luxembourg Presidency reopened negotiations, this time

[38] See Annex to the Joint Action. The UK also added that the action should be 'carried out with the intention of stirring up racial hatred or is likely to do so'.

[39] Council, 'Note de Comité K.4 au Coreper' Ref 7808/1/98 REV 1, 29 April 1998.

[40] EU Treaty, Art 31(1)(e).

[41] COM (2001) 664.

[42] Council, 'Proposal for a Council Framework Decision on combating racism and xenophobia' Ref 5983/02 DROIPEN 4, 6 February 2002.

[43] Council, 'Proposal for a Framework Decision on combating racism and xenophobia' Ref 6229/05 DROIPEN 10, 10 February 2005, 2.

[44] A Triandafyllidou, 'Religious diversity and multiculturalism in Southern Europe—the Italian mosque debate' in T Modood, A Triandafyllidou, and R Zapata-Barrero (eds), *Multiculturalism, Muslims and Citizenship—A European Approach* (London: Routledge, 2006) 117, 129.

encountering general reservations from Italy and Poland.[45] Negotiations recommenced once again under the German Presidency in 2007. The Italian government had changed in spring 2006, removing one of the main political obstacles. In a clear echo of the events leading to the adoption of the Racial Equality Directive, the German Presidency championed the Framework Decision as a political response to the formation in January 2007 of a new far-right political grouping in the European Parliament called 'Identity, Tradition and Sovereignty'.[46] Political agreement on the text was reached by the Council on 19 April 2007; however, as the content had substantially changed since the original proposal, the text was then sent to the European Parliament for re-consultation.[47] Although the Parliament delivered its opinion in November 2007,[48] by July 2008 the Framework Decision had not yet been formally adopted. At the time of writing, some doubts were emerging over whether the 2007 political agreement would be maintained. Elections in Italy in April 2008 returned to government some of those parties which had earlier opposed the Framework Decision, notably the Lega Nord. Nevertheless, a 'final' text was available from the Council's website and the discussion below is based on this document.[49]

The core provision of the Framework Decision, Article 1(1), requires Member States to ensure that four offences are punishable in national criminal law where committed with intent:

(a) publicly inciting to violence or hatred directed against a group of persons or a member of such a group defined by reference to race, colour, religion, descent or national or ethnic origin;
(b) the commission of an act referred to in point (a) by public dissemination or distribution of tracts, pictures or other material;
(c) publicly condoning, denying or grossly trivializing crimes of genocide, crimes against humanity and war crimes as defined in Articles 6, 7, and 8 of the Statute of the International Criminal Court, directed against a group of persons or a member of such a group defined by reference to race, colour, religion, descent or national or ethnic origin when the conduct is carried out in a manner likely to incite to violence or hatred against such a group or a member of such a group;

[45] Council, 'Proposal for a Framework Decision on combating racism and xenophobia' Ref 8994/05 DROIPEN 24, 19 May 2005, 3.

[46] H Mahony, 'German call for EU initiative against right-wing extremism' *EUObserver.com* (9 January 2007) <http://euobserver.com/22/23210/?rk1=1> accessed 15 January 2007. The parliamentary group collapsed in November 2007 following internal disagreements.

[47] Council, 'Re-consultation of the EP' Ref 11523/1/07 REV 1 DROIPEN 69, 20 July 2007.

[48] Resolution on the proposal for a Council Framework Decision on combating certain forms and expressions of racism and xenophobia by means of criminal law, P6_TA-PROV(2007)0552, 29 November 2007.

[49] Council, 'Council Framework Decision on combating certain forms and expressions of racism and xenophobia by means of criminal law' Ref 16771/07 DROIPEN 127, 26 February 2008.

(d) publicly condoning, denying or grossly trivializing the crimes defined in Article 6 of the Charter of the International Military Tribunal appended to the London Agreement of 8 August 1945, directed against a group of persons or a member of such a group defined by reference to race, colour, religion, descent or national or ethnic origin when the conduct is carried out in a manner likely to incite violence or hatred against such a group or a member of such a group.

This list of offences differs in several respects from the Joint Action. First, it does not include incitement to *discrimination*. The Commission contended that this lay within the scope of the legal competence found in EC Treaty, Article 13 (which did not exist when the Joint Action was adopted).[50] Second, there is no requirement to penalize participating in a racist organization. This contrasts with the duty on states under ICERD to 'declare illegal and prohibit organisations... which promote and incite racial discrimination'.[51] Such a provision was opposed from the outset by nearly all states except Germany and so it was deleted from the draft text already in 2002.[52] Third, the provisions relating to historical revisionism have been adjusted. On the one hand, these now go beyond the bare reference to 'denial' or 'condoning' in the Joint Action, extending also to 'grossly trivializing', which reflects German legislation.[53] On the other, the circumstances under which such acts should be criminal offences are more strictly defined. This was a key point of contrast between the Member States. While some, such as Austria and Germany,[54] criminalize Holocaust denial per se, others, such as the UK and Ireland, had no such offence in their national law. By limiting the duty to criminalize such acts to situations where the act is 'likely to incite violence or hatred', the UK government takes the view that it will not need to introduce a specific offence of Holocaust denial.[55]

In addition to narrowing the scope of the offences in comparison to the Joint Action, the Framework Decision introduces a number of significant exceptions. The most contentious is Article 7(2):

This Framework Decision shall not have the effect of requiring Member States to take measures in contradiction to fundamental principles relating to freedom of association and freedom of expression, in particular freedom of the press and the freedom of expression in other media as they result from constitutional traditions or rules governing

[50] Commission, 'Legal reasoning for not referring to the concept of "public incitement to discrimination" in the Commission's proposal for a Council Framework Decision on combating racism and xenophobia' SEC (2002) 375.

[51] Art 4(b).

[52] Council, 'Proposal for a Framework Decision on combating racism and xenophobia' Ref 10338/02 DROIPEN 44, 25 June 2002, 3.

[53] Commission (n 41 above) 8.

[54] EU Network of Independent Experts on Fundamental Rights, 'Combating racism and xenophobia through criminal legislation: the situation in the EU Member States' Opinion 5-2005, 28 November 2005, 79.

[55] Select Committee on European Scrutiny, 'Seventeenth Report' HC (2006–2007) 41-xvii [16.8].

the rights and responsibilities of, and the procedural guarantees for, the press or other media where these rules relate to the determination or limitation of liability.

The Commission has expressed the view that this could be interpreted as meaning that the provisions of the Framework Decision are subject to compliance with pre-existing national law, whereas it reaffirms the principle of the supremacy of EU law.[56] A further exception was inserted in Article 1(2), following pressure especially from the UK:[57] 'Member States may choose to punish only conduct which is either carried out in a manner likely to disturb public order or which is threatening, abusive or insulting'. Despite the various examples provided above, there is at least one respect in which the Framework Decision goes beyond the Joint Action. Article 4 specifies that for all other criminal offences evidence of 'racist or xenophobic motivation' should be taken into account as either an 'aggravating circumstance' or as a matter to be considered by courts in determining the penalty to be applied.

There are many dimensions to the Framework Decision which are worthy of further analysis, notably the overall balance it strikes between freedom of expression and combating 'hate' speech. In the context of this book's inquiry, discussion shall be limited to considering what it reveals about using EU criminal law to combat racism. An initial observation is that the difficult passage of the Framework Decision illustrates the limits of political will in this field. The case of Italy, where the national government includes a political party which deploys extreme rhetoric against immigrants and Muslims, is not a unique example in the enlarged European Union and it reveals that combating racism can encounter strong political resistance. The final text very much resembles a lowest common denominator and it is doubtful whether it will lead to much reform of pre-existing national legislation.[58]

The Framework Decision offers an insight into how racism is conceived within EU criminal law. In the Commission's original proposal, the following definition was suggested: '"racism and xenophobia" shall mean the belief in race, colour, descent, religion or belief, national or ethnic origin as a factor determining aversion to individuals or groups'.[59] Unsurprisingly, this was almost immediately dropped from the text during the Council negotiations.[60] As discussed in Chapter 1, very few legal instruments attempt to define the concept of 'racism', let alone 'xenophobia'. Instead, the final text contains the following statement: '"hatred" refers to hatred based on race, colour, religion, descent or national or ethnic origin'.[61] Significantly, this presents a broader concept of the target group

[56] Declaration to be inserted in the Council minutes at the time of the adoption of the Framework Decision: Council (n 47 above) 5.

[57] Select Committee on European Scrutiny, 'Sixteenth Report' HC (2006–2007) 41-xvi [6.12].

[58] eg all Member States already had provisions on incitement to hatred or violence: EU Network (n 54 above) 42.

[59] Art 3(a), Commission (n 41 above).

[60] Council (n 42 above).

[61] Recital 9, Council (n 49 above).

than that found within the Racial Equality Directive (which is limited to 'racial or ethnic origin'). The inclusion of religion was the most controversial element, with particular reservations from the UK.[62] This led to a compromise provision: 'the reference to religion is intended to cover, at least, conduct which is a pretext for directing acts against a group of persons or a member of such a group defined by reference to race, colour, descent, or national or ethnic origin'.[63] The 'pretext' test has also been used in Council of Europe instruments.[64] It seeks to strike a balance between permitting freedom of expression in relation to religious beliefs, whilst ensuring that offenders cannot escape the scope of anti-racism laws by simply replacing references to ethnicity with religious terms (for example, substituting an attack on Pakistanis by an attack on Muslims). It remains to be seen how this test can function in practice. In recent years, hatred directed towards Muslims has been recognized as closely interlinked with contemporary manifestations of racism.[65] Therefore, a key test for the Framework Decision will be whether its provisions are adequate to protect Muslim communities from incitement to violence and hatred. Even if it leaves a degree of ambiguity, the recognition of the close relationship between ethnicity, national origin, and religion within the Framework Decision offers a more constructive response to intersectionality than the separation of these grounds within EC anti-discrimination legislation.

Cross-border cooperation on combating racist crime

To the extent that the Framework Decision promotes convergence amongst national legal provisions on racist crime, then this may assist in dealing with cross-border police and judicial cooperation. Yet, the minimum standards ultimately adopted, combined with some very broad exceptions, imply that substantial differences will remain in this field. The case of David Irving provides a good example. Whilst he was able to engage lawfully in Holocaust denial in the UK, he committed a criminal offence by doing so in Austria.[66] Even after the Framework Decision, it appears that such conduct will remain permissible in the UK, so long as it is not likely to incite violence or hatred. The persistence of such

[62] This reflected a long-running domestic debate where the UK government tried to amend legislation on racial hatred in order to add religion. After being rejected by Parliament on several occasions, compromise was finally reached with the Racial and Religious Hatred Act 2006. See further, K Goodall, 'Incitement to religious hatred: all talk and no substance?' (2007) 70 MLR 89.

[63] Art 1(3).

[64] Art 2(1), Additional Protocol to the Convention on cybercrime, concerning the criminalisation of acts of a racist and xenophobic nature committed through computer systems (Strasbourg, 28 January 2003; CETS 189).

[65] eg D Diène, 'Report of the Special Rapporteur on contemporary forms of racism, racial discrimination, xenophobia and related intolerance, Doudou Diène, on the manifestations of defamation of religions and in particular on the serious implications of Islamophobia on the enjoyment of all rights' A/HRC/6/6, 21 August 2007.

[66] 'Holocaust denier Irving is jailed' *BBC News* (20 February 2006) <http://news.bbc.co.uk/1/hi/world/europe/4733820.stm> accessed 19 May 2008.

disparities in the content of national laws means that the principle of double criminality, where it is applied, can still be a barrier to cross-border police and judicial cooperation in relation to racist crime. As a result, it may be of equal significance that the Framework Decision has been paralleled by the adoption of various measures to derogate from the principle of double criminality in relation to racism and xenophobia.

The first and most notorious of such instruments is the European arrest warrant.[67] This instrument abolished the traditional extradition procedure within the EU. A European arrest warrant may be issued in order to secure the arrest and surrender of a person located in another Member State, either with a view to criminal prosecution or in order to enforce a custodial sentence.[68] National judicial authorities are, in principle, bound to enforce the warrant with limited possibilities to refuse its execution. Crucially, in respect of 32 listed offences, the principle of double criminality does not apply.[69] In other words, an arrest warrant should be enforced even if the offence to which it relates is not present in the domestic law of the executing judicial authority. The list of offences was largely drawn from the crimes mentioned in the annex to the Europol Convention,[70] so it includes 'racism and xenophobia'. Notably, the derogation from double criminality applies only if the offence is 'punishable in the issuing Member State by a custodial sentence or a detention order for a maximum period of at least three years'.[71] This is significant because the Framework Decision on racism and xenophobia specifies that its principal offences should be punishable by a maximum criminal penalty of at least between one and three years.[72] A state can, therefore, comply with the Framework Decision by punishing the offences concerned with a maximum penalty of one or two years. In such a case, the same state would not be able to rely on the derogation from double criminality within the European arrest warrant.

The mutual recognition approach which underpins the European arrest warrant has since been extended to other spheres, including the enforcement of judicial orders on freezing property or evidence,[73] financial penalties,[74] and

[67] Council Framework Decision (EU) 2002/584 on the European arrest warrant and the surrender procedures between Member States [2002] OJ L190/1. See further, M Plachta and W van Ballegooij, 'The Framework Decision on the European arrest warrant and surrender procedures between Member States of the European Union' in R Blekxtoon and W van Ballegooij (eds), *Handbook on the European Arrest Warrant* (The Hague: TMC Asser Press, 2005) 13.

[68] Art 1(1). [69] Art 2(2).

[70] N Keijzer, 'The double criminality requirement' in R Blekxtoon and W van Ballegooij (eds), *Handbook on the European Arrest Warrant* (The Hague: TMC Asser Press, 2005) 137, 149.

[71] Art 2(2). There is no requirement relating to the penalty applying in the law of the executing state.

[72] Art 3(2), Council (n 49 above).

[73] Council Framework Decision (EU) 2003/577 on the execution in the European Union of orders freezing property or evidence [2003] OJ L196/45.

[74] Council Framework Decision (EU) 2005/214 on the application of the principle of mutual recognition to financial penalties [2005] OJ L76/16.

confiscation orders.[75] In each of these instruments, 'racism and xenophobia' are contained within the list of offences where the principle of double criminality no longer applies. In the Framework Decision on financial penalties, the derogation from double criminality is not subject to any requirement regarding the maximum penalty for the offence in the issuing state, so its application will not be affected by the level of sanctions applied to racist offences in the domestic law.[76]

Perhaps the most important instrument in this field is the proposed 'European evidence warrant'. This would allow a judge, investigating magistrate, or public prosecutor in one state to issue a warrant requiring the relevant authorities in another state to seize and transfer evidence. It was originally proposed by the Commission in 2003[77] and a general approach was agreed by the Council in June 2006.[78] At the time of writing, negotiations were continuing with a view to reaching agreement on a final text. Evidence primarily concerns objects, documents, or data for use in criminal proceedings. It would not extend as far as requiring the executing state to conduct interviews with suspects or witnesses, nor could it contain an order to take evidence from the human body, including DNA.[79] It is not difficult to imagine scenarios where the evidence warrant could be used in relation to racist crime. The Verbeke case, mentioned earlier, concerned leaflets denying the Holocaust being produced in Belgium and then sent to the Netherlands. In such cases, the evidence warrant would allow the Dutch authorities to require the Belgian authorities to seize and transfer documents relevant to the prosecution.

The evidence warrant potentially penetrates deep into domestic legal systems. Concern has been expressed about the potential for the warrant to require executing authorities to enter and search private premises in relation to conduct which is not a criminal offence in that state.[80] In the latest version of the text, the principle of double criminality can be applied where the warrant entails search and seizure operations, but not if it relates to one of the listed offences, which include 'racism and xenophobia'.[81] This creates the potential that search and seizure could be requested in relation to, for example, Holocaust denial, even if

[75] Council Framework Decision (EU) 2006/783 on the application of the principle of mutual recognition to confiscation orders [2006] OJ L328/59.

[76] As regards freezing or confiscation orders, the offence must be punishable with at least a maximum custodial sentence of three years in the issuing state.

[77] Commission, 'Proposal for a Council Framework Decision on the European Evidence Warrant for obtaining objects, documents or data for use in criminal proceedings' COM (2003) 688.

[78] Council, 'Proposal for a Council Framework Decision on the European Evidence Warrant (EEW) for obtaining objects, documents or data for use in criminal proceedings' Ref 10511/07 COPEN 90, 11 June 2007.

[79] Art 4(2), Council, 'Council Framework Decision on the European Evidence Warrant (EEW) for the purpose of obtaining objects, documents or data for use in proceedings in criminal matters' Ref 13076/07 COPEN 132, 21 December 2007. If such evidence already existed (eg DNA information was already recorded), the issuing state can request this to be transferred (Art 4(4)).

[80] Select Committee on European Scrutiny, 'Fourth report' HC (2003-2004) 42-iv [6.4].

[81] Art 14(2), Council (n 79 above).

this was not an offence in the executing state.[82] The German government raised particular objections to the derogation from the principle of double criminality in respect of six offences, including 'racism and xenophobia'. It argued that these categories were not sufficiently clearly defined.[83] Consequently, special provisions have been established relating to Germany. It intends to issue a declaration stating that it will only permit search and seizure in relation to racism and xenophobia insofar as the offences concerned fall within the scope of the 1996 Joint Action. If the offence falls outside the scope of the Joint Action, then Germany will apply the principle of double criminality; that is, the offence must also be prohibited in German law.[84] It is difficult to predict how significant this arrangement will be in practice. The offences covered by the Joint Action are broader than those found within the subsequent Framework Decision on racism and xenophobia. Nevertheless, the episode reveals an underlying sensitivity about cross-border cooperation in relation to racism and xenophobia. Indeed, the specialist European Union committees of the House of Commons and the House of Lords have regularly argued that the category 'racism and xenophobia' is too vague as a basis for derogating from the principle of double criminality.[85]

Combating racist media via the EC Treaty

Although this chapter is focused on criminal law, it is worth briefly drawing attention to some 'flanking' measures which have been taken under the aegis of the EC Treaty. In relation to illegal racist content on the Internet, the Commission has promoted non-legal instruments in a series of 'Safer Internet' action plans.[86] These have encouraged self-regulation by the Internet industry and the development of technological responses, such as filters. The most recent action plan funds hotlines, where illegal content can be reported to Internet service providers or the police.[87] Furthermore, since 1989 the cross-border transmission of racist television broadcasts has been prohibited in the 'Television without

[82] It must be an offence in the state issuing the evidence warrant and punishable with a maximum custodial sentence of at least three years (Art 14(2)).

[83] L Kubosova, 'EU clinches deal on transfer of criminal evidence across borders' *EUObserver.com* (2 June 2006) <http://euobserver.com/9/21751/?rk=1> accessed 5 June 2006.

[84] Council, 'Council Framework Decision on the European Evidence Warrant (EEW) for the purpose of obtaining objects, documents or data for use in proceedings in criminal matters' Ref 6388/1/08 REV 1 COPEN 28, 6 May 2008.

[85] eg Select Committee on European Scrutiny (n 80 above) [6.36]; Select Committee on the European Union, '32nd report—the proposed Framework Decision on racism and xenophobia—an update' HL (2002–2003) 136 [14].

[86] Art 3, EP and Council Decision (EC) 276/1999 adopting a multiannual Community action plan on promoting safer use of the internet by combating illegal and harmful content on global networks [1999] OJ L33/1.

[87] Annex 1, action 1; EP and Council Decision (EC) 854/2005 establishing a multiannual Community programme on promoting safer use of the internet and new online technologies [2005] OJ L149/1.

Frontiers' Directive. Article 22 required Member States to 'ensure that broadcasts do not contain any incitement to hatred on grounds of race, sex, religion or nationality'.[88] Significant reforms to this Directive were made in 2007, with a view to ensuring that the same legal principles applied to nonlinear (on-demand) audiovisual services in the digital television era.[89] There is a presumption in favour of regulation by the 'home' state, that is, the state where the media service provider is established. In order to facilitate free movement of audiovisual services, certain minimum standards are to be guaranteed across all states. This includes a duty on states to ensure that 'audiovisual media services provided by media service providers under their jurisdiction do not contain any incitement to hatred based on race, sex, religion or nationality'.[90]

Racist offences and EU criminal law

At the beginning of this chapter, it was argued that promoting equality for ethnic minorities in the field of criminal law requires activity in two directions: combating racist crime and promoting equal treatment in the criminal justice system. This section has concentrated on the first of these categories. On the one hand, there is ample evidence of EU activism in relation to racist crime. Outside of the Racial Equality Directive, it is the most focused engagement of EU law with the issue of racism. The strongest interventions seem to be in relation to cross-border judicial cooperation and removing obstacles to the investigation of racist offences where these have an extraterritorial dimension. The various mutual recognition instruments adopted so far are still rather young, so it is hard to evaluate their impact. Admittedly, difficulties have been encountered with the implementation of the European arrest warrant.[91] Nonetheless, the fact that the category 'racism and xenophobia' has been embedded within this body of legislation as one of the key areas where the principle of double criminality is not applied can be viewed as concrete evidence of mainstreaming. In contrast, efforts to go beyond mere coordination of the legal systems and to establish minimum standards on racist criminal offences have confronted severe obstacles. Unlike the Racial Equality Directive, it is not clear that the Framework Decision will require wide-ranging reforms of national law relating to racist crime. The standards set compare

[88] Council Directive (EEC) 89/552 on the coordination of certain provisions laid down by law, regulation or administrative action in Member States concerning the pursuit of television broadcasting activities [1989] OJ L298/23. See similarly, Art 3(4)(a)(i), EP and Council Directive (EC) 2000/31 on electronic commerce [2000] OJ L178/1.

[89] EP and Council Directive (EC) 2007/65 amending Council Directive (EEC) 89/552 on the coordination of certain provisions laid down by law, regulation or administrative action in Member States concerning the pursuit of television broadcasting activities [2007] OJ L332/27.

[90] Art 3b.

[91] See further, V Mitsilegas, 'The constitutional implications of mutual recognition in criminal matters in the EU' (2006) 43 CML Rev 1277.

unfavourably to the categories of racist crime which ICERD requires states to prohibit[92] or which ECRI recommends are covered in national law.[93] The difficulty encountered in finding agreement amongst the Member States illustrates how EU policy on racism has oriented towards an anti-discrimination model. Prior to the Racial Equality Directive, there was an identifiable split between those states, such as the UK, Ireland, and the Netherlands, which placed more emphasis on combating discrimination via civil law, and other states, notably France, which viewed criminal law as the central mechanism in this field. The odyssey of the Framework Decision confirms that anti-discrimination is set to remain the dominant instrument within EU anti-racism policy.

C. Promoting Ethnic Equality in the Criminal Justice System

In comparison to the measures taken to combat racist crime, there is very little evidence of steps to promote ethnic equality throughout the criminal justice system, either in relation to those subject to a criminal procedure (such as suspects, accused persons, or convicts) or those who have been the victim of crime (whether racist in nature or not). In the first instance, part of this inaction can be attributed to the limitations on the Union's legal competence in this sphere. As described earlier, the principal role for the EU lies in *coordination* where crime assumes a cross-border dimension, alongside a developing body of substantive criminal law. The Union does not have an explicit legal competence in relation to criminal procedure; indeed, a proposed Framework Decision relating to defendants' rights has encountered substantial opposition from the Member States on grounds of lack of competence.[94] Furthermore, racial discrimination by the police or other branches of the criminal justice system does not fall within the scope of the Racial Equality Directive. It applies 'within the limits of the powers conferred upon the Community',[95] whereas the Union's legal competence relating to police and judicial cooperation exists outside of the EC Treaty, under the EU Treaty. Despite these restrictions, it is not difficult to locate examples of legal initiatives or policy measures in the criminal justice sphere which provide an opportunity for integrating ethnic equality objectives. For instance, the stalled proposal for a Framework Decision on defendants' rights could be welcomed insofar as it includes a right to free translation of documents and interpretation throughout criminal proceedings.[96] At the same time, an express guarantee that all defendants will be treated equally irrespective of racial

[92] Art 4 ICERD.

[93] para 18, General recommendation 7 on national legislation to combat racism and racial discrimination, CRI (2003) 8, 13 December 2002.

[94] Mitsilegas (n 91 above) 1304.

[95] Art 3, Dir 2000/43.

[96] Arts 6–7, Commission, 'Proposal for a Council Framework Decision on certain procedural rights in criminal proceedings throughout the European Union' COM (2004) 328.

or ethnic origin would have been a logical expression of mainstreaming. Similarly, the Framework Decision on the standing of victims in criminal proceedings provides that victims should receive information 'as far as possible in languages commonly understood',[97] yet it lacks any explicit protection for victims against discrimination within the criminal justice system. For reasons of space, it is obviously not possible to subject every single EU instrument relating to criminal justice to detailed analysis. The remainder of this section considers two areas where arguably there is scope for mainstreaming: data collection and funding programmes.

Data collection

Gathering information according to ethnic origin in the criminal justice field can be a double-edged sword. On the one hand, such data can paint an accurate picture of racist crime, as well as exposing unequal treatment of ethnic minorities by bodies such as the police. Chapter 3 underlined the necessity of data collection to establishing an effective approach to mainstreaming. On the other hand, there is a risk that this information is misused. Statistics showing an over-representation of ethnic minority groups in certain criminal acts could be exploited to reinforce stereotypes linking immigration and criminality. Solomos argues that British statistics in the 1970s and 1980s showing a disproportionate number of young black people involved in committing street robberies led to a 'racialization' of this crime in public discourse, with insufficient attention to other factors, such as the socio-economic background of those concerned.[98] Alternatively, increasing attention has been paid to 'ethnic profiling' as a form of institutional racism by law enforcement agencies. ECRI defines this as 'the use by the police, with no objective and reasonable justification, of grounds such as race, colour, language, religion, nationality or national or ethnic origin in control, surveillance or investigation activities'.[99] This might involve collecting data on ethnicity and then using this to subject individuals of a particular background to unjustified police monitoring. In the pending case of *Huber*, Advocate-General Maduro has argued that prevention of crime cannot be a justification for imposing heightened levels of data collection in relation to foreign nationals, because this implies that such nationals are intrinsically more disposed to commit crime.[100] Paradoxically, data collection can also be a tool to combat ethnic

[97] Art 4, [2001] OJ L82/1.

[98] J Solomos, *Race and Racism in Britain* (3rd edn, Houndmills: Palgrave, 2003) 137.

[99] para I(1), ECRI (n 14 above). ECRI uses the term 'racial profiling'.

[100] para 21, Case C-524/06 *Huber v Bundesrepublik Deutschland*, Opinion of 3 April 2008. The case concerns the legality of a national database on foreign nationals which includes information on criminal convictions and suspected criminal activity. There is no equivalent national database for German nationals. The legal challenge relates only to the inclusion of EU citizens within the database.

profiling insofar as it can reveal if the police are, for example, disproportionately using stop and search powers in relation to certain ethnic groups.[101]

So far, the Union's main contribution to data collection has been the EUMC, which strove to compile comparable data on racist crime. As mentioned earlier, its main conclusion was that the existing data were not comparable as many states lacked any data collection system in this area.[102] Whilst the FRA will continue to work on data collection in relation to racism and xenophobia, its mandate is explicitly restricted to the scope of the EC Treaty.[103] Moreover, it possesses no instruments through which states can be compelled to improve their data collection systems. The Commission originally proposed that the Framework Decision on racism and xenophobia would establish a network of national contact points to exchange information.[104] The Parliament amended this in order to create an obligation to submit data to the EUMC on police reports, prosecutions, and convictions for racist and xenophobic offences.[105] No such obligation exists in the final text of the Framework Decision and there is no evidence from the *travaux préparatoires* that either of these proposals was given serious consideration by the Council.

With regard to protecting individuals against the misuse of ethnic data within the criminal justice system, this falls outside the scope of the Data Protection Directive.[106] It would, however, be addressed by a proposed Framework Decision on Data Protection. The scope of this instrument has been significantly narrowed during the course of its negotiation. Whereas the Commission anticipated data protection rules which would apply generally in relation to criminal matters,[107] the Council has reduced this to situations where personal data are transmitted between states or from a state to authorities or information

[101] EU Network of Independent Experts on Fundamental Rights, 'Ethnic profiling' Opinion 4-2006, December 2006, 6; J Goldston, 'Toward a Europe without ethnic profiling' in Open Society Institute Justice Initiative (eds), *Ethnic Profiling by Police in Europe* (New York: Open Society Institute, 2005) 6; O de Schutter and J Ringelheim, 'Ethnic profiling: a rising challenge for European human rights law' (2008) 71 MLR 331.

[102] EUMC, 'Racist violence in 15 EU Member States—a comparative overview of findings from the RAXEN national focal points reports 2001–2004' (Vienna: EUMC, 2005) 15.

[103] Art 3(1), Council Regulation (EC) 168/2007 establishing a European Union Agency for Fundamental Rights [2007] OJ L53/1.

[104] Art 15, Commission (n 41 above). The 1996 Joint Action already contains such an obligation, although no information was located on whether such contact points are actually operational.

[105] Amendment 22, Resolution on the proposal for a Council Framework Decision on combating racism and xenophobia [2003] OJ C271E/558.

[106] This does not apply to activities outside the scope of the EC Treaty, including 'the activities of the State in areas of criminal law': Art 3(2), EP and Council Directive (EC) 95/46 on the protection of individuals with regard to the processing of personal data and on the free movement of such data [1995] OJ L281/31.

[107] Art 3(1), Commission, 'Proposal for a Council Framework Decision on the protection of personal data processed in the framework of police and judicial cooperation in criminal matters' COM (2005) 475.

systems established by the Council.[108] As with the Data Protection Directive, data pertaining to the 'racial or ethnic origin' of an identifiable individual are deemed to be in a special category. The Commission's proposal proceeded from the position that such data could not be processed, subject to exceptions.[109] This is also the approach adopted in all of the Council of Europe's instruments in this area.[110] This presumption has been inverted by the Council, whose text now states that the processing of such data 'shall be permitted only where this is strictly necessary and when the domestic law provides adequate safeguards'.[111] This proposed departure from the norm that the use of racial or ethnic data should be prohibited has been criticized by the European Data Protection Supervisor[112] and the European Parliament.[113]

Funding programmes

Like most areas of EU activity, legal instruments have been accompanied by funding programmes. A variety of initiatives has been taken over the years with a view to promoting cooperation between judicial authorities and law enforcement bodies. Between 2003 and 2007, the main programme in this area was 'AGIS'.[114] The Decision establishing this programme had no specific objectives relating to combating discrimination or promoting equality. Nevertheless, it seems that occasional projects were funded which pursued such goals.[115] During this period, the support for EU-level training of judges and police solidified, with the establishment of the European Judicial Training Network and the European Police College. The former promotes the coordination of judicial training and it is also involved in the organization of specific training and exchange programmes. It is not evident from its website that it has initiated training courses focused on racism or equality, although it promotes access to the training courses on EU anti-discrimination law provided by the Academy of European Law.[116]

[108] Art 1(2), Council, 'Proposal for a Council Framework Decision on the protection of personal data processed in the framework of police and judicial cooperation in criminal matters' Ref 16069/07, 11 December 2007.

[109] Art 6, Commission (n 107 above).

[110] See further, EU Network (n 101 above) 16.

[111] Art 7, Council (n 108 above).

[112] European Data Protection Supervisor, 'Third opinion of the European Data Protection Supervisor on the Proposal for a Council Framework Decision on the protection of personal data processed in the framework of police and judicial co-operation in criminal matters' [2007] OJ C139/1, para 37.

[113] Amendment 27, Resolution on the proposal for a Council Framework Decision on the protection of personal data processed in the framework of police and judicial cooperation in criminal matters, P6_TA-PROV(2007)0230, 7 June 2007.

[114] Council Decision (EU) 2002/630 establishing a framework programme on police and judicial cooperation in criminal matters (AGIS) [2002] OJ L203/5.

[115] In 2006, projects on the effective policing of ethnic minorities and combating hate crimes were funded. See, 'List of selected projects in 2006': <http://ec.europa.eu/justice_home/funding/2004_2007/agis/funding_agis_en.htm#> accessed 19 May 2008.

[116] See: <http://www.ejtn.net> accessed 19 May 2008.

The European Police College has existed since 2001. It organizes around 80–100 courses each year, primarily aimed at senior police officers in order to promote cross-border cooperation.[117] During 2002–2005, the College organized one course each year which specifically addressed issues of racism.[118] It is also in the process of designing a common training curriculum on the 'management of diversity'.[119]

Overall, the above activities seem fairly marginal in scope. The current generation of funding programmes promises to be more extensive. An umbrella 'Fundamental Rights and Justice' programme runs from 2007 to 2013. This includes a 'Fundamental Rights and Citizenship' strand, where one of four general objectives is: 'to fight against racism, xenophobia and anti-Semitism and to promote a better interfaith and intercultural understanding . . . '.[120] This has a budget of almost €94 million, so it is comparable in scale to the anti-discrimination and diversity stream of Progress (see Chapter 4).

D. Conclusions

At first glance, criminal law might be viewed as the area where the objectives of combating racism and promoting equality have been most extensively taken on board. Certainly, it is the only policy field outside anti-discrimination where combating racism has been elevated to the level of a Treaty-mandated objective. It is also over a decade since the adoption of the first legal instrument pertaining to these goals, the 1996 Joint Action. Closer scrutiny, however, suggests that mainstreaming is less advanced in practice.

There is no evidence of any mechanism through which ethnic equality objectives are systematically promoted or taken into account during the law-making or policy formulation process. As with fields examined elsewhere in this book, the Commission's impact assessment procedure would appear to be the primary vehicle through which any disparate impact on ethnic minorities should be identified. Yet, there is little evidence that this considers equality issues in much depth. For example, the impact assessment of the proposal for a Framework Decision on Data Protection does not even discuss the question of collecting ethnic data.[121] Despite the lack of clear procedural mechanisms for mainstreaming, it cannot be denied that issues relating to racism have regularly

[117] See: <http://www.cepol.europa.eu/> accessed 19 May 2008.

[118] ibid. See further 'About CEPOL/History' section of website.

[119] <http://www.cepol.europa.eu/index.php?id=common-curricula> accessed 19 May 2008.

[120] Art 2, Council Decision (EC) 2007/252 establishing for the period 2007–2013 the specific programme 'Fundamental Rights and Citizenship' as part of the general programme 'Fundamental Rights and Justice' [2007] OJ L110/33.

[121] Commission, 'Proposal for a Council Framework Decision on the protection of personal data processed in the framework of police and judicial co-operation in criminal matters—impact assessment' SEC (2005) 1241.

found their way onto the criminal law agenda, both through the Framework Decision and within mutual recognition instruments. The overall balance of measures taken is, though, heavily tilted towards repressing racism rather than promoting equality. Competence constraints have undoubtedly played their role in shaping the direction of EU initiatives in this field, but opportunities to promote equal treatment of ethnic minorities within the criminal justice system have, at times, been overlooked. There is some evidence to suggest that mainstreaming is rendered more difficult given the intergovernmental tendency of the EU Treaty legal framework. The requirement for unanimity allows individual recalcitrant states to hinder the adoption of common measures and to impose a lowest common denominator approach. This is very evident in the Framework Decision on racism and xenophobia or alternatively the German derogation in the proposed European evidence warrant. The obstacles to enforcing EU Treaty legislation raise questions about the ultimate effectiveness of the measures already taken, such as the 1996 Joint Action.

The emphasis in this domain on repressing racist crime reveals a generally narrow conception of what racism entails. The focus is on extreme and overt actions by non-state actors, akin to the concept of scientific racism discussed in Chapter 1. Correspondingly, there is little recognition of the concept of institutional racism. EU coordination in the field of criminal law is built upon the notion of 'mutual trust';[122] Member States are assumed to have confidence in the human rights standards applied by criminal justice systems throughout the Union. It is on this basis that decisions by national courts can be enforced elsewhere, individuals can be surrendered, and (in due course) evidence will be transferred. Examples of racism within the criminal justice system, such as the ECHR cases of police violence and discrimination towards Roma, strike at the heart of this trust and underscore the need for a more extensive commitment from the Union to promoting equality for ethnic minorities in this field.

[122] Mitsilegas (n 91 above) 1309.

Conclusions

The principal research question pursued by this book was to explore the extent to which the objectives of combating racism and promoting equality have been mainstreamed across EU law and policy. To that end, the analysis has examined law and policy in the social field (employment, education, healthcare, and housing), as well as law and policy relating to immigration and crime. As stated in the introduction, there was no expectation that a comprehensive strategy for mainstreaming ethnic equality would be uncovered. Two initial observations can be made. First, the absence of any concerted mainstreaming strategy does not mean that the Union completely fails to address issues relating to racism and equality. On the contrary, there was evidence in all the topics examined of ways in which law and policy were being used to combat racism and promote equality, albeit with varying degrees of intensity or effectiveness. The diverse engagements of EU law and policy with promoting ethnic equality strongly suggest that this is an issue which the Union will inevitably encounter again and again, implying that there is a compelling rationale for an overarching approach.

A second preliminary observation is that some of the infrastructure through which mainstreaming could be advanced is already in existence. Mainstreaming gender equality has been an active EU commitment since the mid-1990s and it is supported by a variety of specialist committees, such as the Expert Group on Gender, Social Inclusion and Employment. Some of its work has begun to examine the situation of minority women,[1] which offers both the prospect of raising awareness of ethnic equality objectives, as well as enhancing sensitivity to intersectionality issues. More generally, the past decade has seen greater attention within the EU institutions to compliance with fundamental rights, which offers a concordant back-drop against which equality mainstreaming can be developed. Political initiatives, such as the Group of Commissioners on Fundamental Rights, Non-Discrimination and Equal Opportunities, and technical instruments, namely the impact assessment process, favour a trajectory towards more emphasis on mainstreaming. The picture which emerges is one of multi-speed mainstreaming with opportunities seized in some contexts, yet overlooked and marginalized elsewhere. In some cases, this can be attributed to broader issues,

[1] eg C Fagan, P Urwin, and K Melling, 'Gender inequalities in the risks of poverty and social exclusion for disadvantaged groups in thirty European countries' (Luxembourg: OOPEC, 2006).

such as constraints on legal competence. For instance, the powers of the EU in relation to policing remain relatively minor. There are, though, other occasions where ethnic equality objectives could be more deeply embedded, but such a perspective has been neglected. The legislation on information and consultation of workers or the public health funding programmes were two such examples.[2]

The introduction identified two sub-questions that nested within the overall research question. The first related to what is meant by 'combating racism and promoting equality', in other words, what concepts of racism and equality are in currency? The second concerned the definition of mainstreaming and the various models which can be adopted. Each of these themes is considered below.

A. Combating Racism and Promoting Equality

Chapter 1 examined the multiple meanings that have been attached to 'racism', a term which has been subject to extensive critique within sociological literature. In summary, it identified three generic forms of racism: scientific, cultural, and institutional. Scientific racism was the narrowest concept, reducing racism to theories about the biological superiority of certain imagined human 'races'. Whilst such ideas reached a zenith during the Second World War, contemporary accounts of racism have tended to focus around cultural or institutional interpretations. Cultural approaches to racism link it to prejudice against individuals or groups from a different cultural background, such as hostility to immigrants.[3] Cultural racism tends to centre on prejudice which may manifest itself in acts of racial discrimination; at its root, therefore, racism is traced back to the mindset of individuals and a rejection of those viewed as culturally different. This can be distinguished from institutional racism, which shifts away from individual acts towards a focus on social outcomes. It links the persistence of ethnic inequality to structural factors, notably the (conscious or unconscious) processes and cultures of institutions which operate to reproduce inequality. In this frame, evidence of unequal outcomes rings alarm bells for the presence of institutional racism.[4]

To some extent, theoretical analyses of equality can be mapped to these different models of racism. The conventional dichotomy between formal and substantive equality loosely reflects scientific and cultural racism on the one hand, and institutional racism on the other. Formal equality is typically manifested in a focus on individualized discrimination claims. Although proof of malevolent intent is not essential, the implied paradigm is where an individual is treated less favourably because of discriminatory prejudice by an employer or service provider. Consequently, formal equality seems to flow from a scientific or

[2] See further Chs 5 and 6 respectively.
[3] A Kundnani, 'In a foreign land: the new popular racism' (2001) 43 *Race & Class* 41, 52.
[4] M Rowe, *Policing, Race and Racism* (Cullompton: Willan Publishing, 2004) 10.

cultural interpretation of racism. In contrast, substantive equality is more concerned with overall social outcomes. Whether the goal adopted is equality of opportunity, or the more radical requirement of equality of results, unequal outcomes are viewed as troubling and indicative of the need for active measures to bring about full equality in practice. This clearly echoes the approach of institutional racism.

Unsurprisingly, influences from all of these concepts can be found within EU law and policy. Scientific racism exercised a strong influence at the outset of EU anti-racism policy, as manifested in concerns about how to combat activities such as Holocaust denial within the context of the internal market. This reflects the prominence in early policy discourse of 'xenophobia' and 'anti-Semitism'. After the introduction of EC Treaty, Article 13, this element of the policy frame waned, with a discernible shift towards 'discrimination' as the major concern. The political agreement reached in 2007 on the Framework Decision on racism and xenophobia could, at first glance, suggest a shift back towards this initial orientation. Nevertheless, its relatively meagre contents and the strong deference to diverse national traditions suggest that EU anti-racism policy will remain predominantly focused on issues relating to discrimination.

The cultural concept of racism seems to be the strongest influence across EU law and policy. There is a recurrent tendency to respond to racism with initiatives designed to promote awareness and understanding of cultural diversity or to assist migrants in cultural adaptation. Examples include the anti-discrimination action programme (with its 'For Diversity, Against Discrimination' campaign), or the typical projects often funded under the European Social Fund (ESF), EU education programmes, or the INTI programme on immigrant integration. The overall impression is that racial discrimination is conceived as prejudicial actions of individuals, usually based around stereotyping or cultural misunderstanding. This model is also present in the Racial Equality Directive, which places a strong accent on individual litigation as the primary instrument for combating discrimination.

There is only limited evidence that an institutional racism perspective has penetrated EU law and policy. An illustration can be found within the open method of coordination (OMC) processes on employment or social inclusion, where a tension was noted between policies designed to combat discrimination and those aimed at promoting integration. The former recognize that inequalities in the labour market, or alternatively unequal outcomes in housing, healthcare, and education, are (at least in part) a reflection of discrimination in the underlying institutions or structures. In contrast, integration policies tend to place the onus on ethnic minorities, attributing inequality to factors such as a lack of educational qualifications or insufficient linguistic skills. The emphasis on integration also conveys a formal concept of equality where minorities must adapt their behaviour to the pre-existing norm. The evidence presented in both Chapters 5 and 6 indicated that integration rather than discrimination remained the dominant perspective within OMC national reports. Similarly, integration by the individual migrant has been an increasing theme within immigration law and policy.

The recent trajectory of anti-discrimination law and policy suggests a subtle shift in favour of substantive equality,[5] which might create space for greater recognition of institutional racism. Two major statements of anti-discrimination policy by the Commission have emphasized the role for positive action, as well as mainstreaming and data collection.[6] It is also true that inequalities faced by immigrants and Roma are receiving more attention within the OMC processes than at their outset, even if this positive direction has been called into question by the 2005 reforms to the employment and social inclusion OMCs.[7] Yet institutional racism as a concept has had almost no perceptible influence on EU measures in the field of police and judicial cooperation.

As mentioned above, both substantive equality and institutional racism place considerable weight on outcomes as an indicator of equality. This constitutes a significant obstacle in the EU context where comparable data on the situation of different ethnic groups remain limited. It is easy to rehearse familiar arguments about different philosophical outlooks on whether ethnic groups exist, the impact of historical experiences from the Second World War, or variations in the interpretation of data protection legislation. Nevertheless, more than a decade after the EU Monitoring Centre on Racism and Xenophobia (EUMC) was created with the express goal of compiling 'objective, reliable and comparable data at European level on the phenomena of racism, xenophobia and anti-Semitism',[8] only limited progress has been made in this direction. This has been particularly influential in marginalizing ethnic inequalities within the OMC processes, which are often characterized by a preoccupation with quantitative targets.

Target groups and intersectionality

Alongside the conceptualization of racism and equality, another key definitional issue is the target group(s) addressed by anti-racism policy. This is important on several levels. First, there needs to be some understanding of who the target groups are in order to inform any process of gathering data and measuring outcomes. Second, racism is not a monolithic concept and it may be experienced in different ways by different groups. As mentioned above, anti-Semitism

[5] E Howard, 'The European Year of Equal Opportunities for All—2007: is the EU moving away from a formal idea of equality?' (2008) 14 ELJ 168, 183.

[6] Commission, 'Non-discrimination and equal opportunities for all—a framework strategy' COM (2005) 224; Commission, 'Non-discrimination and equal opportunities: a renewed commitment' COM (2008) 420/3.

[7] See further Chs 5 and 6.

[8] Art 2(1), Council Regulation (EC) 1035/97 establishing a European Monitoring Centre for Racism and Xenophobia [1997] OJ L151/1.

is often more closely associated with racist ideologies which typify scientific racism rather than the socio-economic inequalities connected to institutional racism. Third, the demographic variations across Europe inevitably mean that the groups vulnerable to racism are, to some extent, geographically contingent. EU anti-racism policy has been predominantly focused on immigrants and communities of immigrant descent. The 2004 and 2007 enlargements altered this picture, bringing into the frame national minorities and Roma communities. Such groups could already be found within western European states; however, they form notably larger proportions of the population of some eastern European states. Moreover, there are heightened political sensitivities due to potential cross-border consequences. These range from troubled relations with the neighbouring 'kin' states of national minorities,[9] to the migration of Roma from eastern to western Europe.[10]

Although national minorities are potentially vulnerable to discrimination on grounds of ethnic origin, they remain a marginal concern in EU anti-racism policy. This seems to be based on the assumption that groups such as Hungarians in Romania or Russians in the Baltic States are not systematically subject to socio-economic disadvantage, for example, in relation to employment rates or educational outcomes. It is difficult to be confident that this implicit assumption is well founded. Whilst there is a growing body of data on migrants within the labour market and, to a lesser extent, other fields of life, there is often little attention to national minorities. This issue was initially raised when the states concerned entered the social inclusion OMC process,[11] but it has not been pursued. Arguably, there is a need for more extensive social research to explore whether national minorities do enjoy broadly similar socio-economic outcomes to the majority ethnic population. Some existing studies in Estonia and Latvia have documented ethnic inequalities (primarily affecting Russian minorities) in average salary, type of employment, and unemployment rate.[12]

In comparison, there has been steadily increasing documentation of the severe socio-economic situation confronted by Roma communities. This has undoubtedly driven their visibility as a specific sub-group within EU anti-racism policy. This was an evident trend in the fields of anti-discrimination, employment, and social inclusion. For example, the Commission established an inter-service group dedicated to Roma issues in 2004; Roma were identified as a key

[9] eg Russia and Estonia.

[10] R Guglielmo and T Walters, 'Migrating towards minority status: shifting European policy towards Roma' (2005) 43 JCMS 763.

[11] Commission, 'Report on social inclusion in the 10 new Member States 2005' (Luxembourg: OOPEC, 2005) 33.

[12] Thanks to Vadim Poleshchuk for drawing my attention to the following sources: K Kasesaru and A Trumm, 'The socio-economic situation of non-Estonians' in M Heidmets (ed), *Estonian Human Development Report 2007* (Tallinn: Eesti Koostöö Kogu, 2008) 46, 53–4; A Aasland, 'Russians and the Economy' in N Muižnieks (ed), *Latvian-Russian Relations: Domestic and International Dimensions* (Riga: LU Akademiskais apgads, 2006) 53.

group in the second round of the Equal programme;[13] and Roma have received mention in the 'key policy priorities' of the social inclusion process.[14] Sensitivity to the specific situation of Roma did not, though, appear to have filtered into law and policy relating to immigration or crime.

At the same time as awareness has grown of diversity within the social groups vulnerable to racism, there has been an incremental rise in discussion of intersectionality. This concept has been given a variety of interpretations,[15] but fundamentally it draws attention to situations where characteristics linked to inequality overlap. Intersectionality issues have been explored within anti-discrimination policy, for instance, through funding projects which simultaneously cover several grounds of discrimination. Projects on migrant women (to take a typical example) can also be found under the ESF. Nonetheless, no concerted engagement with intersectionality was found across the various case studies. This perspective was particularly invisible in relation to immigration policy and criminal law.

Taking an overview, EU anti-racism policy grapples today with more complexity than at its outset, when an undifferentiated group of 'immigrants' was the standard frame of reference. This can create tensions: when should Roma receive different treatment in law and policy from other ethnic minorities? When should measures to promote equality for ethnic minorities be combined with other discrimination grounds? To date, the response of the EU lacks coherence. A signal example was the parallel creation of an Institute for Gender Equality at the same time as the EUMC was transformed into the Fundamental Rights Agency. There is unlikely to be any neat answer to these dilemmas. Several observations can be made. First, the intersection between ethnicity, religion, and nationality is particularly strong, therefore law and policy should, as far as possible, deal with inequalities linked to these grounds in a consistent manner. Currently, inequalities linked to (third country) nationality have been detached and dealt with separately via EC immigration legislation. As discussed in Chapter 7, this has given rise to a highly fragmented legal framework where protection against discrimination based on nationality or immigration status is much weaker than that which exists in relation to ethnic origin. Similarly, both EC anti-discrimination legislation and the Framework Decision on racism and xenophobia have created problematic boundaries between ethnic origin and religion which risk creating gaps in protection, particularly in relation to combating Islamophobia.

Second, recognition of intersectionality issues does not imply that law and policy should be completely uniform in relation to all discrimination grounds.

[13] See Ch 5.

[14] Commission, 'Social inclusion in Europe 2006' (Luxembourg: OOPEC, 2006) 164. See further, Commission, 'Community instruments and policies for Roma inclusion' Commission Staff Working Paper, 2 July 2008.

[15] Commission, 'Tackling multiple discrimination—practices, policies and laws' (Luxembourg: OOPEC, 2007) 17.

It is evident that some issues are more sensitive for some grounds than others. Physical accessibility of buildings and transport is highly salient for disability, whilst the distribution of family responsibilities is a key issue for gender equality. In relation to ethnic equality, immigration is typically an issue of special importance, in terms of how migration is regulated, but also public policy approaches to cultural diversity. Choices made in the arena of integration policy, for example on linguistic diversity or manifestation of religious beliefs, will inform the concept of equality which the state is seeking to pursue. Consequently, it is especially important that the objectives of combating racism and promoting equality are mainstreamed in all aspects of law and policy relating to immigration. This is currently lacking, as witnessed by the Commission's failure to identify any potential negative impacts on ethnic minorities from the proposed Directive on sanctioning employers of irregular migrants.

B. Models of Mainstreaming and Styles of Governance

Although the term mainstreaming has entered into the equality lexicon, it can be interpreted in many different ways. Chapter 3 described how approaches to mainstreaming range from 'integrationist' to 'transformative'. This captures the difference between two extremes. At one end of the spectrum (integrationist), mainstreaming might simply constitute a formalistic bureaucratic requirement. Given the list of other issues which policy-makers have to take into account (burden on business, health and safety, environmental impact, etc), equality mainstreaming could be reduced to one more question on a tick-box form (have you considered the impact of the proposed measure on equality?). Conceived in this way, mainstreaming is unlikely to have more than a marginal impact. At the other end of the spectrum, transformative mainstreaming foresees a genuine mobilization of law and policy in all fields in order to promote equality. Increasingly, this goal has been linked to a wider transformation in the style of policy-making, namely, opening up policy formulation and allowing greater participation by affected groups.[16] In reviewing the first 10 years of gender mainstreaming, Beveridge concluded:

> the Commission's conception of mainstreaming has evolved a little, from the initial technocratic approach towards a (slightly) more open, consultative approach; however, there is still little evidence that this shift is much reflected in the day-to-day routines and practices of the various Directorates-General and services.[17]

[16] J Squires, 'Is mainstreaming transformative? Theorizing mainstreaming in the context of diversity and deliberation' (2005) 12 *Social Politics* 366, 380.

[17] F Beveridge, 'Building against the past: the impact of mainstreaming on EU gender law and policy' (2007) 32 ELR 193, 211.

A similar situation was found in relation to ethnic equality. Where evidence of such mainstreaming could be found, this predominantly reflected the 'integrationist' model. The impact assessment procedure is currently the most obvious mechanism through which mainstreaming could and should take place. It would be incorrect to describe this as a 'tick-box' process; some impact assessments are detailed in their analysis and, where an extended impact assessment takes place, this is intended to include consultation with external actors.[18] Nevertheless, the existing impact assessment procedure has no focus on equality, let alone issues specifically relating to racism or ethnic minorities. Such issues could arise under the rubric of 'social impacts' or, since 2005, the emphasis on fundamental rights compliance.[19] In practice, there is little evidence that the impact assessment procedure does function as a forum to mainstream ethnic equality objectives. Chapter 7 noted the failure of the impact assessment of the employer sanctions Directive to identify any potentially adverse effects on ethnic minorities and Chapter 8 found that the impact assessment of the Framework Decision on Data Protection entirely overlooked the issue of ethnic data collection in relation to crime and policing. Even where the impact assessment does address equality issues, it is unclear how much influence it exerts. The possibility of including equality in the required list of topics for workplace consultation was mentioned in the impact assessment of the revision of the European Works Councils Directive, but this suggestion was then overlooked in the final legislative proposal.[20]

The inter-service groups on racism and Roma issues provide a more focused venue for mainstreaming within the Commission. For the most part, they reflect an expert-bureaucratic model,[21] although relevant NGOs are occasionally invited to give presentations. It is difficult to measure the impact of the inter-service groups, in particular, how far they go beyond the mutual sharing of information between Directorates-General (DGs) and actually promulgate a coordinated strategy. Moreover, there seems a risk that participation is self-selecting; just eight DGs are reported to be involved in the racism inter-service group.[22]

Given the weakness of the current structures for mainstreaming, it is almost inevitable that the goals of combating racism and promoting equality will be pursued inconsistently. One variable which impacts upon opportunities for mainstreaming is the style of governance. As discussed in Chapter 3, a dichotomy exists between traditional regulatory instruments (principally binding legislation) and 'new' or experimental governance (notably the OMC). New governance relies less on rights-based litigation as a lever for change, but instead identifies broad objectives and seeks to pursue these in a flexible manner, for example,

[18] Commission, 'Communication on impact assessment' COM (2002) 276, 7.

[19] Commission, 'Compliance with the Charter of Fundamental Rights in Commission legislative proposals—methodology for systematic and rigorous monitoring' COM (2005) 172.

[20] See Ch 5. [21] See Ch 3.

[22] Interview: Commission official, 12 December 2007.

through setting targets and publicly comparing state performance. Mainstreaming shares some of the characteristics of new governance insofar as it is less court-centred than anti-discrimination legislation and it often has recourse to instruments such as targets, indicators, and reporting procedures.

The case studies under consideration revealed evidence of mainstreaming both in traditional forms of regulation and new governance. Considering the former, the hurdles to getting ethnic equality objectives on the agenda seemed higher. Binding legislation in any given area is typically adopted at irregular intervals, with limited opportunity for amendment during the intervening period. In relation to EC employment legislation, it was suggested that legislation on worker participation was a missed opportunity to promote the mainstreaming of ethnic equality issues within workplace information and consultation mechanisms. Criminal law provided a better example of how the issue of racism had been embedded across a range of legislation on judicial cooperation, whilst the express mandate provided in EU Treaty, Article 29 provided the foundation for the tortuous negotiation of the Framework Decision on racism and xenophobia. The hard bargaining process that habitually surrounds legislation in areas such as crime or immigration can be a practical obstacle to providing a consistent framework for promoting equality. In immigration law, this has produced a highly fragmented set of rights contingent on immigration status.

New governance instruments, such as funding programmes or the OMC processes, seemed easier points of initial entry for mainstreaming initiatives. Although immigrants were initially absent from the European Employment Strategy guidelines, the annual process of revision meant that this deficiency could be addressed at a later stage. Similarly, in the post-enlargement climate, Roma issues filtered into the employment and social inclusion OMC processes relatively quickly. The constant reflection and renegotiation that characterize the OMC processes produce the risk, however, that issues can also slide off the agenda. This was the experience of the 2005 reforms to the employment and social inclusion OMC processes where objectives relating to immigrants became much less visible. More generally, Fredman suggests that the shifting sands of new governance mean that a 'bedrock of fundamental rights' is essential to prevent economic concerns overriding social objectives.[23] In contrast, traditional regulation in the form of binding legislation has the advantage that gains accomplished enjoy a more secure foundation for the future.

Mainstreaming inevitably needs to engage with the methods of both traditional and new governance. This has important consequences for the range of tools to be used. For example, the impact assessment procedure is normally applied to 'all legislative and major policy-defining proposals' from the Commission.[24]

[23] S Fredman, 'Transformation or dilution: fundamental rights in the EU social space' (2006) 12 ELJ 41, 59.

[24] Commission (n 19 above) 2.

Consequently, it will not capture the ongoing operation of a policy, such as the OMC processes or the lifecycle of a funding programme. Despite these limitations, the Commission's 2008 communication on anti-discrimination policy continues to construe mainstreaming as predominantly delivered by impact assessment.[25]

C. Looking to the Future

A number of basic findings can be recapped at this point. First, various areas of EU law and policy are already engaging with the objectives of combating racism and promoting equality. Second, those engagements are currently rather haphazard in nature, lacking consistency or an overall direction. Third, although the institutions have flirted with the idea of mainstreaming ethnic equality objectives, an overarching framework remains to be established. Based on these observations, there is a need for the Union to adopt a more concerted approach to mainstreaming. To this end, a prerequisite is the construction of some basic architecture upon which mainstreaming could be founded. One lesson from the 1998 Action Plan Against Racism is that a purely political commitment can easily dissipate over time. Several EU states have moved in the direction of providing mainstreaming with a legal foundation as a buttress against shifting political priorities. Should it be ratified, the Treaty of Lisbon holds considerable promise. The Treaty on the Functioning of the European Union, Article 10, states:

> In defining and implementing its policies and activities, the Union shall aim to combat discrimination based on sex, racial or ethnic origin, religion or belief, disability, age or sexual orientation.[26]

In addition, Shaw argues that this clause needs to be read alongside the non-discrimination guarantee in the Charter of Fundamental Rights,[27] as well as the Charter's positive duty to 'respect cultural, religious and linguistic diversity'.[28] By themselves, these foundational legal norms will not bring about mainstreaming in practice. They do, though, provide a firm mandate for mainstreaming, in a similar manner to the way in which the existing EC Treaty, Article 3(2) has underpinned gender mainstreaming.

Beyond these overarching commitments, mainstreaming is unlikely to function effectively unless it is supported by a thorough institutional framework for its practical implementation. The current mechanisms are not sufficient; fundamentally, the impact assessment procedure is couched in reactive terms of

[25] Commission (n 6 above) 6–7.

[26] Consolidated version of the TFEU [2008] OJ C115/53.

[27] Art 21.

[28] Art 22; J Shaw, 'Mainstreaming equality and diversity in European Union law and policy' in J Holder and C O'Cinnéide (eds), *Current Legal Problems 2005, Vol 58* (Oxford: OUP, 2006) 255, 273.

compliance and non-infringement,[29] rather than mainstreaming's positive agenda of promoting equality. The experience of gender mainstreaming suggests that better institutional structures are needed both to facilitate and to monitor mainstreaming. The Commission's 2006 gender equality 'roadmap' identified various structures performing different functions. These include an inter-service group on gender equality involving *all* DGs; a 'High Level Group on gender mainstreaming' composed of national experts working with the Council Presidencies; and a separate High Level Group focusing on gender mainstreaming in the structural funds.[30] Furthermore, the Expert Group on Gender, Social Inclusion and Employment provides external academic analysis of gender mainstreaming within the OMC processes. It is not suggested that these committees are exemplars which should be automatically reproduced in respect of ethnic equality mainstreaming, but they do provide an indication of the need for more elaborate structures if mainstreaming is to be more than an ephemeral political initiative.

A key challenge in extending mainstreaming to ethnic equality is finding the right balance with the existing mechanisms on gender mainstreaming and the need to consider also other discrimination grounds. Inevitably, it would be administratively cumbersome and inefficient to create separate mainstreaming structures for each of the discrimination grounds found in EC Treaty, Article 13. Moreover, this would reinforce a compartmentalized mindset which neglects the relevance of intersectionality. There are good reasons, therefore, to design inclusive processes for mainstreaming which try to embrace all discrimination grounds. As mentioned earlier, all-encompassing initiatives should not, though, be so rigid as to prevent space for recognition of divergent policy priorities.

A recent study for the Commission on non-discrimination mainstreaming proposed that all DGs be required to prepare 'equality plans' with an associated periodic reporting procedure.[31] This approach, which echoes that pursued in states such as the UK and Finland, could offer a structured mechanism through which each branch of the Commission would be compelled to explain its approach to mainstreaming and to set targets against which it would be publicly accountable. In this respect, it is worth recalling the vital role that external agencies can play in overseeing the implementation of mainstreaming. Chapter 3 identified that in some Member States this function was attributed to national equality bodies. At EU level, the Fundamental Rights Agency could conceivably be given a mandate as an external evaluator of mainstreaming by the EU institutions.

[29] O de Schutter, 'Mainstreaming human rights in the European Union' in P Alston and O de Schutter (eds), *Monitoring Fundamental Rights in the European Union—The Contribution of the Fundamental Rights Agency* (Oxford: Hart Publishing, 2005) 37, 56.

[30] Commission, 'A roadmap for equality between women and men, 2006–2010' (Luxembourg: OOPEC, 2006) 34.

[31] Centre for Strategy and Evaluation Services, 'Non-discrimination mainstreaming—instruments, case studies and way forwards' (Brussels: Commission, 2007) 31.

One dimension to the evaluation of mainstreaming is measuring progress. This underlines the nexus between mainstreaming and data collection. Throughout this book, the shortage of data, be it in relation to employment, education, or racist crime, regularly featured as a factor hindering the evolution of anti-racism policies. Belated political recognition of the need for data collection came from the Council of Ministers in November 2007:

> The collection of data on discrimination and equality is an essential tool for, firstly, properly assessing the extent and type of discrimination issues which individuals face and, secondly, designing, adapting, monitoring and evaluating policies.[32]

It would be premature to assume that this is a genuine turning point in the debate; however, it is the clearest political recognition to date of the merits of data collection. Unlike grounds such as gender or age, finding a consensus on the relevant categories for ethnic data collection is inherently problematic at pan-European level. Even if the principle of ethnic monitoring were accepted by all states, data will only make sense in the national context if the categories resonate with the domestic demographic profile. The UK is well known as the Member State which collects the most extensive data in relation to ethnic origin, yet the systems used in the UK would not be automatically transferable to other Member States. For example, ethnic categories in the UK do not distinguish between Russians, Estonians, or Latvians, whereas this is a key boundary elsewhere. The UK census data do not specifically include Roma/Travellers, but this is obviously the highest profile issue in many central European states. Although it is unlikely that a harmonized system of ethnic data collection could be easily constructed at European level, there are surrogate characteristics which are less sensitive, such as nationality or country of birth (including country of birth of parents).[33] Ultimately, the key objective might not be precisely comparable data, but rather to ensure that each Member State has effective data collection systems which monitor the ethnic stratifications relevant to the domestic society.

Taking some or all of the steps discussed above will undoubtedly not provide any 'quick-fix' solutions to the complex social challenge of promoting equality; a decade of gender mainstreaming has produced only mixed results.[34] Effective mainstreaming should ensure, as a minimum, that the goals of anti-discrimination legislation are not undermined by law and policy in other fields. More broadly, mainstreaming offers an additional route through which to pursue the long path to achieving equality.

[32] Council Resolution on the follow-up to the European Year of Equal Opportunities for All [2007] OJ C308/1.

[33] Such data are beginning to emerge via the European Survey on Income and Living Conditions: see Ch 6. Data collection based on nationality and country of origin is, though, less useful in measuring the situation of Roma communities.

[34] Beveridge (n 17 above).

Bibliography

A. EUROPEAN UNION OFFICIAL DOCUMENTATION (COMMISSION, COUNCIL, PARLIAMENT)

Commission

'Report on the implementation in the Member States of Directive 77/486/EEC on the education of the children of migrant workers' COM (88) 787

'Communication on racism, xenophobia and anti-Semitism' COM (1995) 653

'Proposal for a Council Directive on the framework agreement on parental leave concluded by UNICE, CEEP, and the ETUC' COM (96) 26

'Incorporating equal opportunities for women and men into all Community policies and activities' COM (1996) 67

'Equality of opportunity for people with disabilities – a new European Community Disability Strategy' COM (1996) 406-1

'Illegal and harmful content on the internet' COM (96) 487

'An action plan against racism' COM (1998) 183

'European Year Against Racism – Directory of Projects' (Luxembourg: OOPEC, 1998)

'1997 European Year Against Racism – closing conference report' (Luxembourg: OOPEC, 1998)

'Countering racism, xenophobia and anti-Semitism in the candidate countries' COM (1999) 256

'Proposal for a Council Directive implementing the principle of equal treatment between persons irrespective of racial or ethnic origin' COM (1999) 566

'Communication establishing guidelines for the Community Initiative Equal concerning transnational cooperation to promote new means of combating all forms of discrimination and inequalities in connection with the labour market' [2000] OJ C127/2

'Mainstreaming equal opportunities in the Structural Funds' (Luxembourg: OOPEC, 2000)

'Towards employment for all – combating racism and promoting the integration of migrants' (Luxembourg: OOPEC, 2000)

'Report on the implementation of the action plan against racism – mainstreaming the fight against racism' (Brussels: Commission, 2000)

'Draft detailed work programme for the follow-up of the report on the concrete objectives of education and training systems' COM (2001) 501

'Proposal for a Framework Decision on combating racism and xenophobia' COM (2001) 664

'Communication on a common policy on illegal immigration' COM (2001) 672

'Assessment of the implementation of the 2001 Employment Guidelines' SEC (2001) 1398

'Employment policies in the EU and in the Member States: Joint Employment Report 2000' (Luxembourg: OOPEC, 2001)

'Green paper on a Community return policy on illegal residents' COM (2002) 175

'Communication on impact assessment' COM (2002) 276

'Taking stock of five years of the European Employment Strategy' COM (2002) 416
'Communication on a Community return policy on illegal residents' COM (2002) 564
'Legal reasoning for not referring to the concept of "public incitement to discrimination" in the Commission's proposal for a Council Framework Decision on combating racism and xenophobia' SEC (2002) 375
'Joint report on social inclusion' (Luxembourg: OOPEC, 2002)
'Compendium: Transnational actions for the exchange of information and good practice' (Brussels: Commission, 2002)
'Impact evaluation of the EES. Background paper: social inclusion' (2002): <http://europa.eu.int/comm/employment_social/employment_strategy/eval/papers/inclusion_en.pdf> accessed 18 June 2008.
'Annual report on equal opportunities for women and men in the European Union 2002' COM (2003) 98
'Proposal for a Council Decision on guidelines for the employment policies of the Member States' COM (2003) 176
'Strengthening the social dimension of the Lisbon Strategy: streamlining open coordination in the field of social protection' COM (2003) 261
'Communication on immigration, integration and employment' COM (2003) 336
'Communication on the activities of the European Monitoring Centre on Racism and Xenophobia, together with proposals to recast Council Regulation (EC) 1035/97' COM (2003) 483
'Proposal for a Council Framework Decision on the European Evidence Warrant for obtaining objects, documents or data for use in criminal proceedings' COM (2003) 688
'Communication establishing the guidelines for the second round of the Community Initiative Equal concerning transnational cooperation to promote new means of combating all forms of discrimination and inequalities in the labour market – "free movement of ideas"' COM (2003) 840
'Employment in Europe 2003' (Luxembourg: OOPEC, 2003)
'Equality, diversity and enlargement' (Luxembourg: OOPEC, 2003)
'Employment policies in the EU and in the Member States: Joint Employment Report 2002' (Luxembourg: OOPEC, 2003)
'Proposal for a Council Framework Decision on certain procedural rights in criminal proceedings throughout the European Union' COM (2004) 328
'Equality and non-discrimination in an enlarged European Union' COM (2004) 379
'Study on the links between legal and illegal migration' COM (2004) 412
'First annual report on migration and integration' COM (2004) 508
'Progress towards the common objectives in education and training – indicators and benchmarks' SEC (2004) 73
'The situation of Roma in an enlarged European Union' (Luxembourg: OOPEC, 2004)
'Joint report on social inclusion 2004' (Luxembourg: OOPEC, 2004)
'Comparative study on the collection of data to measure the extent of discrimination within the United States, Canada, Australia, the United Kingdom and the Netherlands' (Luxembourg: OOPEC, 2004)
'Facing the challenge – the Lisbon strategy for growth and employment' (Luxembourg: OOPEC, 2004).

'Healthier, safer and more confident citizens: a health and consumer protection strategy' COM (2005) 115

'Restructuring and employment: anticipating and accompanying restructuring in order to develop employment – the role of the European Union' COM (2005) 120

'Compliance with the Charter of Fundamental Rights in Commission legislative proposals – methodology for systematic and rigorous monitoring' COM (2005) 172

'Non-discrimination and equal opportunities for all – a framework strategy' COM (2005) 224

'Second annual report on migration and integration' COM (2005) 389

'Proposal for a EP and Council Directive on common standards and procedures in Member States for returning illegally staying third-country nationals' COM (2005) 391

'Proposal for a Council Framework Decision on the protection of personal data processed in the framework of police and judicial cooperation in criminal matters' COM (2005) 475

'Proposal for a Directive amending Council Directive 89/552/EEC on the coordination of certain provisions laid down by law, regulation or administrative action in Member States concerning the pursuit of television broadcasting activities' COM (2005) 646

'Policy plan on legal migration' COM (2005) 669

'Working together, working better: a new framework for the open method of coordination of social protection and inclusion policies in the European Union' COM (2005) 706

'Proposal for a Council Framework Decision on the protection of personal data processed in the framework of police and judicial co-operation in criminal matters – impact assessment' SEC (2005) 1241

'Report on social inclusion in the 10 new Member States 2005' (Luxembourg: OOPEC, 2005)

'Amended proposal for an EP and Council Decision establishing a second programme of Community action in the field of health and consumer protection (2007–2013)' COM (2006) 234

'Communication on policy priorities in the fight against illegal immigration of third-country nationals' COM (2006) 402

'The application of Directive 2000/43/EC of 29 June 2000 implementing the principle of equal treatment between persons irrespective of racial or ethnic origin' COM (2006) 643

'Green paper: modernising labour law to meet the challenges of the 21st century' COM (2006) 708

'Evaluation of the open method of coordination for social protection and social inclusion' SEC (2006) 345

'Employment in Europe 2006' (Luxembourg: OOPEC, 2006)

'Social inclusion in Europe 2006' (Luxembourg: OOPEC, 2006)

'A roadmap for equality between women and men, 2006–2010' (Luxembourg: OOPEC, 2006)

'Joint report on social protection and social inclusion 2006' (Luxembourg: OOPEC, 2006)

'Portfolio of overarching indicators and streamlined social inclusion, pensions and health portfolios' D(2006), 7 June 2006: <http://ec.europa.eu/employment_social/social_inclusion/docs/2006/indicators_en.pdf> accessed 18 June 2008.

'Lifelong Learning Programme: Part 1 – priorities of the 2007 general call for proposals' EAC/61/2006, 20 December 2006

'Proposal for a EP and Council Directive providing for sanctions against employers of illegally staying third-country nationals' COM (2007) 249
'Third annual report on migration and integration' COM (2007) 512
'Stepping up the fight against undeclared work' COM (2007) 628
'Proposal for a Council Directive on the conditions of entry and residence of third-country nationals for the purposes of highly qualified employment' COM (2007) 637
'Proposal for a Council Directive on a single application procedure for a single permit for third-country nationals to reside and work in the territory of a Member State and on a common set of rights for third-country workers legally residing in a Member State' COM (2007) 638
'Joint report on social protection and social inclusion – supporting document' SEC (2007) 329
'Proposal for a EP and Council Directive providing for sanctions against employers of illegally staying third-country nationals – impact assessment' SEC (2007) 603
'Tackling multiple discrimination – practices, policies and laws' (Luxembourg: OOPEC, 2007)
'Joint Report on Social Protection and Social Inclusion 2007' (Luxembourg: OOPEC, 2007)
Impact Assessment Board, Document SG C-2 D(2007) 3497, 18 April 2007
'A common immigration policy for Europe: principles, actions and tools' COM (2008) 359
'A renewed commitment to social Europe: reinforcing the open method of coordination for social protection and social inclusion' COM (2008) 418
'Proposal for a EP and Council Directive on the establishment of a European Works Council or a procedure in Community-scale undertakings and Community-scale groups of undertakings for the purposes of informing and consulting employees (recast)' COM (2008) 419
'Non-discrimination and equal opportunities: a renewed commitment' COM (2008) 420/3
'Migration and mobility: challenges and opportunities for EU education systems' COM (2008) 423
'Proposal for a Council Directive on implementing the principle of equal treatment between persons irrespective of religion or belief, disability, age or sexual orientation' COM (2008) 426
'Proposal for a EP and Council Directive on the establishment of a European Works Council or a procedure in Community-scale undertakings and Community-scale groups of undertakings for the purposes of informing and consulting employees (recast) – impact assessment' SEC (2008) 2166
'Community instruments and policies for Roma inclusion' Commission Staff Working Paper, 2 July 2008
'Report on equality between women and men 2008' (Luxembourg: OOPEC, 2008)
'The social situation in the European Union 2007' (Luxembourg: OOPEC, 2008)

Council

Resolution on school provision for gypsy and traveller children [1989] OJ C153/3
Consultative Commission on Racism and Xenophobia, 'Final Report' Ref 6906/1/95 Rev 1 Limite RAXEN 24 (Brussels: General Secretariat of the Council of the European Union, 1995)

Resolution on the response of educational systems to the problems of racism and xenophobia [1995] OJ C312/1

'Note de Comité K.4 au Coreper' Ref 7808/1/98 REV 1, 29 April 1998

'Report on indicators in the field of poverty and social exclusion' Ref 13509/01 SOC 415, ECOFIN 310, EDUC 126, SAN 138, 5 November 2001

'Proposal for a Council Framework Decision on combating racism and xenophobia' Ref 5983/02 DROIPEN 4, 6 February 2002

'Proposal for a Framework Decision on combating racism and xenophobia' Ref 10338/02 DROIPEN 44, 25 June 2002

'Fight against poverty and social exclusion: common objectives for the second round of National Action Plans' Ref 14164/1/02 SOC 508, 25 November 2002

'Detailed work programme on the follow-up of the objectives of education and training systems in Europe' [2002] OJ C142/1

Resolution on transforming undeclared work into regular employment [2003] OJ C260/1

'Brussels European Council: 12 and 13 December 2003. Presidency Conclusions' POLGEN 2, 5 February 2004

'Press Release: 2618th Council Meeting Justice and Home Affairs' 14615/04 (Presse 321), 19 November 2004

'Proposal for a Framework Decision on combating racism and xenophobia' Ref 6229/05 DROIPEN 10, 10 February 2005

'Proposal for a Framework Decision on combating racism and xenophobia' Ref 8994/05 DROIPEN 24, 19 May 2005

'Working together, working better: a new framework for the open coordination of social protection and inclusion policies in the European Union – Joint Social Protection Committee / Economic Policy Committee Opinion' Ref 6801/06 SOC 96, ECOFIN 67, SAN 45, 27 February 2006

'Joint employment report 2004/2005' Ref 7010/05, SOC 102, ECOFIN 77, 9 March 2005

'Presidency Conclusions – 23/24 March 2006' Ref 7775/06

'Joint Employment Report 2006/07' Ref 6706/07, SOC 74, ECOFIN 89, EDUC 39, 23 February 2007

'Proposal for a Council Framework Decision on the European Evidence Warrant (EEW) for obtaining objects, documents or data for use in criminal proceedings' Ref 9913/07 COPEN 72, 25 May 2007

'Proposal for a Council Framework Decision on the European Evidence Warrant (EEW) for obtaining objects, documents or data for use in criminal proceedings' Ref 10511/07 COPEN 90, 11 June 2007

'Proposal for a Council Framework Decision on combating certain forms and expressions of racism and xenophobia by means of criminal law' Ref 11522/07 DROIPEN 68, 19 July 2007

'Re-consultation of the EP' Ref 11523/1/07 REV 1 DROIPEN 69, 20 July 2007

'Proposal for a Council Framework Decision on the protection of personal data processed in the framework of police and judicial cooperation in criminal matters' Ref 11365/1/07 Rev 1, CRIMORG 118, 21 September 2007

'Health and Migration in the EU' Ref 15609/07, 29 November 2007

'Proposal for a Council Framework Decision on the protection of personal data processed in the framework of police and judicial cooperation in criminal matters' Ref 16069/07, 11 December 2007

'Council Framework Decision on the European Evidence Warrant (EEW) for the purpose of obtaining objects, documents or data for use in proceedings in criminal matters' Ref 13076/07 COPEN 132, 21 December 2007

Resolution on the follow-up of the European Year of Equal Opportunities for All [2007] OJ C308/1

'Key messages to the Spring European Council in the field of education and training' Ref 5586/08 EDU 25 SOC 40, 25 January 2008

'Council Framework Decision on combating certain forms and expressions of racism and xenophobia by means of criminal law' Ref 16771/07 DROIPEN 127, 26 February 2008

'Country-specific integrated recommendations' Ref 6775/08, 26 February 2008

'Joint Employment Report 2007/2008' Ref 7169/08 SOC 143 ECOFIN 95 EDUC 67, 3 March 2008

'Joint Report on Social Protection and Social Inclusion 2008' Ref 7274/08, 4 March 2008

'Council Framework Decision on the European Evidence Warrant (EEW) for the purpose of obtaining objects, documents or data for use in proceedings in criminal matters' Ref 6388/1/08 REV 1 COPEN 28, 6 May 2008

Parliament

'Report of the Committee of Inquiry on Racism and Xenophobia' (Luxembourg: OOPEC, 1991)

'Report on the communication from the Commission on countering racism, xenophobia and anti-Semitism in the candidate countries' [Ludford] A5-55/2000, PE 232.460

Resolution on racism and xenophobia [1993] OJ C342/19

Resolution on the communication from the Commission on racism, xenophobia and anti-Semitism [1996] OJ C152/57

Resolution embodying Parliament's opinion on the proposal for a Council Directive establishing a general framework for informing and consulting employees in the European Community [1999] OJ C219/228

Resolution on the proposal for a Council Directive on implementing the principle of equal treatment between persons irrespective of racial or ethnic origin [2001] OJ C59/271

Resolution on the proposal for a Council Framework Decision on combating racism and xenophobia [2003] OJ C271E/558

Resolution on the situation of Roma in the European Union [2006] OJ C45E/129

Position of the EP adopted at first reading on 16 March 2006 with a view to the adoption of Decision No .../2006/EC of the EP and of the Council establishing a *second* programme of Community action in the field of *health* (2007–2013) [2006] OJ C291E/372

Resolution on the proposal for a Council Framework Decision on the protection of personal data processed in the framework of police and judicial cooperation in criminal matters, P6_TA-PROV(2007)0230, 7 June 2007

Resolution on the proposal for a Council Framework Decision on combating certain forms and expressions of racism and xenophobia by means of criminal law, P6_TA-PROV(2007)0552, 29 November 2007

B. GENERAL BIBLIOGRAPHY

Aasland, A 'Russians and the Economy' in N Muižnieks (ed), *Latvian-Russian Relations: Domestic and International Dimensions* (Riga: LU Akadēmiskais apgāds, 2006) 53.

Ahmed, T and Hervey, T, 'The European Union and cultural diversity: a missed opportunity?' in European Centre for Minority Issues (eds), *European Yearbook of Minority Issues Vol 3, 2003/04* (Leiden: Koninklijke Brill NV, 2005) 43.

Alba, R, Handl, J, and Müller, W, 'Ethnic inequalities in the German school system' in P Schuck and R Munz (eds), *Paths to Inclusion – the Integration of Migrants in the United States and Germany* (Oxford: Berghahn Books, 1998) 115.

Ales, E, 'La lotta all'esclusione sociale attraverso l'open method of co-ordination: prime riflessioni (2000–2002)' in M Barbera (ed), *Nuove forme di regolazione: il metodo aperto di coordinamento delle politiche sociali* (Milan: Giuffrè, 2006) 173.

Ales, E, 'Dalla politica sociale europea alla politica europea di coesione economica e sociale. Considerazioni critiche sugli sviluppi del modello sociale europeo nella stagione del metodo aperto di coordinamento' (2007) Working Paper 51/2007, Centro studi di diritto del lavoro europeo 'Massimo D'Antona', Università degli Studi di Catania.

Alibhai-Brown, Y, *After Multiculturalism* (London: The Foreign Policy Centre, 2000).

Allen, S and Macey, M, 'Race and ethnicity in the European context' (1990) 41 *British Journal of Sociology* 375.

Ambrosini, M and Barone, C, 'Employment and working conditions of migrant workers' (Dublin: European Foundation for the Improvement of Living and Working Conditions, 2007).

Amnesty International, 'Linguistic minorities in Estonia: discrimination must end' (Amnesty International, 2006) <http://web.amnesty.org/library/index/engeur510022006> accessed 16 June 2008.

Anthias, F, 'Anti-racism, multiculturalism and struggles for a multicultural democracy' in M Roche and R Van Berkel (eds), *European Citizenship and Social Exclusion* (Aldershot: Ashgate, 1997) 247.

Armstrong, K, 'Tackling social exclusion through OMC: reshaping the boundaries of EU governance' in T Börzel and R Cichowski (eds), *State of the Union: Law, Politics and Society, Vol 6* (Oxford: OUP, 2003) 170.

Ashiagbor, D, *The European Employment Strategy – Labour Market Regulation and New Governance* (Oxford: OUP, 2005).

Aston, J, Hill, D, and Tackey, N D, 'The experience of claimants in race discrimination Employment Tribunal cases' Employment Relations Research Series No 55 (London: Department of Trade and Industry, 2006).

Atkinson, A, 'Social inclusion and the European Union' (2002) 40 JCMS 625.

Atkinson, A, Marlier, E, and Nolan, B, 'Indicators and targets for social inclusion in the European Union' (2004) 42 JCMS 47.

Audit Commission, 'The journey to race equality – delivering improved services to local communities' (London: Audit Commission, 2004).

Babuisk, F, 'Legitimacy, statistics and research methodology – who is Romani in Hungary today and what are we (not) allowed to know about Roma' (2004) *Roma Rights Quarterly* Issue 2.

Bancroft, A, *Roma and Gypsy-Travellers in Europe – Modernity, Race, Space and Exclusion* (Aldershot: Ashgate, 2005).

Bantekas, I, 'The principle of mutual recognition in EU criminal law' (2007) 32 ELR 365.

Banton, M, *The International Politics of Race* (Cambridge: Polity Press, 2002).

Barbera, M, 'I problemi teorici e pratici posti dal metodo di coordinamento aperto delle politiche sociali' in M Barbera (ed), *Nuove forme di regolazione: il metodo aperto di coordinamento delle politiche sociali* (Milan: Giuffrè, 2006) 1.

Barmes L and Ashtiany, S, 'The diversity approach to achieving equality: potential and pitfalls' (2003) 32 ILJ 274.

Barnard, C, *EC Employment Law* (3rd edn, Oxford: OUP, 2006).

Barnett Donaghy, T, 'Mainstreaming: Northern Ireland's participative-democratic approach' (2004) 32 *Policy & Politics* 49.

Barsa, P, 'Ethnocultural justice in East European states and the case of Czech Roma' in W Kymlicka and M Opalski (eds), *Can Liberal Pluralism be Exported? Western Political Theory and Ethnic Relations in Eastern Europe* (Oxford: OUP, 2001) 243.

Begg, I and Marlier, E, '"Feeding in" and "feeding out", and integrating immigrants and ethnic minorities' (Brussels: Commission, 2007).

Behning, U and Serrano Pascual, A, 'Comparison of the adaptation of gender mainstreaming in national employment strategies' in U Behning and A Serrano Pascual (eds), *Gender Mainstreaming in the European Employment Strategy* (Brussels: European Trade Union Institute, 2001) 321.

Bell, M, 'Mainstreaming equality norms into European Union asylum law' (2001) 26 ELR 20.

——, *Anti-discrimination Law and the European Union* (Oxford: OUP, 2002).

——, 'Combating racial discrimination through the European Employment Strategy' in J Bell and C Kilpatrick (eds), *The Cambridge Yearbook of European Legal Studies, Vol 6, 2003–2004* (Oxford: Hart Publishing, 2005) 55.

——, 'EU anti-racism policy: the leader of the pack?' in H Meenan (ed), *Equality Law in an Enlarged Europe* (Cambridge: Cambridge University Press, 2007) 178.

——, 'Civic citizenship and migrant integration' (2007) 13 EPL 311.

——, Chopin I, and Palmer, F, 'Developing Anti-Discrimination Law in Europe – the 25 EU Member States Compared' (3rd edn, Luxembourg: OOPEC, 2007).

Bell, M and Waddington, L, 'Reflecting on inequalities in European equality law' (2003) 28 ELR 349.

Bernhard, S, 'The European paradigm of social exclusion' (2006) 2 JCER 41.

Bernard Brunhes International, 'EU-wide evaluation of the Community Initiative Equal 2000–2006. Final report – Vol 1' (Brussels: Commission, 2006).

Besselink, L, 'Unequal citizenship: integration measures and equality' in S Carerra (ed), *The Nexus Between Immigration, Integration and Citizenship in the EU* (Brussels: Centre for European Policy Studies, 2006) 14.

Betten, L, 'New equality provisions in European law: some thoughts on the fundamental value of equality as a legal principle' in K Economides, L Betten, J Bridge, A Tettenborn, and V Shrubsall (eds), *Fundamental Values* (Oxford: Hart Publishing, 2000) 69.

Beveridge, F, 'Building against the past: the impact of mainstreaming on EU gender law and policy' (2007) 32 ELR 193.

Beveridge, F and Nott, S, 'Gender auditing – making the Community work for women' in T Hervey and D O'Keeffe (eds), *Sex Equality Law in the European Union* (Chichester: John Wiley & Sons, 1996) 383.

——, 'Mainstreaming: a case for optimism and cynicism' (2002) 10 FLS 299.

Beveridge, F, Nott, S, and Stephen, K, 'Mainstreaming and the engendering of policy-making: a means to an end?' (2000) 7 JEPP 385.

——, 'Setting the scene: the why, what and how of promoting equality between the sexes' in F Beveridge, S Nott and K Stephen (eds), *Making Women Count – Integrating Gender into Law and Policy-making* (Aldershot: Ashgate, 2000) 1.

Beveridge, F and Shaw, J, 'Introduction: mainstreaming gender in European public policy' (2002) 10 FLS 209.

Bhandal, L and Hopkins, L, 'Fighting racism and promoting equal rights in the field of education' (Brussels: ENAR, 2007).

Bhattacharyya, G, Ison, L, and Blair, M, 'Minority ethnic attainment and participation in education and training: the evidence' Research Topic Paper RTP01-03 (London: Department for Education and Skills, 2003).

Bhavnani, R, Safia Mirza, H, and Meetoo, V, *Tackling the Roots of Racism – Lessons for Success* (Bristol: Policy Press, 2005).

Bleich, E, *Race Politics in Britain and France – Ideas and Policymaking Since the 1960s* (Cambridge: Cambridge University Press, 2003).

Bleich, E and Feldmann, M C, 'The rise of race? Europeanization and antiracist policymaking in the EU'. Paper presented at the conference 'The impact of Europeanization on Politics and Policy in Europe: Trends and Trajectories', University of Toronto, 7–9 May 2004.

Blum, A, 'Resistance to identity categorization in France' in D Kertzer and D Arel (eds), *Census and Identity – The Politics of Race, Ethnicity and Language in National Censuses* (Cambridge: Cambridge University Press, 2002) 121.

Boelaert-Suominen, S, 'Non-EU nationals and Council Directive 2003/109/EC on the status of third country nationals who are long-term residents: five places forward and possibly three paces back' (2005) 42 CML Rev 1011.

Bonilla-Silva, E, 'Rethinking racism: towards a structural interpretation' (1996) 62 *American Sociological Review* 465.

Booth, C and Bennett, C, 'Gender mainstreaming in the European Union: towards a new conception and practice of equal opportunities?' (2002) 9 *European Journal of Women's Studies* 430.

Borrillo, D, 'Les instruments juridiques français et européens dans la mise en place du principe d'égalité et de non-discrimination' [2002] *Revue français des affaires sociales* 113.

Bouget, D and Prouteau, L, 'National and supranational government-NGO relations: anti-discrimination policy formation in the European Union' (2002) 22 *Public Administration and Development* 31.

Boyle, K and Baldaccini, A, 'A critical evaluation of international human rights approaches to racism' in S Fredman (ed), *Discrimination and Human Rights – The Case of Racism* (Oxford: OUP, 2001) 135.

Brine, J, *The European Social Fund and the EU – Flexibility, Growth and Stability* (London: Sheffield Academic Press, 2002).

Brown, C, 'The Race Directive: towards equality for *all* the peoples of Europe?' (2002) 21 YEL 195.

Buckner, L, Yeandle, S, and Botcherby, S, 'Ethnic minority women and local labour markets' (Manchester: EOC, 2007).

Caestecker, F, 'Registration of allochthonous persons, the experience of Flanders' in J Cormack (ed), 'Proving discrimination: the dynamic implementation of EU anti-discrimination law – the role of specialised bodies' (Brussels: Migration Policy Group, 2003) 11.

Capacity Global, 'Environmental justice and race equality in the European Union' (London: Capacity Global, 2007): <http://www.capacity.org.uk/downloads/CC-EJ%20in%20EU.pdf> accessed 9 May 2008.

Carrera, S, 'A comparison of integration programmes in the EU – trends and weaknesses' CHALLENGE Papers No 1/March 2006 (Brussels: Centre for European Policy Studies, 2006).

Carrera, S and Guild, E, 'An EU framework on sanctions against employers of irregular immigrants – some reflections on the scope, features and added value' Centre for European Policy Studies (CEPS) Policy Brief, No 140, August 2007.

Carter, R, 'Genes, genomes and genealogies: the return of scientific racism?' (2007) 30 *Ethnic and Racial Studies* 546.

Centre for Enterprise and Economic Development Research, 'Young entrepreneurs, women entrepreneurs, co-entrepreneurs and ethnic minority entrepreneurs in the European Union and Central and Eastern Europe' (Brussels: Commission, 2000).

Centre for Strategy and Evaluation Services, 'Evaluation of the European Monitoring Centre on Racism and Xenophobia' (Brussels: Commission, 2002).

Centre for Strategy and Evaluation Services, 'Non-discrimination mainstreaming – instruments, case studies and way forwards' (Brussels: Commission, 2007).

Chakraborti, N, 'Policing Muslim communities' in M Rowe (ed), *Policing Beyond MacPherson – Issues in Policing, Race and Society* (Cullompton: Willan Publishing, 2007) 107.

Chaney, P, 'The post-devolution equality agenda: the case of the Welsh Assembly's statutory duty to promote equality of opportunity' (2004) 32 *Policy & Politics* 63.

Chiattelli, C, 'The reform of the Lisbon Strategy's governance framework – is "new governance" the way forward?' (2006) 2 JCER 4.

Cholewinski, R, *Irregular Migrants: Access to Minimum Social Rights* (Strasbourg: Council of Europe Publishing, 2005).

——, 'Migrants as minorities: integration and inclusion in the enlarged European Union' (2005) JCMS 695.

Chopin, I, 'The Starting Line Group: a harmonised approach to fight racism and to promote equal treatment' (1999) 1 EJML 111.

Chopin, I and Niessen, J, (eds), 'Proposals for legislative measures to combat racism and to promote equal rights in the European Union' (London: CRE, 1998).

Colgan, F, Creegan, C, McKearney, A, and Wright, T, 'Lesbian, gay and bisexual workers: equality, diversity and inclusion in the workplace' (London: Comparative Organisation and Equality Research Centre, London Metropolitan University, 2006).

Collins, D, *The Operation of the European Social Fund* (London: Croom Helm, 1983).

Collins, H, 'Discrimination, equality and social inclusion' (2003) 66 MLR 16.

Corbett, C and Perepa, P, 'Missing out? Autism, education and ethnicity: the reality for families today' (London: The National Austistic Society, 2007).

Craig, P and de Búrca, G, *EU Law – Text, Cases and Materials* (4th edn, Oxford: OUP, 2008).

CRE, 'A lot done, a lot to do – our vision of an integrated Britain' (London: CRE, 2007).

Crenshaw, K, 'Demarginalizing the intersection of race and sex: a black feminist critique of antidiscrimination doctrine, feminist theory, and antiracist politics' in A Phillips (ed), *Feminism and Politics* (Oxford: OUP, 1998) 314.

Crusaid and National AIDS Trust (NAT), 'Poverty and HIV – findings from the Crusaid Hardship Fund 2006' (London: Crusaid/NAT, 2006).

Cullen, H, 'From migrants to citizens? European Community policy on intercultural education' (1996) 45 ICLQ 109.

Curtin, D and Geurts, M, 'Race discrimination and the European Union Anno 1996: from rhetoric to legal remedy?' (1996) 14 *Netherlands Quarterly of Human Rights* 147.

de Búrca, G, 'The constitutional challenge of new governance in the European Union' (2003) 28 ELR 814.

——, 'New modes of governance and the protection of human rights' in P Alston and O de Schutter (eds), *Monitoring Fundamental Rights in the EU – The Contribution of the Fundamental Rights Agency* (Oxford: Hart Publishing, 2005) 25.

——, 'EU race discrimination law: a hybrid model?' in G de Búrca and J Scott (eds) *Law and New Governance in the EU and the US* (Oxford: Hart Publishing, 2006) 97.

de Búrca, G and Scott, J, 'New governance, law and constitutionalism' in G de Búrca and J Scott (eds), *Law and New Governance in the EU and the US* (Oxford: Hart Publishing, 2006) 1.

de la Porte, C and Pochet, P, 'The European Employment Strategy: existing research and remaining questions' (2004) 14 JESP 71.

de Schutter, O, 'Mainstreaming human rights in the European Union' in P Alston and O de Schutter (eds), *Monitoring Fundamental Rights in the European Union – The Contribution of the Fundamental Rights Agency* (Oxford: Hart Publishing, 2005) 37.

——, 'Positive action' in D Schiek, L Waddington, and M Bell (eds), *Cases, Materials and Text on National, Supranational and International Non-discrimination Law* (Oxford: Hart Publishing, 2007) 757.

de Schutter, O and Ringelheim, J, 'Ethnic profiling: a rising challenge for European human rights law' (2008) 71 MLR 331.

de Schutter, O and Verstichel, A, 'Integrating the Roma into European society: time for a new initiative' in European Centre for Minority Issues (eds), *European Yearbook of Minority Issues, Vol 4, 2004/05* (Leiden: Koninklijke Brill, 2006) 429.

de Witte, B, 'Politics versus law in the EU's approach to ethnic minorities' RSC No 2000/4, EUI Working Papers (Florence: European University Institute, 2000).

Department of Work and Pensions, 'Delivering equality for disabled people – a consultation on the extension of the Disability Discrimination Act to functions of public authorities, and the introduction of a duty to promote equality for disabled persons' (London: The Stationery Office, 2004).

Diène, D, 'Report of the Special Rapporteur on contemporary forms of racism, racial discrimination, xenophobia and related intolerance, Doudou Diène, on the manifestations of defamation of religions and in particular on the serious implications of Islamophobia on the enjoyment of all rights' A/HRC/6/6, 21 August 2007.

Donnelly, M, Mullally, S, and Smith, O, 'Making women count in Ireland' in F Beveridge, S Nott, and K Stephen (eds), *Making Women Count – Integrating Gender into Law and Policy-making* (Aldershot: Ashgate, 2000) 23.

Duvall, M, 'Evidence of ethnic profiling in selected European countries' in Open Society Institute Justice Initiative (eds), *Ethnic Profiling by Police in Europe* (New York: Open Society Institute, 2005) 14.

Dworkin, R, 'Bakke's case: are quotas unfair?' in B Boxill (ed), *Race and Racism* (Oxford: OUP, 2001) 297.

EAPN, 'Strengthening the social dimension of the Lisbon Strategy' (Brussels: EAPN, 2007).

——, 'Light year: hard work! Assessing the impact on poverty' (Brussels: EAPN, 2007).

——, 'Social Inclusion Scoreboard' (Brussels: EAPN, 2008).

Edgar, B, 'Policy measures to ensure access to decent housing for migrants and ethnic minorities' (Dundee: Joint Centre for Scottish Housing Research, Universities of Dundee/St Andrews, 2004).

Edwards, J, 'Mainstreaming equality in Wales: the case of the National Assembly building' (2004) 32 *Policy & Politics* 33.

Ellis, E, 'The principle of non-discrimination in the post-Nice era' in A Arnull and D Wincott (eds), *Accountability and Legitimacy in the European Union* (Oxford: OUP, 2002) 291.

Ellis, E, *EU Anti-Discrimination Law* (Oxford: OUP, 2006).

Employment Taskforce, 'Jobs, jobs, jobs – creating more employment in Europe. Report of the Employment Taskforce chaired by Wim Kok' (Brussels: Commission, 2003).

ENAR, 'The voice of the anti-racist movement in Europe' (Brussels: ENAR, undated).

——, '2005 Annual report' (Brussels: ENAR, 2006).

——, '2006 Annual report' (Brussels: ENAR, 2007).

Entzinger, H, 'The dynamics of integration policies: a multidimensional model' in R Koopmans and P Statham (eds), *Challenging immigration and ethnic relations politics* (Oxford: OUP, 2000) 97.

The Equalities Review, 'Fairness and freedom: the final report of the Equalities Review' (London: Cabinet Office, 2007).

Ernst & Young, '2005 evaluation of the Community action programme to combat discrimination – executive summary' (Brussels: Commission, 2005).

——, 'Évaluation du programme d'action communautaire de lutte contre la discrimination (2001–2006) – bilan final 2006' (Brussels: Commission, 2006).

ERRC, 'Ambulance not on the way – the disgrace of healthcare for Roma in Europe' (Budapest: ERRC, 2006).

——, 'The glass box: exclusion of Roma from employment' (Budapest: ERRC, 2007).

ERRC and Númena Centro de Investigaço em Ciências Sociais e Humanas, 'Social inclusion through social services: the case of Roma and Travellers. Assessing the impact of National Action Plans for Social Inclusion in the Czech Republic, France and Portugal' (Budapest: ERRC and Númena Centro de Investigaço em Ciências Sociais e Humanas, 2007).

EUMC, 'Racism and xenophobia in the EU Member States: trends, developments and good practice' Annual report 2003/2004 – Part 2' (Vienna: EUMC, 2004).

——, 'Racist violence in 15 EU Member States – a comparative overview of findings from the RAXEN national focal points reports 2001–2004' (Vienna: EUMC, 2005).

——, 'Antisemitism: summary overview of the situation in the European Union 2001–2005' (Vienna: EUMC, 2006).

EU Network of Independent Experts on Fundamental Rights, 'Combating racism and xenophobia through criminal legislation: the situation in the EU Member States' Opinion 5-2005, 28 November 2005.

——, 'Ethnic profiling' Opinion 4-2006, December 2006.

European Data Protection Supervisor, 'Third opinion of the European Data Protection Supervisor on the proposal for a Council Framework Decision on the protection of personal data processed in the framework of police and judicial co-operation in criminal matters' [2007] OJ C139/1.

Eurydice, 'Integrating immigrant children into schools in Europe' (Brussels: Eurydice, 2004).

Fagan, C, Grimshaw, S, and Rubery, J, 'The subordination of the gender equality objective: the National Reform Programmes and "making work pay" policies' (2006) 37 IRJ 571.

Fagan, C, Urwin, P, and Melling, K, 'Gender inequalities in the risks of poverty and social exclusion for disadvantaged groups in thirty European countries' (Luxembourg: OOPEC, 2006).

Fenton, S, *Ethnicity* (Cambridge: Polity Press, 2003).

Fernández Esteban, M, 'The internet: a new horizon for hatred?' in S Fredman (ed), *Discrimination and Human Rights – The Case of Racism* (Oxford: OUP, 2001) 77.

Ferrera, M, Matsaganis, M, and Sacchi, S, 'Open coordination against poverty: the new EU social inclusion process' (2002) 12 JESP 227.

FitzGerald, M and Sibbitt, R, 'Ethnic monitoring in police forces: a beginning' Home Office Research Study 173 (London: Home Office, 1997).

Flynn, L, 'The implications of Article 13 EC – after Amsterdam, will some forms of discrimination be more equal than others?' (1999) 36 CML Rev 1127

Focus Consultancy, 'Critical review of academic literature relating to the EU Directives to combat discrimination' (Brussels: Commission, 2004).

Fredman, S, 'Affirmative action at the Court of Justice: a critical analysis' in J Shaw (ed), *Social Law and Policy in an Evolving Union* (Oxford: Hart Publishing, 2000).

——, 'Equality: a new generation?' (2001) 30 ILJ 145.

——, 'Combating racism with human rights: the right to equality' in S Fredman (ed), *Discrimination and Human Rights: The Case of Racism* (Oxford: OUP, 2001) 9.

——, *Discrimination Law* (Oxford: OUP, 2002).

——, 'The future of equality in Britain' EOC Working Paper Series No 5 (Manchester: EOC, 2002).

——, 'The age of equality' in S Fredman and S Spencer (eds), *Age as an Equality Issue* (Oxford: Hart Publishing, 2003) 21.

——, 'Changing the norm: positive duties in equal treatment legislation' (2005) 12 MJ 369.

Fredman, S, 'Double trouble: cumulative discrimination and EU law' (2005) 2 *European Anti-Discrimination Law Review* 13.

——, 'Transformation or dilution: fundamental rights in the EU social space' (2006) 12 ELJ 41.

——, *Human Rights Transformed – Positive Rights and Positive Duties* (Oxford: OUP, 2008).

Fundamental Rights Agency, 'Trends and developments 1997–2005 – combating ethnic and racial discrimination and promoting equality in the European Union' (Hungary: Printer Elanders Hungary, 2007).

Geddes, A, 'Lobbying for migrant inclusion in the European Union: new opportunities for transnational advocacy?' (2000) 7 JEPP 632.

——, 'Integrating immigrants and minorities in a wider and deeper Europe' in W Spohn and A Triandafyllidou (eds), *Europeanisation, National Identities and Migration – Changes in Boundary Constructions between Western and Eastern Europe* (London: Routledge, 2003) 83.

Geddes, A and Guiraudon, V, 'Britain, France and EU anti-discrimination policy: the emergence of an EU policy paradigm' (2004) 27 *West European Politics* 334.

Gelazis, N, 'The European Union and the statelessness problem in the Baltic states' (2004) 6 EJML 225.

Gerards, J, 'Discrimination grounds' in D Schiek, L Waddington, and M Bell (eds), *Cases, Materials and Text on National, Supranational and International Non-discrimination Law* (Oxford: Hart Publishing, 2007) 33.

Gijzen, M, *Selected Issues in Equal Treatment Law: A Multi-layered Comparison of European, English and Dutch Law* (Antwerp: Intersentia, 2006).

Gillberg, M, 'Making women count in Sweden' in F Beveridge, S Nott, and K Stephen (eds), *Making Women Count – Integrating Gender into Law and Policy-making* (Aldershot: Ashgate, 2000) 131.

Giubboni, S, 'Immigrazione e politiche dell'Unione Europea: dal Trattato di Roma alla Costituzione per l'Europa' (2005) no. 106 / anno XXVII *Giornale di diritto del lavoro e di relazioni industriali* 205.

Godwin, K, 'Race equality: an ongoing obligation' (2006) 154 *Equal Opportunities Review* 13.

Goldston, J, 'Toward a Europe without ethnic profiling' in Open Society Institute Justice Initiative (eds), *Ethnic Profiling by Police in Europe* (New York: Open Society Institute, 2005) 6.

Goodall, K, 'Incitement to religious hatred: all talk and no substance?' (2007) 70 MLR 89.

Goodey, J, 'Racist violence in Europe: challenges for official data collection' (2007) 30 *Ethnic and Racial Studies* 570.

Gori, G, *Towards an EU Right to Education* (The Hague: Kluwer Law International, 2001).

Groenendijk, K, 'The Long-Term Residents Directive, denizenship and integration' in A Baldaccini, E Guild, and H Toner (eds), *Whose Freedom, Security and Justice? EU Immigration and Asylum Law and Policy* (Oxford: Hart Publishing, 2007) 429.

Group of Specialists on Mainstreaming, 'Gender mainstreaming – conceptual framework, methodology and presentation of good practice. Final report of activities of the Group of Specialists on Mainstreaming (EG-S-MS)' (Strasbourg: Council of Europe, 1998).

Guglielmo, R and Walters, T, 'Migrating towards minority status: shifting European policy towards Roma' (2005) 43 JCMS 763.

Guild, E, 'The EC Directive on race discrimination: surprises, possibilities and limitations' (2000) 29 ILJ 416.

Guiraudon, V, 'Anti-discrimination policy' in P Graziano and M Vink (eds), *Europeanization – New Research Agendas* (Houndmills, Palgrave Macmillan, 2007) 295.

Guolo, R, *Xenofobi e xenofili – gli italiani e l'islam* (Rome: Editori Laterza, 2003).

Halleskov, L, 'The Long-Term Residents Directive: a fulfillment of the Tampere objective of near-equality?' (2005) 7 EJML 181.

Haney López, I, *White by Law – The Legal Construction of Race* (New York: New York University Press, 1996).

Hannett, S, 'Equality at the intersections: the legislative and judicial failure to tackle multiple discrimination' (2003) 23 OJLS 65.

Hantrais, H, *Social Policy in the European Union* (3rd edn, Houndmills: Palgrave Macmillan, 2007).

Harrison, M, Law, I and Phillips, D, 'Migrants, minorities and housing: exclusion, discrimination and anti-discrimination in 15 Member States of the European Union' (Luxembourg: OOPEC, 2005).

Hatzopoulos, V, 'Why the open method of coordination is bad for you: a letter to the EU' (2007) 13 ELJ 309.

Heintze, H, 'Article 3' in M Weller (ed), *The Rights of Minorities in Europe – A Commentary on the European Framework Convention for the Protection of National Minorities* (Oxford: OUP, 2005) 107.

Hepple, B, 'Race and law in Fortress Europe' (2004) 67 MLR 1.

Hervey, T, *European Social Law and Policy* (London: Longman, 1998).

——, 'Putting Europe's house in order: racism, race discrimination and xenophobia after the Treaty of Amsterdam' in D O'Keeffe and P Twomey (eds), *Legal Issues of the Amsterdam Treaty* (Oxford: Hart, 1999) 329.

——, 'The European Union and the governance of health care' in G de Búrca and J Scott (eds), *Law and New Governance in the EU and the US* (Oxford: Hart Publishing, 2006) 179.

Hervey, T and McHale, J, *Health Law and the European Union* (Cambridge: Cambridge University Press, 2004).

Hervey, T and Trubek, L, 'Freedom to provide health care services within the EU: an opportunity for a transformative Directive' (2007) 13 CJEL 623.

High Level Advisory Group of Experts on the social integration of ethnic minorities and their full participation in the labour market, 'Ethnic minorities in the labour market – an urgent call for social inclusion' (Brussels: European Commission, 2007).

Hinds, B, 'Mainstreaming equality in Northern Ireland' in A Dobrowolsky and V Hart (eds), *Women Making Constitutions – New Politics and Comparative Perspectives* (Houndmills: Palgrave Macmillan, 2003) 185.

Hirschman, C, 'The origins and demise of the concept of race' (2004) 30 *Population and Development Review* 385.

Hollo, L, 'Equality for Roma in Europe – a roadmap for action' (New York: Open Society Institute, 2005).

Home Office, 'Consultation on the implementation of new powers to prevent illegal migrant working in the UK' (London: Home Office, 2007).

——, 'Prevention of illegal working – Immigration, Asylum and Nationality Act 2006. Equality impact assessment' (London: Home Office, 2007)

——, 'Guidance for employers on the avoidance of unlawful discrimination in employment practice whilst seeking to prevent illegal working – Code of Practice' (London: Home Office, 2008).

Howard, E, 'Anti race discrimination measures in Europe: an attack on two fronts' (2005) 11 ELJ 468.

——, 'The case for a considered hierarchy of discrimination grounds in EU law' (2006) 13 MJ 443.

——, 'The road to equality – developing the protection against discrimination on racial or ethnic grounds within the European Union' Ph.D. thesis, Queen Mary, University of London, February 2007.

——, 'The European Year of Equal Opportunities for All – 2007: is the EU moving away from a formal idea of equality?' (2008) 14 ELJ 168.

——, 'Race and racism – why does European law have difficulties with definitions?' (2008) 24 IJCLLIR 5.

Hussain, Y, 'South Asian disabled women: negotiating identities' [2005] *The Sociological Review* 522.

ISTAT, 'La presenza straniera in Italia: caratteristiche socio-demografiche' (Rome: ISTAT, 2007).

Izzi, D, *Eguaglianza e differenze nei rapporti di lavoro – il diritto antidiscriminatorio tra genere e fattori di rischio emergenti* (Napoli: Casa Editrice Jovene, 2005).

Jahan, R, *The Elusive Agenda – Mainstreaming Women in Development* (London: Zed Books, 1995).

Jandl, M, Kraler, A, and Stepien, A, 'Migrants, minorities and employment – exclusion, discrimination and anti-discrimination in 15 Member States of the European Union' (Luxembourg: OOPEC, 2003).

Jones, J,'The Race Directive: redefining protection from discrimination in EU law' [2003] EHRLR 515.

Juss, S, 'Free movement and the world order' (2004) 16 *International Journal of Refugee Law* 289.

Kasesaru, K and Trumm, A, 'The socio-economic situation of non-Estonians' in M Heidmets (ed), *Estonian Human Development Report 2007* (Tallinn: Eesti Koostöö Kogu, 2008) 46.

Kate, M and Niessen, J, 'Locating immigrant integration policy measures in the machinery of the European Commission' (Brussels: Migration Policy Group, 2007).

Keijzer, N, 'The double criminality requirement' in R Blekxtoon and W van Ballegooij (eds), *Handbook on the European Arrest Warrant* (The Hague: TMC Asser Press, 2005) 137.

Kenner, J, 'Employment and macroeconomics in the EC Treaty: a legal and political symbiosis' (2000) 7 MJ 375.

——, *EU Employment law: From Rome to Amsterdam and Beyond* (Oxford: Hart, 2003).

Kilpatrick, C, 'New EU employment governance and constitutionalism' in G de Búrca and J Scott (eds), *Law and New Governance in the EU and the US* (Oxford: Hart Publishing, 2006) 129.

Kimber, C, 'Recent developments in EC equality law' in M Lucey and C Keville (eds), *Irish Perspectives on EC Law* (Dublin: Round Hall Ltd, 2003) 291.

Kingsley, S, 'Creating the climate for diversity and race equality in health care' (2001) 6 *Ethnicity & Health* 255, 261.

Kundnani, A, 'In a foreign land: the new popular racism' (2001) 43 *Race & Class* 41.

Kymlicka, W, *Multicultural Citizenship* (Oxford: OUP, 1995).

——, *Politics in the Vernacular – Nationalism, Multiculturalism, and Citizenship* (Oxford: OUP, 2001).

——, 'Western political theory and ethnic relations in Eastern Europe' in W Kymlicka and M Opalski (eds), *Can Liberal Pluralism be Exported? Western Political Theory and Ethnic Relations in Eastern Europe* (Oxford: OUP, 2001).

Lenschow, A, 'New regulatory approaches in "greening" EU policies' (2002) 8 ELJ 19.

Lentin, A, *Racism and Anti-racism in Europe* (London: Pluto Press, 2004).

Lester, A, 'Thirty years on: the East African Asians case revisited' [2002] PL 52.

Lloyd, C, 'Anti-racist responses to European integration' in R Koopmans and P Satham (eds), *Challenging Immigration and Ethnic Relations Politics* (Oxford: OUP, 2000) 389.

Loenen, T, 'Indirect discrimination: oscillating between containment and revolution' in T Loenen and P Rodrigues (eds), *Non-discrimination Law: Comparative Perspectives* (The Hague: Kluwer, 1999) 195.

Luciak, M, 'Migrants, minorities and education – documenting discrimination and integration in 15 Member States of the European Union' (Luxembourg: OOPEC, 2004).

Lynch, C, 'Racism in Europe – ENAR Shadow Report 2005' (Brussels: ENAR, 2006).

MacPherson, W, 'The Stephen Lawrence Inquiry – report of an inquiry' (Cm 4262-I, 1999).

Makkonen, T, *European Handbook on Equality Data* (Luxembourg: OOPEC, 2006).

——, 'Report on measures to combat discrimination: Directive 2000/43/EC and 2000/78/EC: Finland' (Brussels: European Commission, 2007).

Mantouvalou, V, 'Servitude and forced labour in the 21st century: the human rights of domestic workers' (2006) 35 ILJ 395.

Marlier, E, Atkinson, A, Cantillon, B, and Nolan, B, *The EU and Social Inclusion – Facing the Challenges* (Bristol: Policy Press, 2007).

Martin, P and Miller, M, 'Employer sanctions: French, German and US experiences' International Migration Papers No 36 (Geneva: International Labour Office, 2000).

Mazey, S, 'Integrating gender – intellectual and "real world" mainstreaming' (2000) 7 JEPP 333.

——, 'Gender mainstreaming strategies in the E.U.: delivering on an agenda?' (2002) 10 FLS 227.

McCabe, C and Keyes, F, 'A review of Travellers' health using primary care as a model of good practice' (Dublin: Pavee Point, 2005).

McColgan, A, 'Reconfiguring discrimination law' [2007] PL 74.

McCrudden, C, 'Institutional discrimination' (1982) 2 OJLS 303.

——, 'Equality' in C Harvey (ed), *Human Rights, Equality and Democratic Renewal in Northern Ireland* (Oxford: Hart Publishing, 2001) 75.

——, 'Theorizing European equality law' in C Costello and E Barry (eds), *Equality in Diversity – The New Equality Directives* (Dublin: Irish Centre for European Law, 2003) 1.

——, *Buying Social Justice – Equality, Government Procurement, and Legal Change* (Oxford: OUP, 2007).

McGonagle, T, 'The international and European legal standards for combating racist expression' in ECRI (eds), *Combating Racism While Respecting Freedom of Expression* (Strasbourg: Council of Europe, 2007) 77.

McInerney, S, 'Equal treatment between persons irrespective of racial or ethnic origin: a comment' (2000) 25 ELR 317.

McMaster, N, *Racism in Europe 1870–2000* (Houndmills: Palgrave, 2001).

McVeigh, R and Lentin, R, 'Situated racisms: a theoretical introduction' in R Lentin and R McVeigh (eds), *Racism and Anti-racism in Ireland* (Belfast: Beyond the Pale Publications, 2002).

Meenan, H (ed), *Equality Law in an Enlarged European Union – Understanding the Article 13 Directives* (Cambridge: Cambridge University Press, 2007).

Miles, R and Brown, M, *Racism* (2nd edn, London: Routledge, 2003).

Ministry of Justice, 'Statistics on race and the criminal justice system – 2006' (London: Ministry of Justice, 2007).

Mitsilegas,V, 'Measuring irregular migration: implications for law, policy and human rights' in B Bogusz, R Cholewinski, A Cygan, and E Szyszczak (eds), *Irregular Migrants: Theoretical, European and International Perspectives* (Leiden: Martinus Nijhoff Publishers, 2004) 29.

——, 'The constitutional implications of mutual recognition in criminal matters in the EU' (2006) 43 CML Rev 1277.

——, 'Constitutional principles of the European Community and European criminal law' (2006) 8 *European Journal of Law Reform* 301.

——, 'Immigration, diversity and integration: the limits of EU law' in P Shah (ed), *Law and Ethnic Plurality: Socio-Legal perspectives* (Leiden: Koninklijke Brill NV, 2007) 31.

Modood, T, 'Ethnic diversity and racial disadvantage in employment' in T Blackstone, B Parekh, and P Sanders (eds), *Race Relations in Britain – A Developing Agenda* (London: Routledge, 1998) 53.

——, '"Difference", cultural racism and anti-racism' in B Boxill (ed), *Race and Racism* (Oxford: OUP, 2001).

Moller Okin, S, 'Is multiculturalism bad for women?' in J Cohen, M Howard, and M Nussbaum (eds), *Is Multiculturalism Bad for Women?* (Princeton: Princeton University Press, 1999) 9.

Monod, J, 'Quelle(s) politique(s) d'intégration au sein de l'Union européenne?' (2007) Fondation Robert Schuman Policy Papers, No 53.

Moon, G, 'Multiple discrimination – problems compounded or solutions found?' (London: Justice, 2007).

Mósesdottir, L, 'Moving Europe towards the dual-breadwinner model' in D Foden and L Magnussen (eds), *Five Years' Experience of the Luxembourg Employment Strategy* (Brussels: European Trade Union Institute, 2003) 183.

Neveu, C, 'Is 'black' an exportable category to mainland Europe? Race and citizenship in a European context' in J Rex and B Drury (eds), *Ethnic Mobilization in a Multi-cultural Europe* (Aldershot: Averbury, 1994) 97.

Niessen, J and Huddleston, T, 'Setting up a system of benchmarking to measure the success of integration policies in Europe' (Brussels: European Parliament, 2007).

Niessen, J, Peiro, M J, and Schibel, Y, *Civic Citizenship and Immigrant Inclusion – A Guide for the Implementation of Civic Citizenship Policies* (Brussels: Migration Policy Group, 2005).

Niessen, J and Schibel, Y, *Handbook on integration for policy-makers and practitioners* (Luxembourg: OOPEC, 2004).

Niessen, J and Schibel, Y, *Handbook on integration for policy-makers and practitioners* (2nd edn, Luxembourg: OOPEC, 2007).

Nott, S, 'Accentuating the positive: alternative strategies for promoting gender equality' in F Beveridge, S Nott, and K Stephen (eds), *Making Women Count – Integrating Gender into Law and Policy-making* (Aldershot: Ashgate, 2000) 247.

Numhauser-Henning, A, 'Report on measures to combat discrimination: Directives 2000/43/EC and 2000/78/EC: Sweden' (Brussels: European Commission, 2007).

O'Cinnéide, C, 'Making use of positive equality duties: the UK experience' in C Costello and E Barry (eds), *Equality in Diversity – The New Equality Directives* (Dublin: Irish Centre for European Law, 2003) 75.

——, 'A new generation of equality legislation? Positive duties and disability rights' in A Lawson and C Gooding (eds), *Disability Rights in Europe – From Theory to Practice* (Oxford: Hart Publishing, 2005) 237.

——, 'Positive duties and gender equality' (2005) 8 *International Journal of Discrimination and the Law* 91.

——, 'Positive action and the limits of existing law' (2006) 13 MJ 351.

OECD, 'Where immigrant students succeed – a comparative review of performance and engagement in PISA 2003' (Paris: OECD, 2006).

Olli, E and Kofod Olsen, B, 'Towards common measures for discrimination: exploring possibilities for combining existing data for measuring ethnic discrimination' (Copenhagen: Centre for Combating Ethnic Discrimination and the Danish Institute of Human Rights, 2005).

Open Society Institute Justice Initiative, '"I can stop and search whoever I want" – police stops of ethnic minorities in Bulgaria, Hungary, and Spain' (New York: Open Society Institute, 2007).

Osler, A and Starkey, H, 'Education for citizenship: mainstreaming the fight against racism?' (2002) 37 *European Journal of Education* 143.

Parekh, B, 'Equality in a multicultural society' in J Franklin (ed), *Equality* (London: Institute for Public Policy Research, 1997) 142.

——, 'Integrating minorities' in T Blackstone, B Parekh, and P Saunders (eds), *Race Relations in Britain – A Developing Agenda* (London: Routledge, 1998) 1.

Parmar, S, 'The European Court of Justice and anti-discrimination law: some reflections on the experience of gender equality jurisprudence for the future interpretation of the

Racial Equality Directive' in J Niessen and I Chopin (eds), *The Development of Legal Instruments to Combat Racism in a Diverse Europe* (Leiden: Martinus Nijhoff, 2004) 131.

Peers, S, 'Implementing equality? The Directive on long-term resident third-country nationals' (2004) 29 ELR 437.

——, *EU Justice and Home Affairs Law* (2nd edn, Oxford: OUP, 2006).

——, 'EU Reform Treaty: Analysis 1: Version 3: JHA provisions' <http://www.statewatch.org/news/2007/oct/eu-refrom-treaty-jha-anal-1-ver-3.pdf> accessed 19 May 2008.

——, 'British and Irish opt-outs from EU Justice and Home Affairs law' <http://www.statewatch.org/news/2007/oct/eu-reform-treaty-uk-ireland-opt-outs.pdf> accessed 19 May 2008.

Percy-Smith, J, 'The contours of social exclusion' in J Percy-Smith (ed), *Policy Responses to Social Exclusion – Towards Inclusion?* (Buckingham: Open University Press, 2000) 4.

Peters, M, Seeds, K, and Harding, C, 'Findings from the survey of claimants in race discrimination Employment Tribunal cases' Employment Relations Research Series No 54 (London: Department of Trade and Industry, 2006).

Piper, N and Satterthwaite, M, 'Migrant women' in R Cholewinski, R Perruchoud and E MacDonald (eds), *International Migration Law – Developing Paradigms and Key Challenges* (The Hague: TMC Asser Press, 2007) 237.

Plachta, M and van Ballegooij, W, 'The Framework Decision on the European arrest warrant and surrender procedures between Member States of the European Union' in R Blekxtoon and W van Ballegooij (eds), *Handbook on the European Arrest Warrant* (The Hague: TMC Asser Press, 2005) 13.

Pollack, M and Hafner-Burton, E, 'Mainstreaming gender in the European Union' (2000) 7 JEPP 432.

PRIAE Research Briefing, 'Minority elderly health and social care in Europe' (2004): <http://www.priae.org/docs/MEC%20European%20Summary%20Findings2.pdf> accessed 10 April 2008.

Radcliffe, P, *'Race', Ethnicity and Difference – Imaging the Inclusive Society* (Maidenhead: Open University Press, 2004).

Rees, T, *Mainstreaming Equality in the European Union – Education, Training and Labour Market Policies* (London: Routledge, 1999).

Reuter, N, Makkonen, T, and Oosi, O, 'Study on data collection to measure the extent and impact of discrimination in Europe' (Brussels: Commission, 2004).

Rodrigues, P, 'Cross-border discrimination: private international law, the denial of the Holocaust and the internet' in T Loenen and P Rodrigues (eds), *Non-discrimination Law: Comparative Perspectives* (Kluwer, The Hague, 1999) 397.

Roseberry, L, *The Limits of Employment Discrimination Law in the United States and European Community* (Copenhagen: DJØF Publishing, 1999).

Rowe, M, *Policing, Race and Racism* (Cullompton: Willan Publishing, 2004).

Rubery, J, 'Gender mainstreaming and gender equality in the EU: the impact of the EU employment strategy' (2002) 33 IRJ 500.

——, Grimshaw, D, Fagan, C, Figueiredo, H, and Smith, M, 'Gender equality still on the European agenda – but for how long?' (2003) 34 IRJ 477.

The Runnymede Trust, *The Future of Multi-ethnic Britain – The Parekh Report* (London: Profile Books, 2002).

Ryan, B, 'The European Union and labour migration: regulating admission or treatment?' in A Baldaccini, E Guild, and H Toner (eds), *Whose Freedom, Security and Justice? EU Immigration and Asylum Law and Policy* (Oxford: Hart Publishing, 2007) 489.

Sánchez-Rubio, B, 'A comparative research study on Roma and employment in Spain' (2006) 16 *ENARgy* 27.

Sasse, G, 'EU conditionality and minority rights: translating the Copenhagen criterion into policy' EUI Working Papers, RSCAS No 2005/16 (Florence: European University Institute, 2005).

Schiek, D, 'Torn between arithmetic and substantive equality? Perspectives on equality in German labour law' (2002) 18 IJCLLIR 149.

——, 'A new framework on equal treatment of persons in EC law?' (2002) 8 ELJ 290.

——, 'Broadening the scope and the norms of EU gender equality law: towards a multidimensional conception of equality law' (2005) 12 MJ 427.

——, 'Indirect discrimination' in D Schiek, L Waddington, and M Bell (eds), *Cases, Materials and Text on National, Supranational and International Non-discrimination Law* (Oxford: Hart Publishing, 2007) 323.

Schoukens, P and Carmichael, L, 'Social exclusion in Europe: testing the limits of European integration' in D Mayes, J Berghman, and R Salais (eds), *Social Exclusion and European Policy* (Cheltenham: Edward Elgar, 2001) 76.

Sciarra, S, 'Social values and the multiple sources of European social law' (1995) 1 ELJ 60.

Scott, J and Trubek, D, 'Mind the gap: law and new approaches to governance in the European Union' (2002) 8 ELJ 1.

Select Committee on European Scrutiny, 'Fourth report' HC (2003–2004) 42-iv.

——, 'Sixteenth Report' HC (2006–2007) 41-xvi.

——, 'Seventeenth Report' HC (2006–2007) 41-xvii.

Select Committee on the European Union, '32nd report – the proposed Framework Decision on racism and xenophobia – an update' HL (2002–2003) 136.

Shaw, J, 'The European Union and gender mainstreaming: constitutionally embedded or comprehensively marginalised?' (2002) 10 FLS 213.

——, 'Mainstreaming equality in European Union law and policymaking' (Brussels: ENAR, 2004).

——, 'Mainstreaming equality and diversity in European Union law and policy' in J Holder and C O'Cinnéide (eds), *Current Legal Problems 2005, Vol 58* (Oxford: OUP, 2006) 255.

Sigona, N, 'Locating "the Gypsy problem". The Roma in Italy: stereotyping, labelling and "nomad camps"' (2005) 31 *Journal of Ethnic and Migration Studies* 741.

Simon, P, '"Ethnic" statistics and data protection in the Council of Europe countries' (Strasbourg: Council of Europe, 2007).

Skidmore, P, 'The European Employment Strategy and labour law: a German case-study' (2004) 29 ELR 52.

Skordas, A, 'Immigration and the market: the Long-Term Residents Directive' (2006) 13 CJEL 201.

Sobotka, E, 'Targeting and mainstreaming the integration of Roma at the EU and European level' (2005) 16 *Equal Voices* 4.

Solomos, J, *Race and Racism in Britain* (3rd edn, Houndmills: Palgrave, 2003).

Solomos, J and Schuster, L, 'Citizenship, multiculturalism and the politics of identity: contemporary dilemmas and policy agendas' in R Koopmans and P Statham (eds), *Challenging Immigration and Ethnic Relations Politics* (Oxford: OUP, 2000).

Soysal, Y, *Limits of Citizenship – Migrants and Postnational Membership in Europe* (Chicago: University of Chicago Press, 1994).

Spencer, S, 'The impact of immigration policy on race relations' in T Blackstone, B Parekh, and P Sanders (eds), *Race Relations in Britain – A Developing Agenda* (London: Routledge, 1998) 74.

Squires, J, 'Is mainstreaming transformative? Theorizing mainstreaming in the context of diversity and deliberation' (2005) 12 *Social Politics* 366.

Squires, J and Wickham-Jones, M, 'New Labour, gender mainstreaming and the Women and Equality Unit' (2004) 6 *British Journal of Politics and International Relations* 81.

Staudt, K, 'Gender mainstreaming: conceptual links to institutional machineries' in S M Rai (ed), *Mainstreaming Gender, Democratising the State? Institutional Mechanisms for the Advancement of Women* (Manchester: Manchester University Press, 2003) 40.

Stephen, K, 'Catalysts for change? The effectiveness of state agencies in promoting equality' in F Beveridge, S Nott, and K Stephen (eds), *Making Women Count – Integrating Gender into Law and Policy-making* (Aldershot: Ashgate, 2000) 223.

Strazzardi, D, 'Nuove strategie di lotta alla discriminazione razziale nell'UE e in Gran Bretagna: il cosidetto principio di *mainstreaming* e il parternatario sociale. Verso un diverso approccio della legislazione antidiscriminatoria?' [2002] *Diritto pubblico comparato ed europeo* Part 1: 161.

Szyszczak, E, 'The evolving European Employment Strategy' in J Shaw (ed), *Social Law and Policy in an Evolving Union* (Oxford: Hart Publishing, 2000) 197.

——, 'Experimental governance: the open method of coordination' (2006) 12 ELJ 486.

Terence Higgins Trust (THT), 'Prejudice, discrimination and HIV' (London: THT, 2001).

Tobler, C, 'Positive action under the revised second equal treatment Directive' in Association française des femmes juristes and European Women Lawyers Association (eds), *L'égalité entre les femmes et hommes et la vie professionnelle – le point sur les développements actuels en Europe* (Paris: Dalloz, 2003) 59.

Toggenburg, G, 'The Race Directive: a new dimension in the fight against ethnic discrimination in Europe' (2001/2) 1 *European Yearbook of Minority Issues* 231.

——, 'Who is managing ethnic and cultural diversity in the European condominium? The moments of entry, integration and preservation' (2005) 43 JCMS 717.

Toner, H, 'Impact assessments and fundamental rights protection in EU law' (2006) 31 ELR 316.

——, 'Impact assessments: a useful tool for "better lawmaking" in EU migration policy?' in A Baldaccini, E Guild, and H Toner (eds), *Whose Freedom, Security and Justice? EU Immigration and Asylum Law and Policy* (Oxford: Hart Publishing, 2007) 109.

Tratar, M and Hot, M, 'Report on measures to combat discrimination: Slovenia' (Brussels: European Commission, 2007).

Triandafyllidou, A, 'Religious diversity and multiculturalism in Southern Europe – the Italian mosque debate' in T Modood, A Triandafyllidou, and R Zapata-Barrero (eds), *Multiculturalism, Muslims and Citizenship – A European Approach* (London: Routledge, 2006) 117.

Tyler, K, 'The genealogical imagination: the inheritance of interracial identities' [2005] *The Sociological Review* 476.

Tyson, A, 'The negotiation of the European Community Directive on racial discrimination' (2001) 3 EJML 199.

Urth, H, 'Building momentum for the integration of third country nationals in the European Union' (2005) 7 EJML 163

Vandenbrouke, F, 'Preface' in A Atkinson, B Cantillon, E Marlier, and B Nolan (eds), *The EU and Social Inclusion* (Oxford: OUP, 2002) v.

Velluti, S, 'What European Union strategy for integrating migrants? The role of OMC soft mechanisms in the development of an EU immigration policy' (2007) 9 EJML 53.

Verloo, M, 'Gender mainstreaming: practice and prospects' Report EG (1999) 13 (Strasbourg: Council of Europe, 1999).

——, 'Making women count in the Netherlands' in F Beveridge, S Nott, and K Stephen (eds), *Making Women Count – Integrating Gender into Law and Policy-making* (Aldershot: Ashgate, 2000) 49.

——, 'Multiple inequalities, intersectionality and the European Union' (2006) 13 *European Journal of Women's Studies* 211.

——, 'Understanding institutional racism' in The Evens Foundation (eds), *Europe's New Racism: Causes, Manifestations and Solutions* (Oxford: Berghahn Books, 2002) 27.

Waddington, L, 'Testing the limits of the EC Treaty Article on non-discrimination' (1999) 28 ILJ 133.

——, 'The expanding role of the equality principle in European Union law' Policy Papers (Series on Constitutional Reform of the EU) 2003/04 (Florence: European University Institute, 2003).

——, 'Taking stock and looking forward: the Commission Green Paper on equality and non-discrimination in an enlarged European Union' (2004) 33 ILJ 367.

Waddington, L and Hendriks, A, 'The expanding concept of employment discrimination in Europe: from direct and indirect discrimination to reasonable accommodation discrimination' (2002) 18 IJCLLIR 403.

Ware, L, 'Strict scrutiny, affirmative action, and academic freedom: the University of Michigan cases' (2004) 78 *Tulane Law Review* 2097.

Watt, P, 'An intercultural approach to "integration"' (2006) 1 *Translocations – The Irish Migration, Race and Social Transformation Review* 154.

Weissbrodt, D, 'The protection of non-citizens in international human rights law' in R Cholewinski, R Perruchoud, and E MacDonald (eds), *International Migration Law – Developing Paradigms and Key Challenges* (The Hague: TMC Asser Press, 2007) 221.

White, R, 'Free movement, equal treatment and citizenship of the Union' (2005) 54 ICLQ 885.

Wieviorka, M, 'Racisme, racialisation et ethnicisation en France' (1996) 1195 *Hommes & Migrations* 27.

Wincott, D, 'Beyond social regulation? New instruments and/or a new agenda for social policy at Lisbon?' (2003) 81 *Public Administration* 533.

Woodward, A, 'Too late for mainstreaming?: dealing with difference in Brussels', European Consortium of Political Research Joint Sessions, Granada, 14–19 April 2005.

Wrench, J, *Preventing Racism at the Workplace – A Report on 16 European Countries* (Luxembourg: OOPEC, 1996).

——, 'Diversity management can be bad for you' (2005) 46 *Race & Class* 73.

Xanthaki, A, 'Hope dies last: an EU Directive on Roma integration' (2005) 11 EPL 515.

Index